Three.js Cookbook

Over 80 shortcuts, solutions, and recipes that allow you to create the most stunning visualizations and 3D scenes using the Three.js library

Jos Dirksen

BIRMINGHAM - MUMBAI

Three.js Cookbook

Copyright © 2015 Packt Publishing

First published: January 2015

Production reference: 1220115

Published by Packt Publishing Ltd.
Livery Place
35 Livery Street
Birmingham B3 2PB, UK.

ISBN 978-1-78398-118-2

www.packtpub.com

Credits

Author

Jos Dirksen

Reviewers

Cameron Chamberlain

Josh Marinacci

Felix Palmer

Commissioning Editor

Ashwin Nair

Acquisition Editor

Owen Roberts

Content Development Editor

Adrian Raposo

Technical Editor

Mohita Vyas

Copy Editors

Rashmi Sawant

Stuti Srivastava

Project Coordinator

Kinjal Bari

Proofreaders

Simran Bhogal

Maria Gould

Ameesha Green

Paul Hindle

Indexer

Priya Sane

Graphics

Sheetal Aute

Abhinash Sahu

Production Coordinator

Nitesh Thakur

Cover Work

Nitesh Thakur

About the Author

Jos Dirksen has worked as a software developer and an architect for more than a decade. He has a lot of experience in a large range of technologies that range from backend technologies, such as Java and Scala, to frontend development using HTML5, CSS, and JavaScript. Besides working with these technologies, Jos also regularly speaks at conferences and likes to write about new and interesting technologies on his blog. He also likes to experiment with new technologies and see how they can best be used to create beautiful data visualizations, the results of which you can see on his blog at http://www.smartjava.org/.

He is currently working as an independent contractor for ING, a large Dutch financial institution, through his own company Smartjava. Previously, he worked as an enterprise architect for Malmberg, a large Dutch publisher of educational material. He helped to create the new digital platform for the creation and publication of educational content for primary, secondary, and vocational education. He has also worked in many different roles in the private and public sectors, ranging from private companies such as Philips and ASML to organizations in the public sector, such as the Department of Defense.

He has also written two other books on Three.js: *Learning Three.js*, *Packt Publishing*, which provides an in-depth description of all the features Three.js provides, and *Three.js Essentials*, *Packt Publishing*, which shows you how to use the core features of Three.js through extensive examples. Besides his interest in frontend JavaScript and HTML5 technologies, he is also interested in backend service development using REST and traditional web service technologies. He has already written two books on this subject. He is the coauthor of the book *Open Source ESBs in Action*, *Manning Publications* and author of the book *SOA Governance in Action*, *Manning Publications*. This book is on how to apply SOA governance in a practical and pragmatic manner.

Acknowledgments

Writing a book isn't something you do by yourself. A lot of people have helped and supported me when I was writing this book.

A special thanks to all the guys from Packt Publishing who have helped me during the writing, reviewing, and laying out part of the process. Great work guys!

I would also like to thank Ricardo Cabello, also known as Mr.dò_ób, for creating the great Three.js library.

Many thanks go to the reviewers. They provided me with great feedback and comments that really helped improve the book. Their positive remarks really helped me shape the book!

Also, I'd like to thank my family: my wife, Brigitte, for supporting me, and my two girls, Sophie and Amber, who can always find reasons to pull me away from the keyboard and computer.

About the Reviewers

Cameron Chamberlain is a frontend developer from Australia. He was awarded a first class honors degree in visual arts (digital media) from the Australian National University, where he focused on character animation. He has taught several media units at the University of Canberra and is now working in the user experience team at an international start-up based in Melbourne. His passions for both web development and computer graphics combine when exploring new web technology such as WebGL.

Josh Marinacci is an engineer, author, speaker, designer, and general UI wrangler. He has written books for O'Reilly Media, built IDEs, coded app stores, authored developer content, and prototyped an endless array of amusing interfaces. He is currently working as a researcher at Nokia. He previously traveled the world teaching webOS, JavaFX, Swing, and HTML canvas. He works from home in rainy but green Eugene, Oregon, with his wife and 3-year-old son.

Felix Palmer comes from a physics background and got into software by writing games in Flash. Since then he has spent time working in London and Silicon Valley, working with a wide range of technologies from mobile to cloud, server to web. He enjoys combining the visual and technical aspects and is excited about the opportunities WebGL brings.

Currently he lives in Prague, spending his time building things with WebGL, speaking at conferences, and writing on `www.pheelicks.com`. He is the creator of `www.piste.io`.

www.PacktPub.com

Support files, eBooks, discount offers, and more

For support files and downloads related to your book, please visit www.PacktPub.com.

Did you know that Packt offers eBook versions of every book published, with PDF and ePub files available? You can upgrade to the eBook version at www.PacktPub.com and as a print book customer, you are entitled to a discount on the eBook copy. Get in touch with us at service@packtpub.com for more details.

At www.PacktPub.com, you can also read a collection of free technical articles, sign up for a range of free newsletters and receive exclusive discounts and offers on Packt books and eBooks.

https://www2.packtpub.com/books/subscription/packtlib

Do you need instant solutions to your IT questions? PacktLib is Packt's online digital book library. Here, you can search, access, and read Packt's entire library of books.

Why Subscribe?

- Fully searchable across every book published by Packt
- Copy and paste, print, and bookmark content
- On demand and accessible via a web browser

Free Access for Packt account holders

If you have an account with Packt at www.PacktPub.com, you can use this to access PacktLib today and view 9 entirely free books. Simply use your login credentials for immediate access.

Table of Contents

Preface

Each year, web browsers become more powerful, increase in features, and improve in performance. Throughout the last couple of years, browsers have emerged as a great platform to create immersive, complex, and beautiful applications. Most of the current applications that are being built use modern HTML5 features such as web sockets, local storage, and advanced CSS techniques for styling.

Most modern browsers, however, also have support for a technology that can be used to create beautiful, 3D graphics and animations that use the GPU to achieve maximal performance. This technology is called WebGL and is supported by the latest versions of Firefox, Chrome, Safari, and Internet Explorer. With WebGL, you can create 3D scenes that run directly in your browser, without the need for any plugins. Support on the desktop for this standard is great, and most modern devices and mobile browsers fully support this standard.

To create WebGL applications, however, you need to learn a new language (called GLSL) and understand how vertex and fragment shaders can be used to render your 3D geometries. Luckily, though, there are a number of JavaScript libraries available that wrap the WebGL internals and provide a JavaScript API that you can use without having to understand the most complex features of WebGL. One of the most mature and feature-rich of those libraries is Three.js.

Three.js started in 2010 and provides a large number of easy-to-use APIs that expose all the features of Three.js and allows you to quickly create complex 3D scenes and animations in your browser.

Through its APIs, you can do pretty much everything that you want with Three.js. However, because it has so many features, it's sometimes difficult to find the right way to accomplish something. Throughout the years, Three.js has been under heavy development, but it is stabilizing now. So many examples and tutorials that you find online are outdated and don't work anymore. In this book, we'll provide you with a large number of recipes that you can follow to accomplish some common tasks with Three.js. Each example is accompanied with a runnable example that you can examine to better understand the recipe or adapt for your own purposes.

What this book covers

Chapter 1, Getting Started, covers the basic recipes that you can use when you create new Three.js-based applications. We'll show you how you can set up a basic Three.js skeleton using any of the available Three.js renderers. We'll further show you WebGL detection, loading resources, setting up an animation loop, adding drag and drop support, and controlling your scene through the keyboard.

Chapter 2, Geometries and Meshes, shows you a number of recipes that focus on creating, working with and manipulating geometries and meshes. We'll go into detail on how to rotate meshes in different ways, manipulate them using matrix transformations, generate geometries programmatically, and load models from Blender and in other formats.

Chapter 3, Working with the Camera, focuses on recipes that manipulate the cameras available in Three.js. It shows you how to work with the perspective and the orthogonal camera. This chapter also shows you recipes that explain how to rotate a camera, center a camera, and follow objects around.

Chapter 4, Materials and Textures, contains recipes that explain how to get good results working with the materials provided by Three.js. It has recipes on transparency, reflections, UV mapping, face materials, bump and normal maps and also explains how the various blend modes work.

Chapter 5, Lights and Custom Shaders, has recipes that deal with the workings of the different light sources in Three.js and shows you how to work with WebGL shaders. It shows you how to correctly set up shadows, create a sun-like lighting source, and goes into the differences between spot lights, point lights, and directional lights. In this chapter, we'll also provide you with a couple of recipes that explain how to create a custom vertex shader and a custom fragment shader.

Chapter 6, Point Clouds and Postprocessing, provides you with recipes that show you how to set up postprocessing. With postprocessing, you can enhance your scene with blurring, coloring, or other types of effects. This chapter also contains recipes that explain features of a particle system, such as animation and particle materials.

Chapter 7, Animation and Physics, shows you a number of recipes that help you in animating the objects in your scene and show you how to add physics (such as gravity and collision detection) to your scene.

What you need for this book

The only thing that you need for this book is a simple text editor to experiment with the provided recipes and a modern web browser to run the examples. For some of the advanced recipes, it is preferred to have a locally installed web server or disable some security settings in your browser. In *Chapter 1, Getting Started*, recipes are provided that explain how to set up such a server and disable the relevant security settings.

Who this book is for

This book is for everyone who has a basic understanding of JavaScript and Three.js but wants to learn how to use more advanced features of Three.js You don't need to understand advanced math concepts or have in depth knowledge of WebGL. The recipes in this book will explain the various features of Three.js step-by-step and we also provide all the recipes as ready to use HTML sources.

Sections

In this book, you will find several headings that appear frequently (Getting ready, How to do it, How it works, There's more, and See also).

To give clear instructions on how to complete a recipe, we use these sections as follows:

Getting ready

This section tells you what to expect in the recipe, and describes how to set up any software or any preliminary settings required for the recipe.

How to do it...

This section contains the steps required to follow the recipe.

How it works...

This section usually consists of a detailed explanation of what happened in the previous section.

There's more...

This section consists of additional information about the recipe in order to make the reader more knowledgeable about the recipe.

See also

This section provides helpful links to other useful information for the recipe.

Conventions

In this book, you will find a number of styles of text that distinguish between different kinds of information. Here are some examples of these styles, and an explanation of their meaning.

Code words in text, database table names, folder names, filenames, file extensions, pathnames, dummy URLs, user input, and Twitter handles are shown as follows: " One interesting thing to note is the addition of `texture.needsUpdate = true` to the `ondrop` event handler."

A block of code is set as follows:

```
step1(function (value1) {
  step2(value1, function(value2) {
    step3(value2, function(value3) {
      step4(value3, function(value4) {
        // Do something with value4
      });
    });
  });
});
```

When we wish to draw your attention to a particular part of a code block, the relevant lines or items are set in bold:

```
var y = camera.position.y;
camera.position.y = y * Math.cos(control.rotSpeed) +
  z * Math.sin(control.rotSpeed);
camera.position.z = z * Math.cos(control.rotSpeed) -
  y * Math.sin(control.rotSpeed);
```

New terms and **important words** are shown in bold. Words that you see on the screen, in menus or dialog boxes for example, appear in the text like this: "On this screen, just click on the **I'll be careful, I promise!** button."

 Warnings or important notes appear in a box like this.

Tips and tricks appear like this.

Reader feedback

Feedback from our readers is always welcome. Let us know what you think about this book—what you liked or may have disliked. Reader feedback is important for us to develop titles that you really get the most out of.

To send us general feedback, simply send an e-mail to feedback@packtpub.com, and mention the book title through the subject of your message.

If there is a topic that you have expertise in and you are interested in either writing or contributing to a book, see our author guide on www.packtpub.com/authors.

Customer support

Now that you are the proud owner of a Packt book, we have a number of things to help you to get the most from your purchase.

Downloading the example code

You can download the example code files from your account at http://www.packtpub.com for all the Packt Publishing books you have purchased. If you purchased this book elsewhere, you can visit http://www.packtpub.com/support and register to have the files e-mailed directly to you.

Downloading the color images of this book

We also provide you with a PDF file that has color images of the screenshots/diagrams used in this book. The color images will help you better understand the changes in the output. You can download this file from `https://www.packtpub.com/sites/default/files/downloads/1182OS.pdf`.

Errata

Although we have taken every care to ensure the accuracy of our content, mistakes do happen. If you find a mistake in one of our books—maybe a mistake in the text or the code—we would be grateful if you could report this to us. By doing so, you can save other readers from frustration and help us improve subsequent versions of this book. If you find any errata, please report them by visiting `http://www.packtpub.com/submit-errata`, selecting your book, clicking on the **Errata Submission Form** link, and entering the details of your errata. Once your errata are verified, your submission will be accepted and the errata will be uploaded to our website or added to any list of existing errata under the Errata section of that title.

To view the previously submitted errata, go to `https://www.packtpub.com/books/content/support` and enter the name of the book in the search field. The required information will appear under the **Errata** section.

Piracy

Piracy of copyright material on the Internet is an ongoing problem across all media. At Packt, we take the protection of our copyright and licenses very seriously. If you come across any illegal copies of our works, in any form, on the Internet, please provide us with the location address or website name immediately so that we can pursue a remedy.

Please contact us at `copyright@packtpub.com` with a link to the suspected pirated material.

We appreciate your help in protecting our authors, and our ability to bring you valuable content.

Questions

If you have a problem with any aspect of this book, you can contact us at `questions@packtpub.com`, and we will do our best to address the problem.

1
Getting Started

In this chapter, we'll cover the following recipes:

- Getting started with the WebGL renderer
- Getting started with the Canvas renderer
- Getting started with the CSS 3D renderer
- Detecting WebGL support
- Setting up an animation loop
- Determining the frame rate for your scene
- Controlling the variables used in the scene
- Setting up a local web server with Python
- Setting up a local web server with Node.js
- Setting up a local web server using Mongoose
- Solving cross-origin-domain error messages in Chrome
- Solving cross-origin-domain error messages in Firefox
- Adding keyboard controls
- Loading textures asynchronously
- Loading models asynchronously
- Loading models asynchronously with progress
- Loading other resources asynchronously with progress
- Waiting until resources are loaded
- Dragging a file from the desktop to the scene

Introduction

In this chapter we'll show you a number of recipes that introduce the basic usage of Three.js. We'll start with a number of simple recipes that you can use as a starting point for your Three.js projects. Next, we'll show you a couple of features that you can add to your project, such as WebGL detection and defining an animation loop. We'll end with a number of more advanced features such as adding drag and drop support, and loading resources synchronously and asynchronously.

Getting started with the WebGL renderer

When you want to create an initial Three.js project that uses WebGL for rendering, you always have to set up the same couple of variables. You need a `THREE.WebGLRenderer` object, a `THREE.Scene` object, a camera, and some way to render the scene. In this recipe, we'll provide you with a standard template that you can use in your own projects to quickly get started with the WebGL renderer.

Getting ready

Make sure that you download the sources for this book. You can either do this in the following two ways:

 ▸ Firstly, you can do this by cloning the Git repo that you can find at `https://github.com/josdirksen/threejs-cookbook`.

 ▸ Alternatively, you can download the sources from Packt Publishing website. When you extract the ZIP file or clone the repository you'll find a set of directories; one for each chapter of this book. For this recipe, you can use 0 as a reference.

You can directly view the end result of this recipe by opening the previously mentioned file in your browser. When you open this example in the browser, you'll see the following screenshot:

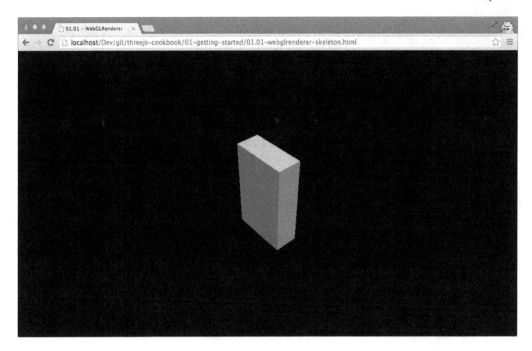

This is a minimal scene, rendered with the THREE.WebGLRenderer object.

How to do it...

Creating a skeleton that you can use as a base for your projects is easy. With a couple of simple steps, you'll get your first WebGLRenderer-based Three.js scene up and running:

1. Let's first define the basic HTML that we'll use:

```
<!DOCTYPE html>
<html>
  <head>
    <title>01.01 - WebGLRenderer - Skeleton</title>
    <script src="../libs/three.js"></script>
    <style>
      body {
      margin: 0;
      overflow: hidden;
      }
    </style>
  </head>
  <body>
```

```
    <script>
       . . .
    </script>
  </body>
</html>
```

Downloading the example code

You can download the example code files from your account at `http://www.packtpub.com` for all the Packt Publishing books you have purchased. If you purchased this book elsewhere, you can visit `http://www.packtpub.com/support` and register to have the files e-mailed directly to you.

As you can see this is use a simple page, with a `script` tag in the body that'll contain our Three.js code. The only interesting part is the CSS style.

We will add this style to the body element to make sure that our Three.js scene will run in fullscreen mode and won't show any scrollbars.

2. Next, let's start by filling in the script tag. The first thing that we will do is create a number of global variables that are used throughout this recipe:

```
// global variables
var renderer;
var scene;
var camera;
```

The `renderer` variable will hold a reference to the `THREE.WebGLRenderer` object that we're going to create in the next step. The `scene` variable is the container for all the objects that we want to render, and the `camera` variable determines what we will see when we render the scene.

3. Usually, you'd want to wait for all the HTML elements to finish loading, before you start running your JavaScript. For this, we use the following JavaScript:

```
// calls the init function when the window is done
   loading.
window.onload = init;
```

With this code, we tell the browser to call the `init` function, once the complete page has loaded. In the next step, we'll show the content of this `init` function.

4. For your skeleton to work, you need to add the `init` function, which looks as follows:

```
function init() {

    // create a scene, that will hold all our elements
    // such as objects, cameras and lights.
    scene = new THREE.Scene();
    // create a camera, which defines where we looking
      at.
    camera = new THREE.PerspectiveCamera(45,
      window.innerWidth / window.innerHeight, 0.1, 1000);
    // position and point the camera to the center
    camera.position.x = 15;
    camera.position.y = 16;
    camera.position.z = 13;
    camera.lookAt(scene.position);

    // create a renderer, set the background color and
      size
    renderer = new THREE.WebGLRenderer();
    renderer.setClearColor(0x000000, 1.0);
    renderer.setSize(window.innerWidth,
      window.innerHeight);

    // create a cube and add to scene
    var cubeGeometry = new THREE.BoxGeometry(
      10 * Math.random(),
      10 * Math.random(),
      10 * Math.random());

    var cubeMaterial = new THREE.MeshNormalMaterial();

    var cube = new THREE.Mesh(cubeGeometry,
      cubeMaterial);
    scene.add(cube);

    // add the output of the renderer to the html element
    document.body.appendChild(renderer.domElement);

    // call the render function
    renderer.render(scene, camera);

}
```

In this `init` function, we first created a `THREE.Scene` object with the container for all the objects that we want to render. Next, we created a camera, which determines the field of the view that will be rendered. Next, we created the `THREE.WebGLRenderer` object, which is used to render the scene using WebGL. The `THREE.WebGLRenderer` object has many properties. In this recipe, we used the `setClearColor` property to set the background of our scene to black, and we told the renderer to use the complete window for its output, using the `window.innerWidth` and `window.innerHeight` properties. To see whether our skeleton page is working, we then added a simple `THREE.Mesh` object with a `THREE.BoxGeometry` object to the scene. At this point, we can add the output of the WebGL, as a child of the HTML body element. We do this by appending the renderer's DOM element to the document body. Now, all that is left to do is render the scene by calling `renderer.render()`.

With these steps, you've created a basic `WebGLRenderer` based Three.js scene, which you can use as a basic starting point for all your Three.js experiments.

See also

▸ The `THREE.WebGLRenderer` object only works when your browser supports WebGL. Even though most modern desktop browsers (and even a large number of mobile browsers) support WebGL, in some cases, you might need to look for an alternative. Three.js provides a couple of other renderers, which you can use. To get an up-to-date overview of which browsers support WebGL, you can check out the information on this topic at `http://caniuse.com/webgl`.

▸ Besides using the `THREE.WebGLRenderer` object to render your scene, you can use the `THREE.CanvasRenderer` object, which is explained in *Getting started with the Canvas renderer* recipe or the `THREE.CSS3DRenderer` object, which is explained in the *Getting started with the CSS 3D renderer* recipe.

Getting started with the Canvas renderer

If your system doesn't support WebGL, there is an alternative renderer that you can use to render your scenes: the `CanvasRenderer` object. This renderer doesn't use WebGL to render the output, but directly uses JavaScript to draw the HTML5 canvas element.

Getting ready

In the r69 Version of Three.js, the canvas renderer has been removed from the default distribution. To use this renderer, we have to first import the following two files:

```
<script src="../libs/CanvasRenderer.js"></script>
<script src="../libs/Projector.js"></script>
```

For this recipe, you can take a look at the `01.02-canvasrenderer-skeleton.html` example from the sources in this chapter. If you open this example in your browser, you'll see a cube, pretty much like the one in the previous recipe:

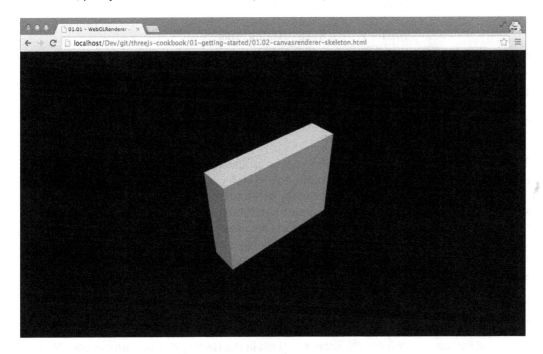

This time, however, this cube is rendered with the HTML5 canvas element. HTML5 canvas is supported on many devices, but provides less performance than the WebGL- based solution.

How to do it...

To set up the WebGL renderer, you will follow exactly the same steps as we showed in the previous recipe, *Getting started with the WebGL renderer,* so we won't go into the details in this section but we'll just list down the differences:

1. To get started with the `THREE.CanvasRenderer` object, the only thing we need to change is the following:

    ❑ Replace the `THREE.WebGLRenderer` object in the following piece of code:

    ```
    renderer = new THREE.WebGLRenderer();
    renderer.setClearColor(0x000000, 1.0);
    renderer.setSize(window.innerWidth,
      window.innerHeight);
    ```

❏ Replace the THREE.WebGLRenderer object with the `THREE.CanvasRenderer` object as follows:

```
renderer = new THREE.CanvasRenderer();
renderer.setClearColor(0x000000, 1.0);
renderer.setSize(window.innerWidth,
    window.innerHeight);
```

And that's it. With this change, we move from rendering using WebGL to rendering on the HTML5 canvas.

How it works...

The main difference between the HTML5 canvas renderer and the WebGL renderer is that this approach uses JavaScript to directly draw to the HTML5 canvas for rendering your 3D scene. The main issue with this approach is the lousy performance. When you use the `THREE.WebGLRenderer` object, you can use hardware-accelerated rendering. However, with the `THREE.CanvasRenderer` object, you have to completely rely on software-based rendering, which will result in lower performance. An added disadvantage of `THREE.CanvasRenderer` is that you can't use the advanced materials and features of Three.js, as that relies on WebGL specific functionality.

See also

▸ If you can use the WebGL approach given in the *Getting started with the WebGL renderer* recipe, you should really use it. It provides more features than those that are available with the canvas-based approach, and has much better performance.

▸ In the following recipe, *Getting started with the CSS 3D renderer*, this will also show a different approach where we use the CSS 3D-based renderer to animate the HTML elements. CSS 3D also provides hardware accelerated rendering, but only has support for a limited set of Three.js features.

Getting started with the CSS 3D renderer

HTML and CSS are getting more and more powerful each day. Modern browsers, both mobile and desktop variants, have great support for these two standards. The latest versions of CSS also support 3D transformations. With the `THREE.CSS3DRenderer` object, we can directly access these CSS 3D features and transform an arbitrary HTML element in 3D space.

Getting ready

To use the CSS 3D renderer, we first have to download the specific JavaScript file from the Three.js site, as it hasn't been included in the standard Three.js distribution. You can download this file directly from GitHub at `https://raw.githubusercontent.com/mrdoob/three.js/master/examples/js/renderers/CSS3DRenderer.js` or look in the lib directory of the sources provided with this book.

To see the `CSS3DRenderer` scene in action, you can open the example `01.03-cssrenderer-skeleton.html` in your browser:

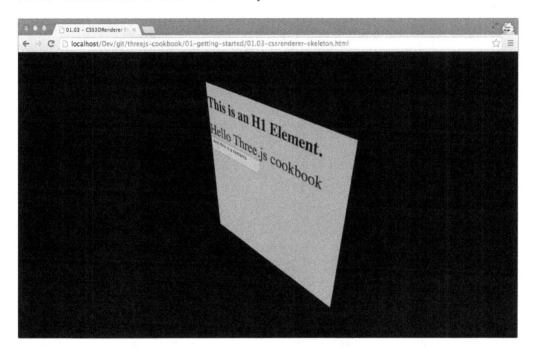

What you see here is a standard HTML div element, rendered in 3D with the `THREE.CSS3DRenderer` object.

How to do it...

To set up a `THREE.CSS3DRenderer` based scene, we need to perform a couple of simple steps:

1. Before we get started with the `THREE.CSS3DRenderer` specific information, first, you have to set up a simple basic HTML page as we did in the *Getting started with the WebGL renderer* recipe. So walk through the first three steps of that recipe, and then continue with the next step.

2. After the initial setup, the first thing that we need to do is to add the correct JavaScript to our head element:

   ```
   <script src="../libs/CSS3DRenderer.js"></script>
   ```

   Next, we'll start with the definition of the global variables that we need:

   ```
   var content = '<div>' +
     '<h1>This is an H1 Element.</h1>' +
     '<span class="large">Hello Three.js cookbook</span>'
       +
     '<textarea> And this is a textarea</textarea>' +
   '</div>';

   // global variables, referenced from render loop
   var renderer;
   var scene;
   var camera;
   ```

3. What we define here is a string representation of the element that we want to render. As the `THREE.CSS3DRenderer` object works with the HTML elements, we won't use any of the standard Three.js geometries here, but just plain HTML. The renderer, scene, and camera are simple variables for the corresponding Three.js elements, so that we can easily access them from the `render()` function, which we'll see later on.

4. Similar to the other skeletons we will initialize the scene in the `init()` function. The function that you need to add to the `THREE.CSS3DRenderer` object is shown as follows:

   ```
   function init() {

     scene = new THREE.Scene();
     camera = new THREE.PerspectiveCamera(45,
       window.innerWidth / window.innerHeight, 0.1, 1000);
   ```

```
// create a CSS3DRenderer
renderer = new THREE.CSS3DRenderer();
renderer.setSize(window.innerWidth, window.innerHeight);
document.body.appendChild(renderer.domElement);

// position and point the camera to the center of the
   scene
camera.position.x = 500;
camera.position.y = 500;
camera.position.z = 500;
camera.lookAt(scene.position);

var cssElement = createCSS3DObject(content);
cssElement.position.set(100, 100, 100);
scene.add(cssElement);

render();
}
```

5. We'll focus on the highlighted parts in this code fragment. For an explanation of the other parts of this function, we will take a look at the _Getting started with the WebGL renderer_ recipe. As you can see in this fragment, this time we will create a THREE. CSS3DRenderer object. Just as we did with the other renderers, we also need to set the size. Since we want to fill the screen, we will use the window.innerwidth and window.innerheight properties. The rest of the code stays the same.

6. Now, all we need to do to finish this skeleton is add an element. With the CSS 3D renderer, we can only add THREE.CSS3DObject elements. For this step, just add the following function:

```
function createCSS3DObject(content)
    {
    // convert the string to dome elements
    var wrapper = document.createElement('div');
    wrapper.innerHTML = content;
    var div = wrapper.firstChild;

    // set some values on the div to style it.
    // normally you do this directly in HTML and
    // CSS files.
    div.style.width = '370px';
    div.style.height = '370px';
    div.style.opacity = 0.7;
    div.style.background = new THREE.Color(Math.random()
       * 0xffffff).getStyle();
```

```
        // create a CSS3Dobject and return it.
        var object = new THREE.CSS3DObject(div);
        return object;
}
```

This function takes an HTML string as the input, converts it to an HTML element, sets some CSS styles, and uses this as the input to create a `THREE.CSS3DObject` object, which is added to the scene.

If you open this file in your browser, you'll see something that resembles the example we showed in the *Getting ready* section of this recipe. You can use the HTML page and JavaScript as a template for the entirety of your CSS 3D renderer project.

How it works...

With CSS 3D, you can apply all kinds of transformations to the HTML elements. For instance, you can apply a specific rotation around an axis using the transform property. The interesting thing is that you can also apply matrix transformations. Three.js uses matrix transformations internally to position and rotate the elements. With the `THREE.CSS3DRenderer` object, Three.js hides the internal CSS 3D specific transformations and styles and provides a nice abstraction level, which you can use to work with the HTML elements in 3D.

See also

▶ If you can use the WebGL approach from the *Getting started with the WebGL renderer* recipe, you should really use it. It provides more features than those that are available with the CSS-based approach, but has less support for mobile devices. If, on the other hand, you're looking to manipulate the HTML elements on screen, the `THREE.CSS3DRenderer` object is a great solution.

Detecting WebGL support

Not all browsers currently support WebGL. When you create a page that uses the `THREE.WebGLRenderer` object, it is a good idea to make sure that the browser supports WebGL. If a browser doesn't support it, this will result in all kinds of strange JavaScript errors in the JavaScript console and an empty screen for the end user. To make sure that your WebGL projects work as expected, we'll explain how to detect WebGL support in a browser in this recipe.

Getting ready

In this recipe, as an example, we will use the `01.04-detect-webgl-support.html` file, which you can find in the sources provided with this book. If you open this file, you'll see the following result if your browser doesn't support WebGL:

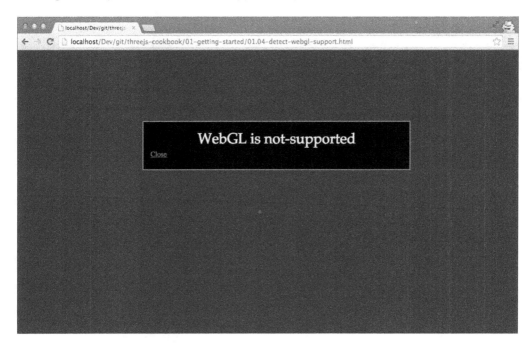

Let's take a look at the recipe to create the preceding example.

How to do it...

To detect WebGL and create the message **WebGL is not-supported**, we need to perform the following steps:

1. First, we'll create the CSS for the pop up to show when WebGL isn't supported.
2. Then, we need to detect whether the browser WebGL is supported. For this, we'll write a method that returns the values true or false.
3. Finally, we'll use the result from the previous step to either show the pop up or just continue.

    In the following section, we'll look at these steps in detail:

4. The first thing you need to do is set up the CSS that we'll use:

```html
<!DOCTYPE html>
<html>
  <head>
    <style>
      .black_overlay {
        display: none;
        position: absolute;
        top: 0;
        left: 0%;
        width: 100%;
        height: 100%;
        background-color: black;
        z-index: 1001;
        opacity: .80;
      }

      .white-content {
        display: none;
        position: absolute;
        top: 25%;
        left: 25%;
        width: 50%;
        height: 70px;
        padding: 16px;
        border: 2px solid grey;
        background-color: black;
        z-index: 1002;
      }

      .big-message {
        width: 80%;
        height: auto;
        margin: 0 auto;
        padding: 5px;
        text-align: center;
        color: white;

        font-family: serif;
        font-size: 20px;
      }
    </style>
    <title></title>
  </head>
  <body>
```

As you can see, there is nothing special in this CSS. The only thing that we will do here is create a number of classes that we'll use to create a pop-up message and hide the background. Next, we will define the HTML that is used to create the pop ups.

5. The following snippet shows you the HTML code, which will contain the message. Using the CSS that we previously defined we can show or hide this element:

```html
<!-- Lightbox to show when WebGL is supported or not
  -->
<div id="lightbox" class="white-content">
<div class="big-message" id="message">

</div>
<a href="javascript:void(0)"
  onclick="hideLightbox()">Close</a>
</div>
<div id="fade" class="black_overlay"></div>
```

As you can see, we just create a number of `div` elements that are currently hidden. When we detect that WebGL isn't supported this will be shown by the two `div` elements by changing their visibility.

6. Next, let's take a look at the JavaScript you need to add to detect WebGL. We'll create the following function for it:

```javascript
// loosely based on the http://get.webgl.org
  function detectWebGL() {

  // first create a canvas element
  var testCanvas = document.createElement("canvas");
  // and from that canvas get the webgl context
  var gl = null;

  // if exceptions are thrown, indicates webgl is null
  try {
    gl = testCanvas.getContext("webgl");
  } catch (x) {
    gl = null;
  }

  // if still null try experimental
  if (gl == null) {
    try {
    gl = testCanvas.getContext("experimental-webgl");
    } catch (x) {
    gl = null;
    }
  }
  // if webgl is all good return true;
  if (gl) {
    return true;
  } else {
    return false;
  }
}
```

As you can see, we create an HTML `canvas` element and then try to create a WebGL context with the `getContext` function. If this fails, the `gl` variable is set to null but if it succeeds, the `gl` variable will contain the WebGL context. If the `gl` variable isn't null, it will return true. On the hand, if it is, it will return false.

7. Now that we're able to detect whether a browser supports WebGL or not, we'll use this function to show a pop up. For this recipe, we'll also show you a pop up when WebGL is supported:

```
var hasGl = detectWebGL();
if (hasGl) {
  showLightbox("WebGL is supported");
} else {
showLightbox("WebGL is not-supported");
}

function showLightbox(message) {
  var lightBox = document.getElementById('light');
  lightBox.style.display = 'block';

  var fadeBox = document.getElementById('fade');
  fadeBox.style.display = 'block'

  var msg = document.getElementById('message');
  msg.textContent = message;
}

function hideLightbox() {
  var lightBox = document.getElementById('light');
  lightBox.style.display = 'none';

  var fadeBox = document.getElementById('fade');
  fadeBox.style.display = 'none'
}
```

And that is it for this recipe. If we add this to a web page, a browser that supports WebGL shows a pop up with **WebGL is supported**, if no WebGL is available, a pop up is shown with the text **WebGL isn't supported**. Besides this approach, you can also use the detector object provided by Three.js at `https://github.com/mrdoob/three.js/blob/master/examples/js/Detector.js`. If you include this file in your JavaScript, you can detect WebGL by checking the `webgl` attribute of the `Detector` object.

Setting up an animation loop

In the recipes at the beginning of this chapter, we showed you how to set up a basic Three.js scene, using one of the available renderers. If you want to add animations to your Three.js scene, for instance, to move the camera around or rotate an object, you'll need to call the `render` function multiple times. In the old days of JavaScript, you had to control this yourself using the `setTimeout` or `setInterval` JavaScript functions. The problem with these functions is that they don't take into account what is happening in your browser. For instance, your page will be hidden or the Three.js scene might be scrolled out of view. A better solution for animations, and the one that we'll use in this recipe, is `requestAnimationFrame`. With this function, your browser determines when it is the best time to call the animation code.

Getting ready

For this recipe, we will use the `01.05-setup-animation-loop.html` example HTML file. To see the animation in action, just open this file in your browser:

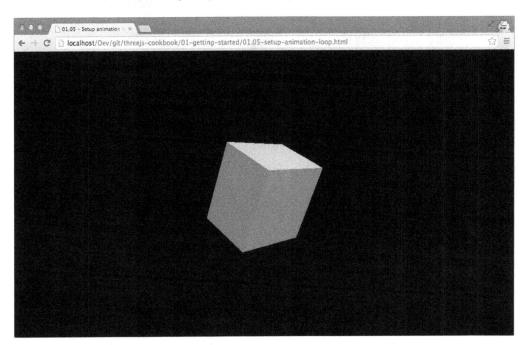

This example uses the WebGL renderer. You can of course apply this same recipe to the other renderers we've discussed in this chapter.

Let's take a look at the steps we need to take to set up such an animation loop.

How to do it...

To create an animation loop you don't have to change much in your existing code:

1. Let's first look at how to use `requestAnimationFrame` for rendering. For this, we've created a render function:

   ```
   function render() {
       renderer.render(scene, camera);
       scene.getObjectByName('cube').rotation.x += 0.05;
       requestAnimationFrame(render);
   }
   ```

   As you can see, we pass the render function as an argument to request a frame for animation. This will cause the `render` function to be called at a regular interval. In the `render` function, we will also update the rotation of the x axis of the cube to show you that the scene is re-rendered.

2. To use this function in the recipes, which we saw at the beginning of this chapter, we just have to replace this call:

   ```
   function init() {
       ...
       // call the render function
       renderer.render(scene, camera);
   }
   ```
   With the following:
   ```
   function init() {
       ...
       // call the render function
       render();
   }
   ```

3. You will now have your own animation loop, so any changes made to your model, camera, or other objects in the scene can now be done from within the `render()` function.

See also

► We mentioned that in this recipe, we've used the `THREE.WebGLRenderer` object as an example. You can of course also apply this to the skeletons from the *Getting started with the Canvas renderer* recipe or *Getting started with the CSS 3D renderer* recipe.

► What will be of interest to you also is the *Determining the frame rate of your scene* recipe, where we'll add additional functionality to the skeletons so you can easily see how often the render function is called by `requestAnimationFrame`.

Determining the frame rate for your scene

When you create large Three.js applications with many objects and animations, it is good to keep an eye on the frame rate at which the browser can render your scene. You can do this yourself using log statements from your animation loop, but luckily, there is already a good solution available that integrates great with Three.js (which isn't that strange since it was originally written for Three.js).

Getting ready

For this recipe, we'll use the `stats.js` JavaScript library that you can download from its GitHub repository at `https://github.com/mrdoob/stats.js/`. To use this library, you have to include it at the top of your HTML file such as this:

```
<script src="../libs/stats.min.js"></script>
```

We've also provided a ready to use example for this recipe. If you open the `01.06-determine-framerate.html` file in your browser, you can directly see how this library shows the current framerate, which you can see at the top-left of the browser, as shown in the following screenshot:

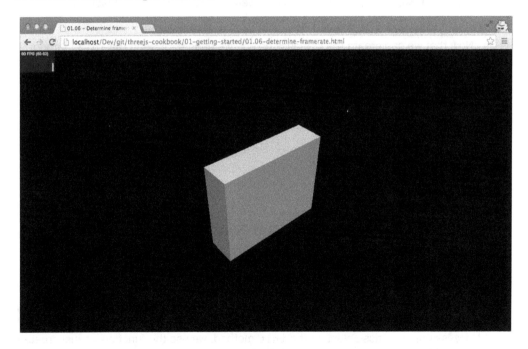

Let's take a look at the steps you need to take to add this to your Three.js application.

How to do it...

Adding this functionality to your scene only takes a couple of small steps, which are as follows:

1. Firstly, we have to create the `stats` object and position it. For this, we create a simple function:

```
function createStats() {
  var stats = new Stats();
  stats.setMode(0);

  stats.domElement.style.position = 'absolute';
  stats.domElement.style.left = '0';
  stats.domElement.style.top = '0';

  return stats;
}
```

We create the statistics object by calling `new Stats()`. The `Stats.js` library supports two different modes that we can set with the `setMode` function. If we pass `0` as an argument, you see the frames rendered in the last second, and if we set the mode to `1`, we see the milliseconds that were needed to render the last frame. For this recipe, we want to see the framerate, so we set the mode to `0`.

2. Now that we can create the statistics object, we need to append the `init` method we've seen in the skeleton recipes:

```
// global variables
var renderer;
var scene;
var camera;
var stats;

function init() {
  ...
  stats = createStats();
  document.body.appendChild( stats.domElement );

  // call the render function
  render();
}
```

As you can see we created a new global variable called `stats`, which we'll use to access our statistics object. In the `init` method, we use the function we just created, and add the `stats` object to our HTML body.

3. We're almost there. The only thing we need to do now is make sure that we update the stats object whenever the render function is called. This way, the stats object can calculate either the framerate or the time it took to run the render function:

```
function render() {
  requestAnimationFrame(render);

  scene.getObjectByName('cube').rotation.x+=0.05;
  renderer.render(scene, camera);
  stats.update();
}
```

How it works...

We mentioned that Stats.js provides two modes. It either shows the framerate or the time it took to render the last frame. The Stats.js library works by simply keeping track of the time passed between calls and its update function. If you're monitoring the framerate, it counts how often the update was called within the last second, and shows that value. If you're monitoring the render time, it just shows the time between calls and the update function.

Controlling the variables used in the scene

When you're developing and writing JavaScript, you often need to tune some variables for the best visualization. You might need to change the color of a sphere, change the speed of an animation, or experiment with more complex material properties. You can just change the source code, and reload the HTML, but that becomes tedious and time consuming. In this recipe, we'll show you an alternative way to quickly and easily control the variables in your Three.js scene.

Getting ready

For this recipe, we also need an external JavaScript library called dat.gui. You can download the latest version from https://code.google.com/p/dat-gui/, or look into the libs directory of the sources provided with this book. To use this library, you first have to include it in the top of your HTML file:

```
<script src="../libs/dat.gui.min.js"></script>
```

In the source folder of this chapter, there is also a ready-to-use example, which we'll explain in the following sections. When you open the `01.07-control-variables.html` file, you'll see the following:

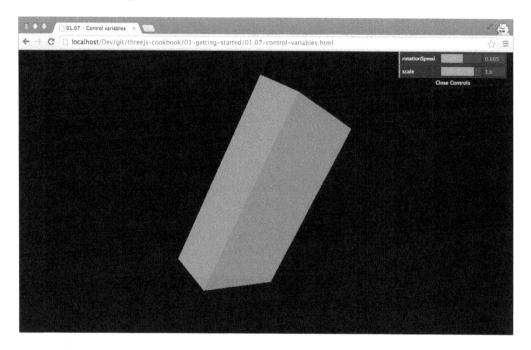

As you can see in the preceding screenshot, a menu is available in the top-right corner that you can use to control the rotation speed and the scaling of the cube.

How to do it...

To use this library for yourself, you only need to do a couple of small things:

1. The first thing you need to do is define a JavaScript object that contains the properties you want to control. In this case, you need to add it to the `init` function and create a new global JavaScript variable with the name, `control`:

```
...
var control;
function init() {

  ...

  control = new function() {
    this.rotationSpeed = 0.005;
    this.scale = 1;
  };
```

```
        addControls(control);

        // call the render function
        render();
    }
```

2. The control object in the preceding code contains two properties: `rotationSpeed` and `scale`. In the `addControls` function, we'll create the UI component that is shown in the preceding screenshot:

```
function addControls(controlObject) {
    var gui = new dat.GUI();
    gui.add(controlObject, 'rotationSpeed', -0.1, 0.1);
    gui.add(controlObject, 'scale', 0.01, 2);
}
```

In this `addControls` function, we use the provided argument that contains the `rotationSpeed` and `scale` properties in order to create the control GUI. For each variable, we specify four arguments:

1. **Object**: The first argument is the JavaScript object that contains the variables. In our case, it's the object passed to the `addControls` function.

2. **Name**: The second argument is the name of the variable we want to add. This should point to one of the variables (or functions) available in the object that is provided in the first argument.

3. **Minimum value**: The third argument is the minimum value that should be shown in the GUI.

4. **Maximum value**: The last argument specifies the maximum value that should be shown.

3. At this point, we've got a GUI that can be used to control the variables, as you can see in the following screenshot:

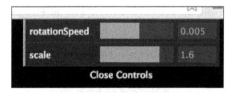

The only thing we now need to do is make sure that we update our object in the render loop, which is based on the variables from the GUI. We can do this easily in the `render` function, which is as follows:

```
function render() {
    renderer.render(scene, camera);
```

```
scene.getObjectByName('cube').rotation.x+=
  control.rotationSpeed;
scene.getObjectByName('cube')
  .scale.set
  (control.scale,
  control.scale,
  control.scale);

requestAnimationFrame(render);
}
```

There's more...

In this recipe, we've just used `dat.gui` to change the numeric values. The `dat.gui` library also allows you to add controls for other types of values as follows:

 ▸ If the variable you add is a Boolean, a checkbox will be shown

 ▸ If the variable is a string, you can add an array of valid values

 ▸ If the variable is a color, you can use add color to create a color picker

 ▸ If the variable is a function, you get a button that fires the selected function

Besides this, you can add different kinds of event listeners to fire custom callbacks when a value managed by `dat.gui` changes. For more information, see the `dat.gui` library documentation which you can find at `http://workshop.chromeexperiments.com/examples/gui/#1--Basic-Usage`.

Setting up a local web server with Python

The best way to test your Three.js applications, or any JavaScript application for that matter, is to run it on a local web server. This way, you have the best representation of how your users will eventually see your Three.js visualization. In this chapter, we will show you three different ways in which you can run a web server locally. The three different ways to set up a local web server are:

 ▸ One way to do this is via a Python-based approach that you can use if you've got Python installed

 ▸ Another way is to do if you use Node.js or have already played around with Node.js, you can use the `npm` command to install a simple web server

 ▸ A third option is if you don't want to use the `npm` command or Python, you can also use **Mongoose**, which is a simple portable web server, that runs on OS X and Windows

This recipe will focus on the Python-based approach (the first bullet point).

Getting ready

If you've got Python installed, you can very easily run a simple web server. You will first need to check whether you've got Python installed. The easiest way to do this is just type in `python` on a console and hit *enter*. If you see an output as follows, you are ready to begin:

```
> python
Python 2.7.3 (default, Apr 10 2013, 05:09:49)
[GCC 4.7.2] on linux2
Type "help", "copyright", "credits" or "license" for more information.
>>>
```

How to do it...

1. Once Python (`http://python.org`) has been installed, you can run a simple web server by just executing the following Python command. You will need to do this in the directory from where you want to host the files:

    ```
    > python -m SimpleHTTPServer
    ```

2. The following output shows the web server running on port 8000:

    ```
    Serving HTTP on 0.0.0.0 port 8000...
    ```

If you don't have Python installed, take a look at one of the following two recipes for alternative options.

Setting up a local web server with Node.js

If you would like to test your Three.js applications, then as described in the *How to set up a local web server with Python* recipe, you can run it in three different ways. This recipe will focus on the Node.js approach.

Getting ready

To run a local web server with Node.js (`https://nodejs.org`), we first have to check whether we've got `npm` (the node package manager, which is installed together with Node.js) installed. You can check this by running the `npm` command from the command line:

```
> npm
```

If the output is similar to the following code snippet, you've got `npm` installed and you are ready to begin the recipe:

```
Usage: npm <command>
where ...
```

How to do it...

1. You can use it to run a simple web server using:

   ```
   Usage: npm <command>...
   ```

2. Now, you are ready to install a web server by running:

   ```
   > npm install -g http-server
   ```

3. Finally, you are ready to start the web server by running `http-server` from the command line:

   ```
   > http-server
   Starting up http-server, serving ./ on port: 8080
   Hit CTRL-C to stop the server
   ```

A final recipe for running your own web server is presented in the next section. In that recipe you don't need Python or Node.js installed, but we will show you how to download a portable web server that you can run without requiring any installation.

Setting up a local web server using Mongoose

If you would like to test your Three.js applications, then as described in the *How to set up a local web server with Python* recipe, you can run it in three different ways. If the first two approaches fail, you can always use a simple portable web server using Mongoose. This recipe will focus on the Mongoose approach.

Getting ready

Before you run Mongoose, you first have to download it. You can download Mongoose from https://code.google.com/p/mongoose/downloads/list.

How to do it...

1. The platform you are using will affect how you run Mongoose. If you're running Windows, you can just copy the downloaded file (an executable) to the folder from where you want to host your files from (for example, the directory where you extracted the sources for this book), and double-click on the executable to start the web server on port 8080.

2. For Linux or OS X platforms, you will also need to have a copy of the downloaded file in the directory where your files are located, but you have to start Mongoose from the command line.

See also

▸ If you can't install a local web server, you can take a look at the *Solving cross-origin-domain error messages in Chrome* recipe. This recipe provides you with an alternative way of running the more advanced Three.js examples.

Solving cross-origin-domain error messages in Chrome

When you are developing Three.js applications, the simplest way of testing your application is to just open the file in your browser. For a lot of scenarios, this will work, until you start loading textures and models. If you try to do this, you'll be presented with an error that looks something like this:

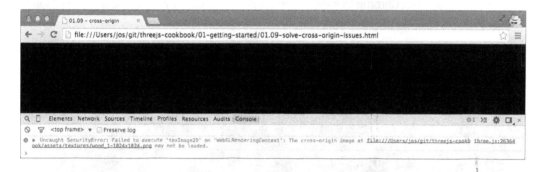

This error, which you can easily reproduce yourself by just dragging `01.09-solve-cross-origin-issues.html` to your browser, will have the terms **cross-origin** or **SecurityError** in its message. What this error means is that the browsers prevents the current page loading a resource from a different domain. This is a necessary feature to avoid maleficent websites access to personal information. During development, however, this can be a bit incovenient. In this recipe, we'll show you how you can circumvent these kinds of errors by tweaking the security settings of your browser.

We'll take a look at how to disable the security checks for the two browsers that have the best support for WebGL: Chrome and Firefox. In this recipe, we'll look at how to do this in Chrome, and in the next recipe, we'll show you how to do this in Firefox. An important note, though, before we go on with the recipe. If you can, run a local web server. It's much more secure and doesn't result in low security settings in your browser.

How to do it...

1. After the installation of Chrome is complete, we will then need to disable the security settings in Chrome, for which we have to pass a command line parameter. Each operating system, however, does this slightly differently:

    ❑   For Windows, you call the following (from the command line):

        ```
        chrome.exe --disable-web-security
        ```

    ❑   On Linux, do the following:

        ```
        google-chrome --disable-web-security
        ```

    ❑   And on Mac OS, you disable the settings by starting Chrome using:

        ```
        open -a Google\ Chrome --args --disable-web-security
        ```

2. When you start Chrome this way, even running it directly from the filesystem will load the resources correctly to give you the following result:

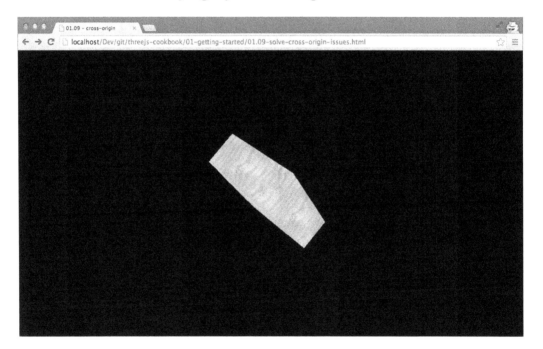

3. Do remember to restart the browser normally after you're done experimenting or developing with Three.js, since you've lowered the security settings of your browser.

4. For Firefox users, we explain how to solve these cross-origin issues for this browser in the following recipe.

Solving cross-origin-domain error messages in Firefox

In the previous recipe, we explained that cross-origin error messages can occur when you run Three.js applications from the filesystem. In this recipe, we showed you how to solve these kind of issues on Chrome. In this recipe, we look at how to solve these issues in another popular browser: Firefox.

How to do it...

1. For Firefox, we will then need to disable the security settings directly from the browser. If you type about:config in the URL bar, you will see the following:

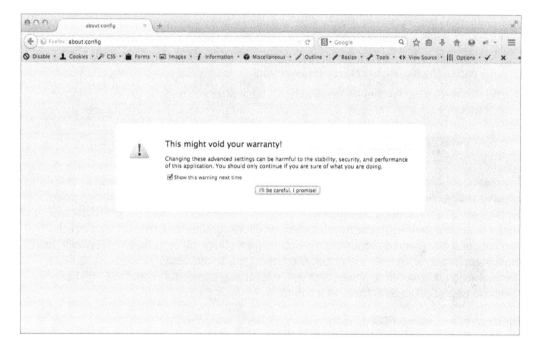

2. On this screen, just click on the **I'll be careful, I promise!** button. This will bring you to an overview page that shows you all the internal properties available in Firefox.

3. Following this, in the search box on this screen type `security.fileuri.strict_origin_policy` and change its value, as shown in the following screenshot:

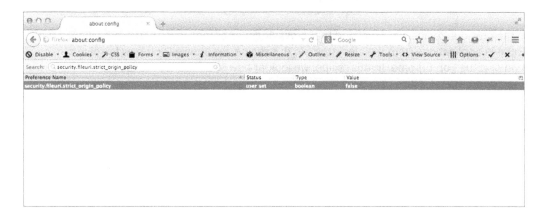

4. Now, when you open a file directly in the browser, even the resources loaded through one of the asynchronous loaders will work.

5. Do remember to change these settings back after you're done experimenting or developing with Three.js, since you've lowered the security settings of your browser.

How it works...

The reason we have to set these properties is that, by default, the modern browser checks whether you're allowed to request a resource from a different domain than the one you're running on. When you use Three.js to load a model or a texture, it uses an `XMLHTTPRequest` object to access that resource. Your browser will check for the availability of the correct headers, and since you're requesting a resource from your local system, which doesn't provide the correct headers, an error will occur. Even, though with this recipe, you can circumvent this restriction, it is better to always test with a local web server, since that will most closely resemble how your users will access it online.

For more information on CORS, refer to `http://www.w3.org/TR/cors/`.

See also

▸ As we mentioned in the previous section, a better way to handle these kinds of errors is by setting up a local web server. The *Setting up a local web server with Python* recipe, explains how to accomplish this.

Adding keyboard controls

If you want to create games or more advanced 3D scenes, you often need a way to control elements in your scene using keyboard controls. For instance, you might make a platform game where the user uses the arrows on the keyboard to move through your game. Three.js in itself doesn't provide a specific functionality to handle keyboard events, since it is very easy to connect the standard HTML JavaScript event handling to Three.js.

Getting ready

For this recipe, we included an example where you can rotate a cube around its *x* and *z* axes using the arrows on your keyboard. If you first open an example `01.10-keyboard-controls.html` in your browser, you'll see a simple cube:

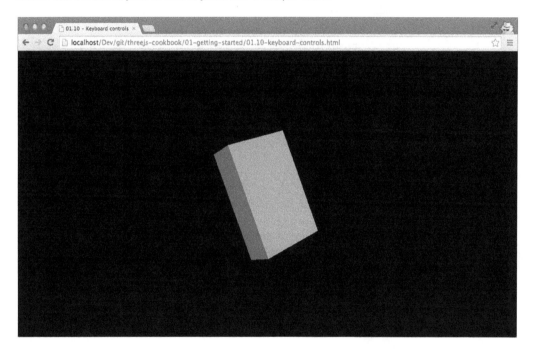

With the up, down, left, and right arrows on your keyboard, you can rotate this cube. With this file open, you are now ready to begin.

How to do it...

Adding a key support in your browser is very easy; all you have to do is assign an event handler to `document.onkeydown`.

1. To do this we need to assign a function to the `document.onkeydown` object This function will get called whenever a key is pressed. The following code, wrapped in the `setupKeyControls` function, registers this listener:

    ```
    function setupKeyControls() {
        var cube = scene.getObjectByName('cube');
        document.onkeydown = function(e) {
          switch (e.keyCode) {
            case 37:
            cube.rotation.x += 0.1;
            break;
            case 38:
            cube.rotation.z -= 0.1;
            break;
            case 39:
            cube.rotation.x -= 0.1;
            break;
            case 40:
            cube.rotation.z += 0.1;
            break;
          }
        };
    }
    ```

2. In this function, we use the `keyCode` property from the passed event `e` in order to determine what to do. In this example, if a user presses the left arrow key that corresponds to key code `37`, we change the `rotation.x` property of the Three.js object in our scene. We apply the same principle to the up arrow key(`38`), the right arrow (`39`), and the down arrow (`40`).

How it works...

Using event handlers is a standard HTML JavaScript mechanism, they are a part of the DOM API. This API allows you to register functions for all kinds of different events. Whenever that specific event occurs, the provided function is called. In this recipe, we chose to use the `KeyDown` event. This event is triggered when the user presses a key. There is also a `KeyUp` event available that is triggered when the user releases a key, which one to use depends on your use case. Note that there is also a `KeyPress` event available. This event, though, is meant to be used with characters and doesn't register any noncharacter key press.

There's more...

In this recipe, we only showed the key code values for the arrows. There is, of course, a separate key code for each key on your keyboard. A good explanation of how the various keys are mapped (especially, the special ones such as the function keys) can be found at `http://unixpapa.com/js/key.html`. If you want to know the key value of a specific key, and you don't feel like looking up the value in a list, you can also use just the following simple handler to output the key codes to the JavaScript console:

```
function setupKeyLogger() {
  document.onkeydown = function(e) {
    console.log(e);
  }
}
```

This small handler logs the complete event. In the output to the console, you can then see the key code that is used, as shown in the following screenshot:

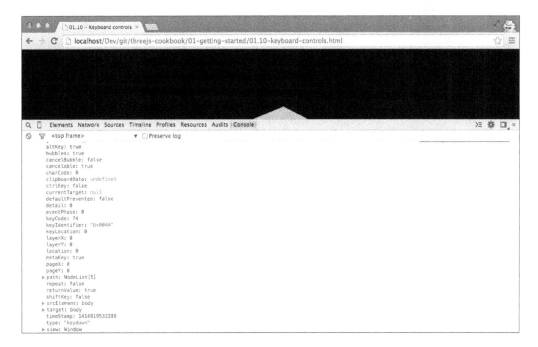

As you can see, you also see a lot of other interesting information. For instance, you can see whether the *shift* or *Alt* keys were also pressed at the same time of the event.

See also

> ▶ If you want to learn more about key events, Mozilla provides a good overview of all the events that are available at `https://developer.mozilla.org/en-US/docs/Web/Events`.

Loading textures asynchronously

When you create Three.js scenes, you often need to load resources. There might be textures you want to load for your objects, you might have some external models you want to include in your scene, or maybe some CSV data that you want to use as an input for your visualization. Three.js offers a number of different ways of loading these resources asynchronously, which we'll explore in this and the following recipes.

To run these recipes and experiment with them, we included a simple sample in the source folder of this chapter that shows this loading in action. If you open an example `01.11-load-async-resources.html` in your browser, and open the JavaScript console, you'll see the progress and the result of loading resources asynchronously.

Please note that since we are loading files directly from the browser, you need to have either a local web server installed (see the *Setting up a local web server with Python* recipe or the *Setting up a local web server with Node.js* recipe) or disable some security checks as explained in the *Solving cross-origin-domain error messages in Chrome* recipe or the *Solving cross-origin-domain error messages in Firefox* recipe.

In these first of the five recipes, we'll show you how you can load textures asynchronously with Three.js.

Getting ready

Before looking at the steps in this recipe, you will need to create a number of standard callbacks that can be used by all the different loaders. These callbacks are used to inform you when a resource is loaded, when loading fails and, if available, the progress of the current request.

So for loading resources, we need to define three different callbacks:

- The `onload` callback: Whenever a resource is loaded, this callback will be called with the loaded resource as an argument.

- The `onprogress` callback: Some loaders provide progress during the loading of a resource. At specific intervals, this callback will be called to inform you how much of the resource has been loaded.

- The `onerror` callback: If something goes wrong during the loading of the resource, this callback is used to inform you about the error that occurred.

For all the recipes dealing with asynchronous loading, we'll use the same set of loaders. These loaders just output some information to the console, but you can of course customize these callbacks for your specific use case.

First, we define the `onLoadCallback` function, which is called when a resource is loaded:

```
function onLoadCallback(loaded) {
  // just output the length for arrays and binary blobs
  if (loaded.length) {
    console.log("Loaded", loaded.length);
  } else {
    console.log("Loaded", loaded);
  }
}
```

As you can see from the function definition, we just output the passed argument to the console. The other two callbacks, `onProgressCallback` and `onErrorCallback`, work exactly in the same manner as they are presented:

```
function onProgressCallback(progress) {
  console.log("Progress", progress);
}

function onErrorCallback(error) {
  console.log("Error", error)
}
```

In the following sections and recipes, we'll reference these callbacks when we use the Three.js provided functionality to load resources.

How to do it...

1. To load a texture asynchronously, we use the `loadTexture` function from `THREE.ImageUtils`:

```
function loadTexture(texture) {
    var texture = THREE.ImageUtils.loadTexture(textureURL, null,
        onLoadCallback, onErrorCallback);
    console.log("texture after loadTexture call", texture);
}
```

2. The `loadTexture` function from `THREE.ImageUtils` takes the following four arguments:

   - The first one points to the location of the image you want to load

   - The second one can be used to provide a custom UV mapping (a UV mapping is used to determine which part of a texture to apply to a specific face)

   - The third argument is the callback to be used when the textures have been loaded

   - The final argument is the callback to be used in case of an error

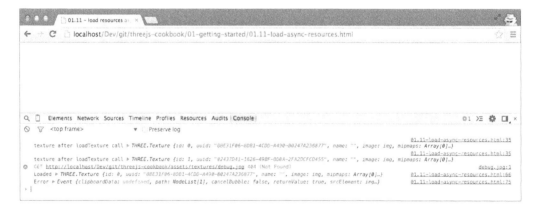

3. Note that the first console output also shows a valid texture object. Three.js does this, so you can immediately assign this object as a texture to a material. The actual image inside the texture, however, is only loaded after the `onLoadCallback` function is called.

How it works...

Three.js provides a nice wrapper to load textures. Internally, Three.js uses the standard way of loading resources from an XMLHTTPRequest web page With an XMLHTTPRequest web page, you can make an HTTP request for a specific resource and process the result. If you don't want to use the Three.js provided functionality, you can also implement an XMLHTTPRequest function yourself.

See also

▸ To run these examples and load resources asynchronously, we need to either run a web server locally, as explained in the *Setting up a local web server using Python* recipe or the *Setting up a web server using Node.js* recipe, or disable some security settings, as explained in the *Solving cross-origin-domain error messages in Chrome* recipe or the *Solving cross-origin-domain error messages in Firefox* recipe.

▸ Alternatively, if you don't want to load resources asynchronously, but wait for all the resources to load, before you initialize your scene you can look at the next *Waiting until resources are loaded* recipe.

Loading models asynchronously

In the *Loading textures asynchronously* recipe, we explained that Three.js offers helper functions to load different types of resources asynchronously. In this recipe, we'll look at how you can use the THREE.JSONLoader object to load models asynchronously.

Getting ready

Before you get started with this recipe, make sure that you've walked through the steps explained in the *Getting ready* section of the *Loading textures asynchronously* recipe. In the following section, we'll reference the JavaScript callbacks defined in the *Getting ready* section of that recipe.

How to do it...

1. Three.js also allows you to easily load external models. The following function shows you how to do this for the JSON models' Three.js uses. The same, however, applies to any of the other model loaders:

```
function loadModel(modelUrl) {
  var jsonLoader = new THREE.JSONLoader();
  jsonLoader.load(modelUrl, onLoadCallback, null);
}
```

2. The `jsonLoader.load` function takes the following three arguments:

    ❏   The first one is the location of the model you want to load

    ❏   The second is the callback to call when the model is successfully loaded

    ❏   The final parameter is the one that we can specify the path from where the texture images should be loaded

3. When we call this function, you'll see the following output on the console:

There is more...

With this approach, the `JSONLoader` object doesn't provide any feedback on how much it has loaded. If you want to load large models, it is nice to know something about the progress. The `JSONLoader` object also provides an alternative way of loading models that also provides progress. In the *Load model asynchronously with progress* recipe, we show you how to load a model and provide feedback on the progress. Besides the `THREE.JSONLoader` object, which loads Three.js' own proprietary models, Three.js is also shipped with a large number of loaders that you can use for other model formats. For an overview of what is provided by Three.js, please refer to `https://github.com/mrdoob/three.js/tree/master/examples/js/loaders`.

Loading models asynchronously with progress

In the previous section, the *Loading models asynchronously* recipe, we loaded a model asynchronously without providing feedback about the progress. In this recipe, we'll explain how you can add progress feedback to that scenario.

Getting started

Before you get started with this recipe, make sure that you've walked through the steps explained in the *Getting ready* section of the *Loading textures asynchronously* recipe. In the following section, we'll reference the JavaScript callbacks defined in the *Getting ready* section of that recipe.

How to do it...

1. To load models and to also show progress, we have to use a different method apart from THREE.JSONLoader. If we use the loadAjaxJSON function, we can also specify a progress callback instead of just the load callback:

```
function loadModelWithProgress(model) {
  var jsonLoader = new THREE.JSONLoader();
  jsonLoader.loadAjaxJSON(jsonLoader, model, onLoadCallback,
    null, onProgressCallback);
}
```

2. If we now load the same model as the previous one, we see the loading progress as follows:

Loading other resources asynchronously with progress

Besides loading specific resources, Three.js also provides a simple helper object to load any type of resource asynchronously. In this recipe, we'll explain how you can use the `THREE.XHRLoader` object to load any type of resource asynchronously.

Getting ready

Before you get started with this recipe, make sure that you've walked through the steps explained in the *Getting ready* section of the *Loading textures asynchronously* recipe. In the following section, we'll reference the JavaScript callbacks defined in the *Getting ready* section of that recipe.

How to do it...

1. The final resource loader we want to show in this recipe is the `THREE.XHRLoader` object. This loader allows you to load any resource that you might need in your Three.js scene:

   ```
   function loadOthers(res) {
       var xhrLoader = new THREE.XHRLoader();
       xhrLoader.load(res, onLoadCallback,
         onProgressCallback, onErrorCallback);
   }
   ```

2. The arguments for the `XHRLoader.load` function should look pretty familiar by now, as it's pretty much the same as for the other loaders. First, we pass the location of the resource we want to load, and then we specify the various callbacks. The output from this function looks like this:

In the preceding screenshot, you can also see the progress while the resource is being loaded.

Waiting until resources are loaded

In the *Load resources asynchronously* recipe, we showed how you can load external Three.js resources asynchronously. For many sites and visualization, loading resources asynchronously is a good approach. Sometimes, however, you want to make sure that all the resources you require in your scene have been loaded beforehand. For instance, when you're creating a game, you might want to load all the data for a specific level beforehand. A common method of loading resources synchronously is nesting the asynchronous callbacks we've seen in the previous recipe. This, however, quickly becomes unreadable and very hard to manage. In this recipe, we'll use a different approach and work with a JavaScript library called Q.

Getting ready

As for all the external libraries that we use, we need to include the Q library in our HTML. You can download the latest version of this library from its GitHub repository at `https://github.com/kriskowal/q`, or use the version provided in the `libs` folder in the sources for this book. To include this library in your HTML page, add the following in the `head` element of your HTML page:

```
<script src="../libs/q.js"></script>
```

In the sources for this chapter, you can also find an example where we load resources synchronously. Open `01.12-wait-for-resources.html` in your browser and open the JavaScript console:

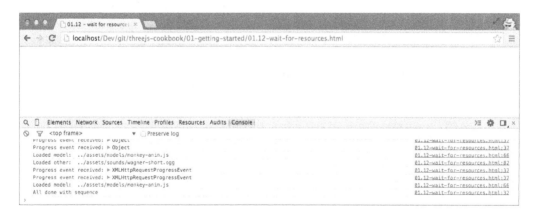

On the console output, you'll see that the required resources and models are loaded one after another.

How to do it...

1. Let's first take a look at what we're aiming for in this recipe. We want to load resources synchronously, using the Q library, in the following manner:

```
loadModel(model)
  .then(function(result) {return loadTexture(texture)})
  .then(function(result) {return loadModel(m)})
  .then(function(result) {return loadTexture(texture)})
  .then(function(result) {return loadOthers(resource)})
  .then(function(result) {return loadModelWithProgress(m)})
  .then(function(result) {return loadModel(model)})
  .then(function(result) {return loadOthers(resource)})
  .then(function(result) {return loadModel(model)})
  .then(function() {console.log("All done with sequence")})
  .catch(function(error) {
    console.log("Error occurred in sequence:",error);
  })
  .progress(function(e){
    console.log("Progress event received:", e);
  });
```

2. What this code fragment means is that:

   1. Firstly, we want to call `loadModel(model)`.

   2. Once the model is loaded, we load, using the `then` function, a texture using the `loadTexture(texture)` function. Once this texture is loaded, we will then load the next resource and so on. In this code fragment, you can also see that we also call a `catch` and a `progress` function. If an error occurs during loading, the function provided to `catch()` will be called. The same goes for `progress()`. If one of the methods wants to provide information about its progress, the function passed into `progress()` will be called.

   3. However, you will then find out that this won't work with the functions from our previous recipe. To get this to work, we have to replace the callbacks from these functions with a special Q construct that is called a deferred function:

```
function loadTexture(texture) {

  var deferred = Q.defer();
  var text = THREE.ImageUtils.loadTexture
  (texture, null, function(loaded) {
    console.log("Loaded texture: ", texture);
```

```
      deferred.resolve(loaded);
    }, function(error) {
      deferred.reject(error);
    });

    return deferred.promise;
}
```

4. In this code snippet, we create a new JavaScript object with the name `deferred`. The `deferred` object will make sure that the results of the callbacks, this time defined as anonymous functions, are returned in such a way that we can use the `then` function we saw at the beginning of this chapter. If the resource is loaded successfully, we use the `deferred.resolve` function to store the result; if the resource was loaded unsuccessfully, we store the error using the `deferred.reject` function.

5. We use the same approach for the `loadModel`, `loadOthers`, and `loadModelWithProgress` functions:

```
function loadModel(model) {

    var deferred = Q.defer();
    var jsonLoader = new THREE.JSONLoader();
    jsonLoader.load(model, function(loaded) {
      console.log("Loaded model: ", model);
      deferred.resolve(loaded);
    }, null);

    return deferred.promise;
}

function loadOthers(res) {
    var deferred = Q.defer();

    var xhrLoader = new THREE.XHRLoader();
    xhrLoader.load(res, function(loaded) {
      console.log("Loaded other: ", res);
      deferred.resolve(loaded);
    }, function(progress) {
      deferred.notify(progress);
    }, function(error) {
      deferred.reject(error);
    });

    return deferred.promise;
}
```

6. In the `loadOthers` function, we are also provided with the progress information. To make sure that the progress callback is handled correctly, we use the `deferred.notify()` function and pass in the `progress` object:

```
function loadModelWithProgress(model) {
  var deferred = Q.defer();

  var jsonLoader = new THREE.JSONLoader();
  jsonLoader.loadAjaxJSON(jsonLoader, model,
  function(model) {
    console.log("Loaded model with progress: ", model);
    deferred.resolve(model)
  }, null,
  function(progress) {
    deferred.notify(progress)
  });

  return deferred.promise;
}
```

7. With these changes, we can now load the resources synchronously.

How it works...

To understand how this works, you have to understand what Q does. Q is a promises library. With promises, you can replace the nested callbacks (also called the Pyramid of doom at `http://calculist.org/blog/2011/12/14/why-coroutines-wont-work-on-the-web/`) with simple steps. The following example for the Q site nicely shows what this accomplishes:

```
step1(function (value1) {
  step2(value1, function(value2) {
    step3(value2, function(value3) {
      step4(value3, function(value4) {
        // Do something with value4
      });
    });
  });
});
```

Using promises, we can flatten this to the following (just like we did in this recipe):

```
Q.fcall(promisedStep1)
then(promisedStep2)
then(promisedStep3)
then(promisedStep4)
then(function (value4) {
  // Do something with value4
})
catch(function (error) {
  // Handle any error from all above steps
})
done();
```

If we were to rewrite the Three.js library, we could have used promises in Three.js internally, but since Three.js already uses callbacks, we had to use the `Q.defer()` function provided by Q to convert these callbacks to promises.

There is more...

We only touched a small part of what is possible with the Q promises library. We used it for synchronous loading, but Q has many other useful features. A very good starting point is the Q wiki available at `https://github.com/kriskowal/q/wiki`.

See also

> ▶ Just like every recipe that loads resources you have to make sure that you run it either with a local web server, see the *Setting up a local web server using Python* recipe or the *Setting up a web server using Node.js* recipe, or disable some security settings (see the *Solving cross-origin-domain error messages in Chrome* recipe or the *Solving cross-origin-domain error messages in Firefox* recipe). If you want to load resources asynchronously, you can take a look at the *Load any resource asynchronously* recipe.

Dragging a file from the desktop to the scene

When you create visualizations, it is a nice feature to let your users provide their own resources. For instance, you might want to let the user specify their own textures or models. You can implement this with a traditional upload form, but with HTML5, you also have the option to let the user drag and drop a resource directly from the desktop. In this recipe, we'll explain how to provide this drag and drop functionality to your users.

Getting ready

The easiest way to prepare for this recipe is by first looking at the example we created for you. Open an example `01.14-drag-file-to-scene.html` in your browser.

[Please note that this only works when running your own web server, or with security exceptions disabled.]

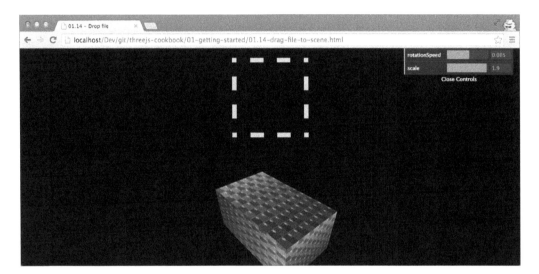

When you drag and drop an image file onto the drop area (the dashed square), you'll immediately see that the texture of the rotating box is changed and the image that you provide is used.

In the following section, we'll explain how you can create this functionality.

How to do it...

To do this, please carry out the following steps:

1. First, we have to set up the correct CSS and define the drop area. To create the dashed drop area, we add the following CSS to the `style` element in the `head` element of our page:

   ```
   #holder { border: 10px dashed #ccc;
   width: 150px; height: 150px;
   margin: 20px auto;}
   #holder.hover { border: 10px dashed #333; #333}
   ```

As you can see in this CSS, we style the HTML element with ID `holder` to have a dashed border. The HTML for the `holder div` element is shown next:

```
<body>
  <div id="holder"></div>
</body>
```

The drop area has been defined, so the next step is to add drag and drop the functionality to it.

2. Then, we have to assign the correct event handlers so that we can respond to the various drag and drop related events.

3. Just as in our previous recipes, we defined a function that contains all the required logic:

```
function setupDragDrop() {
  var holder = document.getElementById('holder');

  holder.ondragover = function() {
    this.className = 'hover';
    return false;
  };
  holder.ondragend = function() {
    this.className = '';
    return false;
  };
  holder.ondrop = function(e) {
    ...
  }
}
```

In this code fragment, we defined three event handlers. The `holder.ondragover` event handler sets the class on the div element to `'hover'`. This way, the user can see that they are allowed to drop the file there. The `holder.ondragend` event handler is called when the user moves away from the drop area. In the event handler, we remove the class of the `div` element. Finally, if the user drops a file in the designated area, the `holder.ondrop` function is called, which we use to process the dropped image.

4. The final step is to process the dropped resource and update the material of our box. When a user drops a file, the following piece of code is executed:

```
this.className = '';
e.preventDefault();

var file = e.dataTransfer.files[0],
var reader = new FileReader();
```

```
reader.onload = function(event) {
  holder.style.background =
  'url(' + event.target.result + ') no-repeat
    center';

  var image = document.createElement('img');
  image.src = event.target.result;
  var texture = new THREE.Texture(image);
  texture.needsUpdate = true;

  scene.getObjectByName('cube').material.map =
    texture;
};
reader.readAsDataURL(file);
return false;
```

The first thing that happens is that we call `e.preventDefault()`. We need to do this to make sure that the browser doesn't just show the file, since that is its normal behavior. Next, we look at the event and retrieve the dropped file using `e.dataTransfer.files[0]`. We can't really do much with the file itself, since Three.js can't work directly with those, so we have to convert it to an `img` element. For this, we use a `FileReader` object. When the reader is done loading, we use the content to create this `img` element. This element is then used to create the `THREE.Texture` object, which we set as material for our box.

How it works...

Drag and drop functionality isn't something that is supported by Three.js out of the box. As we saw in the previous section, we use the standard HTML5 drag and drop related events. A good overview of what events are available can be found in the official HTML5 documentation at `http://www.w3.org/TR/html5/editing.html#drag-and-drop-processing-model`.

One interesting thing to note is the addition of `texture.needsUpdate = true` to the `ondrop` event handler. The reason we need to set this property of the texture is to inform Three.js that our texture has changed. This is needed because WebGL and also Three.js caches textures for performance reasons. If we change a texture, we have to set this property to `true` to make sure that WebGL knows what to render.

2

Geometries and Meshes

In this chapter, we'll cover the following recipes:

- ▶ Rotating an object around its own axis
- ▶ Rotating an object around a point in space
- ▶ Informing Three.js about updates
- ▶ Working with a large number of objects
- ▶ Creating geometries from height maps
- ▶ Pointing an object to another object
- ▶ Writing text in 3D
- ▶ Rendering 3D formulas as 3D geometries
- ▶ Extending Three.js with a custom geometry object
- ▶ Creating a spline curve between two points
- ▶ Creating and exporting a model from Blender
- ▶ Using OBJMTLLoader with multiple materials
- ▶ Applying matrix transformations

Introduction

Three.js comes with a large number of geometries that you can use out of the box. In this chapter, we'll show you some recipes that explain how you can transform these standard geometries. Besides that, we'll also show you how to create your own custom geometries and load geometries from external sources.

You can access all of the example code within all recipes in this cookbook from the GitHub repository created at `https://github.com/josdirksen/threejs-cookbook`.

Rotating an object around its own axis

There are many ways in which you can change the appearance of a mesh. For example, you can change its position, scale, or material. Often, you'll also need to change the rotation of `THREE.Mesh`. In this first recipe on rotation, we'll show you the simplest way to rotate an arbitrary mesh.

Getting ready

To rotate a mesh, we first need to create a scene that contains an object you can rotate. For this recipe, we provide an example, `02.01-rotate-around-axis.html`, that you can open in your browser. When you open this recipe, you'll see something similar to the following screenshot in your browser:

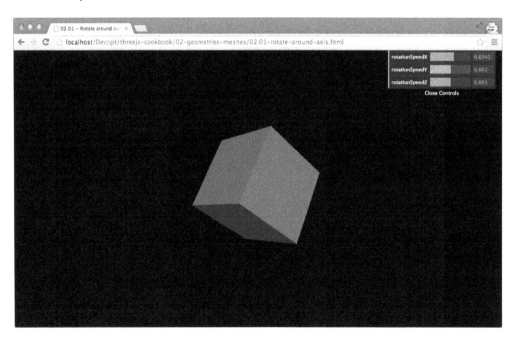

In this demo, you can see a 3D cube slowly rotating around its axis. Using the control GUI in the upper-right corner, you can change the speed at which the object rotates.

How to do it...

To rotate the cube from this example around its axis like we showed you in the previous screenshot, you have to take a couple of steps:

1. For the first step in this recipe, we'll set up the control GUI, as we've shown in *Chapter 1, Getting Started*, in the *Controlling the variables used in the scene* recipe, which you can see in the top-right corner. This time, we'll use the following as the control object:

```
control = new function() {
  this.rotationSpeedX = 0.001;
  this.rotationSpeedY = 0.001;
  this.rotationSpeedZ = 0.001;
};
```

With this `control` object, we'll control the rotation around any of the three axes. We pass this control object to the `addControls` function:

```
function addControls(controlObject) {
  var gui = new dat.GUI();
  gui.add(controlObject, 'rotationSpeedX', -0.2, 0.2);
  gui.add(controlObject, 'rotationSpeedY', -0.2, 0.2);
  gui.add(controlObject, 'rotationSpeedZ', -0.2, 0.2);
}
```

Now when we call the `addControls` function, we'll get the nice GUI that you saw in the screenshot at the beginning of this recipe.

2. Now that we can control the rotation through the GUI, we can use these values to directly set the rotation of our object. In this example, we continuously update the `rotation` property of the mesh, so you get the nice animation you can see in the example. For this, we define the `render` function like this:

```
function render() {
  var cube = scene.getObjectByName('cube');
  cube.rotation.x += control.rotationSpeedX;
  cube.rotation.y += control.rotationSpeedY;
  cube.rotation.z += control.rotationSpeedZ;
  renderer.render(scene, camera);
  requestAnimationFrame(render);
}
```

In this function, you can see that we increase the `rotation` property of the `THREE.Mesh` object with the value set in the control GUI. This results in the animation you can see in the screenshot in the *Getting ready* section. Note that the rotation property is of the `THREE.Vector3` type. This means that you can also set the property in one statement using `cube.rotation.set(x, y, z)`.

How it works...

When you set the rotation property on THREE.Mesh, as we do in this example, Three.js doesn't directly calculate the new positions of the vertices of the geometry. If you print out these vertices to the console, you'll see that regardless of the rotation property, they will stay exactly the same. What happens is that when Three.js actually renders THREE.Mesh in the renderer.render function, it is at that exact point that its exact position and rotation is calculated. So when you translate, rotate, or scale THREE.Mesh, the underlying THREE.Geometry object stays the same.

See also

There are different ways to rotate an object besides the one we showed here:

> ▶ In the upcoming *Rotating an object around a point in space* recipe, we'll show you how you can rotate an object around an arbitrary point in space instead of its own axis, as we showed in this recipe

Rotating an object around a point in space

When you rotate an object using its rotate property, the object is rotated around its own center. In some scenarios, though, you might want to rotate an object around a different object. For instance, when modeling the solar system, you want to rotate the moon around the earth. In this recipe, we'll explain how you can set up Three.js objects in such a way that you can rotate them around one another or any point in space.

Getting ready

For this recipe, we've also provided an example you can experiment with. To load this example, just open 02.02-rotate-around-point-in-space.html in a browser. When you open this file, you'll see something similar to the following screenshot:

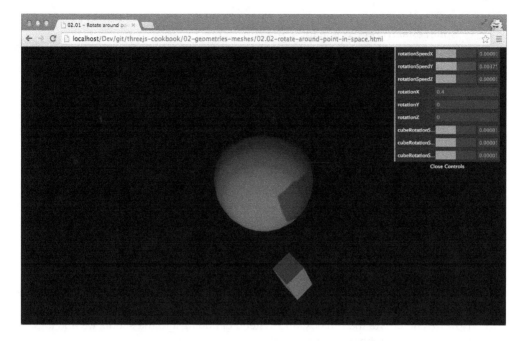

With the controls on the right-hand side, you can rotate various objects around. By changing the **rotationSpeedX**, **rotationSpeedY**, and **rotationSpeedZ** properties, you can rotate the red box around the center of the sphere.

To best demonstrate the rotation of an object around another one, you should rotate around that object's *y* axis. To do this, change the **rotationSpeedY** property.

How to do it...

Rotating an object around another object takes a couple of additional steps compared to the rotation we showed in the previous recipe:

1. Let's first create the central blue sphere you can see in the screenshot. This is the object that we'll rotate the little red box around:

    ```
    // create a simple sphere
    var sphere = new THREE.SphereGeometry(6.5, 20, 20);
    var sphereMaterial = new THREE.MeshLambertMaterial({
      color: 0x5555ff
    });
    ```

```
var sphereMesh = new THREE.Mesh(sphere, spherMaterial);
sphereMesh.receiveShadow = true;
sphereMesh.position.set(0, 1, 0);
scene.add(sphereMesh);
```

So far, there's nothing special in this code snippet. You can see a standard `THREE.Sphere` object from which we create `THREE.Mesh` and add it to the scene.

2. The next step is to define a separate object, which we'll use as the pivot point for our box:

```
// add an object as pivot point to the sphere
pivotPoint = new THREE.Object3D();
sphereMesh.add(pivotPoint);
```

The `pivotPoint` object is a `THREE.Object3D` object. This is the parent object of `THREE.Mesh` and can be added to a scene without a geometry or a material. In this recipe, however, we don't add it to the scene but add it to the sphere we created in step 1. So, if the sphere rotates or changes position, this `pivotPoint` object will also change its position and rotation since we added it as a child to the sphere.

3. Now we can create the red box, and instead of adding it to the scene, we add it to the `pivotPoint` object we just created:

```
// create a box and add to scene
var cubeGeometry = new THREE.BoxGeometry(2, 4, 2);
var cubeMaterial = new THREE.MeshLambertMaterial();
cubeMaterial.color = new THREE.Color('red');
cube = new THREE.Mesh(cubeGeometry, cubeMaterial);
// position is relative to it's parent
cube.position.set(14, 4, 6);
cube.name = 'cube';
cube.castShadow = true;
// make the pivotpoint the cube's parent.
pivotPoint.add(cube);
```

Now we can rotate `pivotPoint` and the cube will follow the rotation of `pivotPoint`. For this recipe, we do this by updating the `rotation` property of `pivotPoint` in the `render` function:

```
function render() {
  renderer.render(scene, camera);
  pivotPoint.rotation.x += control.rotationSpeedX;
  pivotPoint.rotation.y += control.rotationSpeedY;
  pivotPoint.rotation.z += control.rotationSpeedZ;
  requestAnimationFrame(render);
}
```

How it works...

When you create `THREE.Mesh` in Three.js, you normally just add it to `THREE.Scene` and position it individually. In this recipe, however, we've made use of the `THREE.Mesh` feature, which extends from `THREE.Object3D` itself and can also contain children. So when the parent object is rotated, this will also affect the children.

A really interesting aspect of using the approach explained in this recipe is that we can now do a couple of interesting things:

- We can rotate the box itself by updating the `cube.rotation` property like we did in the *Rotating an object around its own axis* recipe
- We can also rotate the box around the sphere by changing the rotation property of the sphere, as we added `pivotPoint` as a child of the sphere mesh
- We can even combine everything, we can rotate `pivotPoint`, `sphereMesh`, and `cube`—all separately—and create very interesting effects

See also

In this recipe, we've used the fact that we can add children to meshes as a way to rotate an object around another object. However, after reading the following recipes, you will learn more about this:

- In the *Rotating an object around its own axis* recipe, we showed you how you can rotate an object around its own axis

Informing Three.js about updates

If you've worked a bit longer with Three.js, you'll probably have noticed that sometimes, it seems that changes you make to a certain geometry doesn't always result in a change onscreen. This is because for performance reasons, Three.js caches some objects (such as the vertices and faces of a geometry) and doesn't automatically detect updates. For these kinds of changes, you'll have to explicitly inform Three.js that something has changed. In this recipe, we'll show you what properties of a geometry are cached and require explicit notification to Three.js to be updated. These properties are:

- `geometry.vertices`
- `geometry.faces`

- ▸ geometry.morphTargets

- ▸ geometry.faceVertexUvs

- ▸ geometry.faces[i].normal and geometry.vertices[i].normal

- ▸ geometry.faces[i].color and geometry.vertices[i].color

- ▸ geometry.vertices[i].tangent

- ▸ geometry.lineDistances

Getting ready

An example is available that allows you to change two properties that require an explicit update: face colors and vertex positions. If you open up the 02.04-update-stuff.html example in your browser, you'll see something similar to the following screenshot:

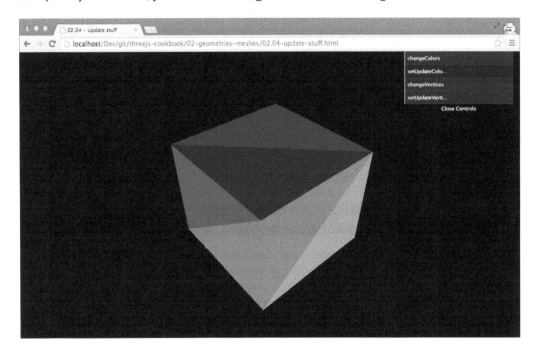

With the menu in the top-right section, you can change two properties of this geometry. With the **changeColors** button, you can set the colors of each individual face to a random color, and with **changeVertices**, you change the position of each vertex of this cube. To apply these changes, you have to push the **setUpdateColors** button or the **setUpdateVertices** button, respectively.

How to do it...

There are a number of properties where you have to explicitly tell Three.js about the update. This recipe will show you how to inform Three.js about all possible changes. Depending on the change you're making, you can jump in at any step of the recipe:

1. Firstly, if you want to add vertices or change the values of an individual vertex of a geometry, you can use the `geometry.vertices` property. Once you've added or changed an element, you need to set the `geometry.verticesNeedUpdate` property to `true`.

2. Following this, you might want the face definition within a geometry to be cached as well, which will require you to use the `geometry.faces` property. This means that when you add `THREE.Face` or update one of the existing properties, you need to set `geometry.elementsNeedUpdate` to `true`.

3. You might then want to morph targets that can be used to create animations, where one set of vertices morph into another set of vertices. This will require the `geometry.morphTargets` property. To do this, when you add a new morph target or update an existing one, you need to set `geometry.morphTargetsNeedUpdate` to `true`.

4. Then, the next step would be to add `geometry.faceVertexUvs`. With this property, you define how textures are mapped onto the geometry. If you add or change elements in this array, you need to set the `geometry.uvsNeedUpdate` property to `true`.

5. You might also want to change the vertices or faces' normals by changing the `geometry.faces[i].normal` and `geometry.vertices[i].normal` properties. When you do this, you have to set `geometry.normalsNeedUpdate` to `true` to inform Three.js about this. Besides the normal, there is also a `geometry.vertices[i].tangent` property. This property is used to calculate shadows and also calculate when textures are rendered. If you make manual changes, you have to set `geometry.tangentsNeedUpdate` to `true`.

6. Next, you can define individual colors on the vertices or the faces. You do this by setting these color properties: `geometry.faces[i].color` and `geometry.vertices[i].color`. Once you've made changes to these properties, you have to set `geometry.colorsNeedUpdate` to `true`.

7. As a final step, you can choose to change textures and materials during runtime. When you want to change one of these properties of a material, you need to set `material.needsUpdate` to `true`: texture, fog, vertex colors, skinning, morphing, shadow map, alpha test, uniforms, and lights. If you want to update the data behind a texture, you need to set the `texture.needsUpdate` flag to `true`.

How it works...

As a summary, steps 1 to 7 apply to geometries and any resulting Three.js objects that are based on geometries.

To get the most performance out of your 3D scene, Three.js caches certain properties and values that usually don't change. Especially when working with the WebGL renderer, a lot of performance is gained by caching all these values. When you set one of these flags to true, Three.js knows, very specifically, which part it needs to update.

See also

▶ There are recipes within this book that are similar to this. If you look at the source code for the *Applying matrix transformations* recipe, you can see that we've used the `verticesNeedUpdate` property after we applied some matrix transformations to the geometry.

Working with a large number of objects

If you have scenes with large numbers of objects, you will start noticing some performance issues. Each of the meshes you create and add to the scene will need to be managed by Three.js, which will cause slowdowns when you're working with thousands of objects. In this recipe, we'll show you how to merge objects together to improve performance.

Getting ready

There are no additional libraries or resources required to merge objects together. We've prepared an example that shows you the difference in performance when using separate objects compared to a merged object. When you open up the `02.05-handle-large-number-of-object.html` example, you can experiment with the different approaches.

You will see something similar to the following screenshot:

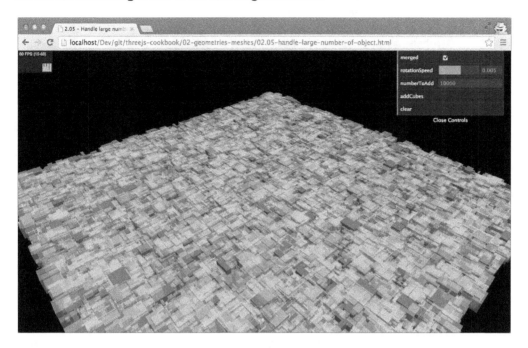

In the preceding screenshot, you can see that with a merged object approach, we still get 60 fps when working with 120,000 objects.

How to do it...

Merging objects in Three.js is very easy. The following code snippet shows you how to merge the objects from the previous example together. The important step here is to create a new `THREE.Geometry()` object named `mergedGeometry` and then create a large number of `BoxGeometry` objects, as shown in the highlighted code sections:

```
var mergedGeometry = new THREE.Geometry();
for (var i = 0; i < control.numberToAdd; i++) {
  var cubeGeometry = new THREE.BoxGeometry(
    4*Math.random(),
    4*Math.random(),
    4*Math.random());
```

```
    var translation = new THREE.Matrix4().makeTranslation(
      100*Math.random()-50,
      0, 100*Math.random()-50);
    cubeGeometry.applyMatrix(translation);
    mergedGeometry.merge(cubeGeometry);
  }
  var mesh = new THREE.Mesh(mergedGeometry,
    new THREE.MeshNormalMaterial({
    opacity: 0.5,
    transparent: true
  }));
  scene.add(mesh);
```

We merge each `cubeGeometry` object into the `mergedGeometry` object by calling the `merge` function. The result is a single geometry that we use to create `THREE.Mesh`, which we add to the scene.

How it works...

When you call the `merge` function on a geometry (let's call it `merged`) and pass in the geometry to be merged (let's call this one `toBeMerged`), Three.js takes the following steps:

1. First, Three.js clones all the vertices from the `toBeMerged` geometry and adds them to the vertices array of the `merged` geometry.

2. Next, it walks through the faces from the `toBeMerged` geometry and creates new faces in the `merged` geometry, copying the original normal and colors.

3. As a final step, it copies the `uv` mapping from `toBeMerged` into the `uv` mapping of the `merged` geometry.

The result is a single geometry that, when added to the scene, looks like multiple geometries.

See also

▶   The main issue with this approach is that it gets harder to color, style, animate, and transform the objects that are merged together independently. For Three.js, after the merge, it counts as a single object. It is, however, possible to apply specific materials to each face. We show you how to do this in the *Using separate materials for faces* recipe in *Chapter 4, Materials and Textures*.

Creating geometries from height maps

With Three.js, it is easy to create your own geometries. For this recipe, we're going to show you how to create your own geometry based on a terrain height map.

Getting ready

To convert a height map into a 3D geometry, we first need to have a height map. In the source files provided with this book, you can find a height map for a portion of the Grand Canyon. The following image shows you what this looks like:

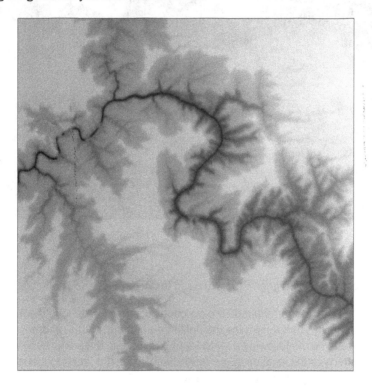

If you're familiar with the Grand Canyon, you'll probably recognize the distinct shape. The final result we'll have at the end of this recipe can be viewed by opening up the `02.06-create-terrain-from-heightmap.html` file in your browser. You'll see something similar to the following screenshot:

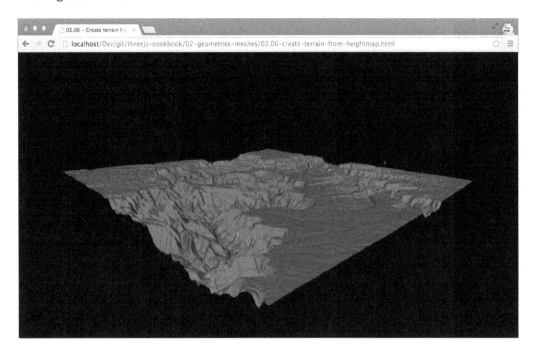

How to do it...

To create a heightmap-based geometry, you need to perform these steps:

1. Before we look at the required Three.js code, we first need to load the image and set some properties that determine the final size and height of the geometry. This can be done by adding the following code snippet and loading the image by setting the `img.src` property to the location of our height map. Once the image is loaded, the `img.onload` function will be called, where we convert the image data to `THREE.Geometry`:

```
var depth = 512;
var width = 512;
var spacingX = 3;
var spacingZ = 3;
var heightOffset = 2;
var canvas = document.createElement('canvas');
canvas.width = 512;
canvas.height = 512;
```

```
var ctx = canvas.getContext('2d');
var img = new Image();
img.src = "../assets/other/grandcanyon.png";
img.onload = function () {...}
```

2. Once the image is loaded in the `onload` function, we need the value of each pixel and convert it to `THREE.Vector3`:

```
// draw on canvas
ctx.drawImage(img, 0, 0);
var pixel = ctx.getImageData(0, 0, width, depth);
var geom = new THREE.Geometry();
var output = [];
for (var x = 0; x < depth; x++) {
  for (var z = 0; z < width; z++) {
    // get pixel
    // since we're grayscale, we only need one element
    // each pixel contains four values RGB and opacity
    var yValue = pixel.data
      [z * 4 + (depth * x * 4)] / heightOffset;
    var vertex = new THREE.Vector3(
      x * spacingX, yValue, z * spacingZ);
    geom.vertices.push(vertex);
  }
}
```

As you can see in this code snippet, we process each of the image pixels, and based on the pixel value, we create `THREE.Vector3`, which we add to the vertices array of our custom geometry.

3. Now that we've defined the vertices, the next step is to use these vertices to create faces:

```
// we create a rectangle between four vertices, and we do
// that as two triangles.
for (var z = 0; z < depth - 1; z++) {
  for (var x = 0; x < width - 1; x++) {
    // we need to point to the position in the array
    // a - - b
    // |  x  |
    // c - - d
    var a = x + z * width;
    var b = (x + 1) + (z * width);
    var c = x + ((z + 1) * width);
    var d = (x + 1) + ((z + 1) * width);
```

```
      var face1 = new THREE.Face3(a, b, d);
      var face2 = new THREE.Face3(d, c, a);
      geom.faces.push(face1);
      geom.faces.push(face2);
   }
}
```

As you can see, each set of four vertices is converted into two `THREE.Face3` elements and added to the `faces` array.

4. Now all we need to do is to let Three.js calculate the vertex and face normals, and we can create `THREE.Mesh` from this geometry and add it to the scene:

```
geom.computeVertexNormals(true);
geom.computeFaceNormals();
var mesh = new THREE.Mesh(geom, new
   THREE.MeshLambertMaterial({color: 0x666666}));
scene.add(mesh);
```

 If you render this scene, you might need to play around with the camera position and the scale of the final mesh to get the correct size.

How it works...

Height maps are a way to embed the height information into an image. Each pixel value of the image represents the relative height measured at that point. In this recipe, we've processed this value, together with its *x* and *y* values, and converted it into a vertex. If we do this for each point, we get an exact 3D representation of the 2D height map. In this case, it results in a geometry that contains 512 * 512 vertices.

There's more...

When we create a geometry from scratch, there are a few interesting things we can add. We can, for instance, color each individual face. This can be done by doing the following:

1. Firstly, add the `chroma` library (you can download the source from https://github.com/gka/chroma.js):

   ```
   <script src="../libs/chroma.min.js"></script>
   ```

2. You can then create a color scale:

   ```
   var scale = chroma.scale(['blue', 'green', red])
     .domain([0, 50]);
   ```

3. Set the face colors based on the height of the face:

```
face1.color = new THREE.Color(
    scale(getHighPoint(geom, face1)).hex());
face2.color = new THREE.Color(
    scale(getHighPoint(geom, face2)).hex())
```

4. Finally, set `vertexColors` of the material to `THREE.FaceColors`. The result looks something like this:

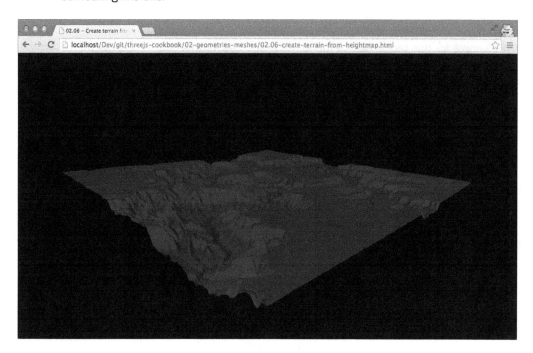

You can also apply different kinds of materials to really create a terrain-like effect. For more information on this, see *Chapter 4, Materials and Textures*, on materials.

See also

▶ In this sample, we've used a height map to create a geometry. You can also use a heightmap as a bump map to add depth detail to a model. We show you how to do this in *Chapter 4, Materials and Textures*, in the *Adding depth to a mesh with bump map* recipe.

Pointing an object to another object

A common requirement for many games is that cameras and other objects follow each other or be aligned to one another. Three.js has standard support for this using the lookAt function. In this recipe, you'll learn how you can use the lookAt function to point an object to look at another object.

Getting ready

The example for this recipe can be found in the sources for this book. If you open 02.07-point-object-to-another.html in your browser, you see something similar to the following screenshot:

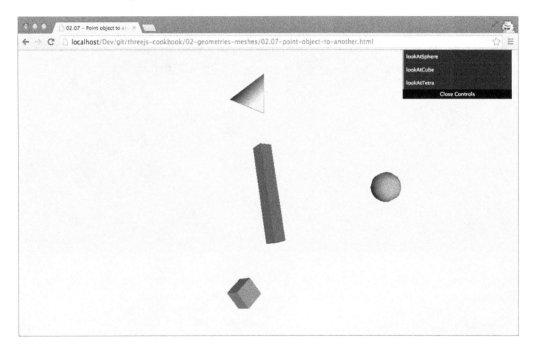

With the menu, you can point the large blue rectangle to look at any of the other meshes in the scene.

How to do it...

Creating the `lookAt` functionality is actually very simple. When you add `THREE.Mesh` to the scene, you can just call its `lookAt` function and point it to the position it should turn to. For the example provided for this recipe, this is done as follows:

```
control = new function() {
  this.lookAtCube = function() {
    cube.lookAt(boxMesh.position);
  };
  this.lookAtSphere = function() {
    cube.lookAt(sphereMesh.position);
  };
  this.lookAtTetra = function() {
    cube.lookAt(tetraMesh.position);
  };
};
```

So when you push the `lookAtSphere` button, the rectangle's `lookAt` function will be called with the sphere's position.

How it works...

Using this code, it is very easy to line up one object with another. With the `lookAt` function, Three.js hides the complexity that is needed to accomplish this. Internally, Three.js uses matrix calculations to determine the rotation it needs to apply to the object to align it correctly with the object you're looking at. The required rotations are then set on the object (to the `rotation` property) and shown in the next render loop.

There's more...

In this example, we showed you how to align one object to another. With Three.js, you can use the same approach for other types of objects. You can point the camera to center on a specific object using `camera.lookAt(object.position)`, and you can also direct a light to point to a specific object using `light.lookAt(object.position)`.

You can also use `lookAt` to follow a moving object. Just add the `lookAt` code in the render loop, and the object will follow the moving object around.

See also

▶ The lookAt function uses matrix calculations internally. In the last recipe of this chapter, *Applying matrix transformations*, we show you how you can use matrix calculations to accomplish other effects.

Writing text in 3D

A cool feature of Three.js is that it allows you to write text in 3D. With a couple of simple steps, you can use any text, even with font support, as a 3D object in your scene. This recipe shows you how to create 3D text and explains the different configuration options available to style the result.

Getting ready

To work with 3D text, we need to include some additional JavaScript in our pages. Three.js provides a number of fonts you can use, and they are provided as individual JavaScript files. To add all the available fonts, include the following scripts:

```
<script src="../assets/fonts/gentilis_bold.typeface.js">
</script>
<script src="../assets/fonts/gentilis_regular.typeface.js">
</script>
<script src="../assets/fonts/optimer_bold.typeface.js"></script>
<script src="../assets/fonts/optimer_regular.typeface.js">
</script>
<script src="../assets/fonts/helvetiker_bold.typeface.js">
</script>
<script src="../assets/fonts/helvetiker_regular.typeface.js">
</script>
<script src=
  "../assets/fonts/droid/droid_sans_regular.typeface.js">
</script>
<script src=
  "../assets/fonts/droid/droid_sans_bold.typeface.js">
</script>
<script src=
  "../assets/fonts/droid/droid_serif_regular.typeface.js">
</script>
<script src="..
  /assets/fonts/droid/droid_serif_bold.typeface.js">
</script>
```

We've already done this in the `02.09-write-text-in-3D.html` example. If you open this in your browser, you can play around with the various fonts and properties available when creating text in Three.js. When you open the specified example you will see something similar to the following screenshot:

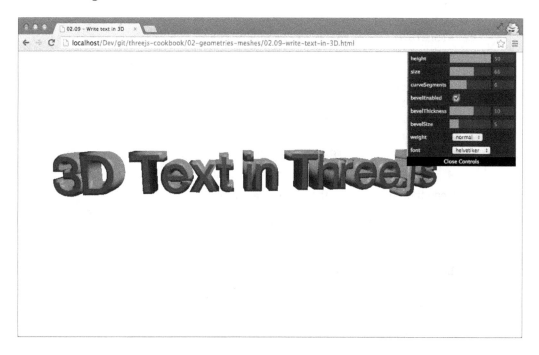

How to do it...

Creating 3D text in Three.js is very easy. All you have to do is create `THREE.TextGeometry` like this:

```
var textGeo = new THREE.TextGeometry(text, params);
textGeo.computeBoundingBox();
textGeo.computeVertexNormals();
```

The `text` property is the text we want to write, and `params` define how the text is rendered. The `params` object can have many different parameters, which you can look at in more detail in the *How it works...* section.

In our example, however, we've used the following set of parameters (which point to the GUI in the top-right section):

```
var params = {
  material: 0,
  extrudeMaterial: 1,
  bevelEnabled: control.bevelEnabled,
  bevelThickness: control.bevelThickness,
  bevelSize: control.bevelSize,
  font: control.font,
  style: control.style,
  height: control.height,
  size: control.size,
  curveSegments: control.curveSegments
};
```

This geometry can then be added to the scene like any other geometry:

```
var material = new THREE.MeshFaceMaterial([
  new THREE.MeshPhongMaterial({
    color: 0xff22cc,
    shading: THREE.FlatShading
  }), // front
  new THREE.MeshPhongMaterial({
  color: 0xff22cc,
  shading: THREE.SmoothShading
  }) // side
]);
var textMesh = new THREE.Mesh(textGeo, material);
textMesh.position.x = -textGeo.boundingBox.max.x / 2;
textMesh.position.y = -200;
textMesh.name = 'text';
scene.add(textMesh);
```

There is one thing you need to take into account when working with `THREE.TextGeometry` and materials. As you can see from the code snippet, we add two material objects instead of one. The first material is applied to the front of rendered text, and the second one is applied to the side of the rendered text. If you just pass in one material, it is applied to both the front and the side.

How it works...

As mentioned, there is a variety of different parameters:

Parameter	Description
`height`	The height property defines the depth of the text, in other words, how far the text is extruded to make it 3D.
`size`	With this property, you set the size of the final text.
`curveSegments`	If a character has curves (for example, the letter *a*), this property defines how smooth the curves will be.
`bevelEnabled`	A bevel provides a smooth transition from the front of the text to the side. If you set this value to true, a bevel will be added to the rendered text.
`bevelThickness`	If you've set `bevelEnabled` to `true`, it defines how deep the bevel is.
`bevelSize`	If you've set `bevelEnabled` to `true`, it defines how high the bevel is.
`weight`	This is the weight of the font (normal or bold).
`font`	This is the name of the font to be used.
`material`	When an array of materials is provided, this should contain the index of the material to be used for the front.
`extrudeMaterial`	When an array of materials is provided, this should contain the index of the materials to be used for the side.

When you create `THREE.TextGeometry`, Three.js internally uses `THREE.ExtrudeGeometry` to create the 3D shapes. `THREE.ExtrudeGeometry` works by taking a 2D shape and extrudes it along the *Z* axis to make it 3D. To create a 2D shape from a text string, Three.js uses the JavaScript files that we included in the *Getting ready* section of this recipe. These JavaScript files, based on `http://typeface.neocracy.org/fonts.html`, allow you to render text as 2D paths, which we then can convert to 3D.

There's more...

If you want to use a different font, you can convert your own fonts at `http://typeface.neocracy.org/fonts.html`. All you need to do to use these fonts is include them on your page and pass in the correct `name` and `style` values as parameters to `THREE.TextGeometry`.

Rendering 3D formulas as 3D geometries

Three.js offers many different ways to create geometries. You can use the standard Three.js objects, such as `THREE.BoxGeometry` and `THREE.SphereGeometry`, create geometries completely from scratch, or just load models created by external 3D modeling programs. In this recipe, we will show you another way to create geometries. This recipe shows you how to create geometries based on math formulas.

Getting ready

For this recipe, we'll be using the `THREE.ParametricGeometry` object. As this is available from the standard Three.js distribution, there is no need to include additional JavaScript files.

To see the end result of this recipe, you can look at `02.10-create-parametric-geometries.html`, you'll see something similar to the following screenshot:

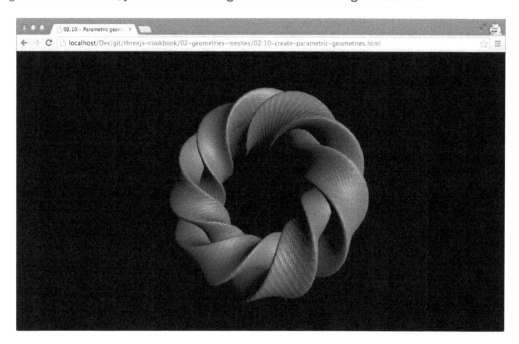

This figure shows you a *Gray's Kleinbottle*, which is rendered based on a couple of simple math formulas.

How to do it...

Generating geometries using math formulas with Three.js is very easy and only takes two steps:

1. The first thing we need to do is create the function that will create the geometry for us. This function will take two arguments: u and v. When Three.js uses this function to generate a geometry, it will call this function with u and v values, starting at 0 and ending at 1. For each of these u and v combinations, this function should return a `THREE.Vector3` object, which represents a single vertex in the final geometry. The function that creates the figure you saw in the previous section is shown next:

    ```
    var paramFunction = function(u, v) {
      var a = 3;
      var n = 3;
      var m = 1;
      var u = u * 4 * Math.PI;
      var v = v * 2 * Math.PI;
      var x = (a + Math.cos(n * u / 2.0)
        * Math.sin(v) - Math.sin(n * u / 2.0)
        * Math.sin(2 * v)) * Math.cos(m * u / 2.0);
      var y = (a + Math.cos(n * u / 2.0)
        * Math.sin(v) - Math.sin(n * u / 2.0)
        * Math.sin(2 * v)) * Math.sin(m * u / 2.0);
      var z = Math.sin(n * u / 2.0)
        * Math.sin(v) + Math.cos(n * u / 2.0)
        * Math.sin(2 * v);
      return new THREE.Vector3(x, y, z);
    }
    ```

    You can provide functions of your own as long as you return a new `THREE.Vector3` object for each value of u and v.

2. Now that we've got the function that creates our geometry, we can use this function to create `THREE.ParametricGeometry`:

    ```
    var geom = new THREE.ParametricGeometry(paramFunction
      , 100, 100);
    var mat = new THREE.MeshPhongMaterial({
      color: 0xcc3333a,
      side: THREE.DoubleSide,
      shading: THREE.FlatShading
    });
    var mesh = new THREE.Mesh(geom, mat);
    scene.add(mesh);
    ```

You can clearly see that three arguments have been applied to the constructor of `THREE.ParametricObject`. This is discussed in more detail in the *How it works...* section.

All you have to do after creating the geometry is create `THREE.Mesh` and add it to the scene just like any other Three.js object.

How it works...

From step 2 in the preceding code snippet, you can see that we provide three arguments to the constructor of `THREE.ParametricObject`. The first one is the function we showed you in step 1, the second determines in how many steps we divide the `u` parameter, and the third one determines in how many steps we divide the `v` parameter. The higher the number, the more vertices will be created, and the smoother the final geometry will look. Note, though, that a very high amount of vertices has an adverse effect on performance.

When you create `THREE.ParametricGeometry`, Three.js will call the provided function a number of times. The amount of times the function is called is based on the second and third parameters. This results in a set of `THREE.Vector3` objects, which are then automatically combined into faces. This results in a geometry that you can use just like any other geometry.

There's more...

There are many different things you can do with these kinds of geometries than what is shown in this recipe. In the `02.10-create-parametric-geometries.html` source file, you can find a couple of other functions that create interesting-looking geometries such as the one shown in the following screenshot:

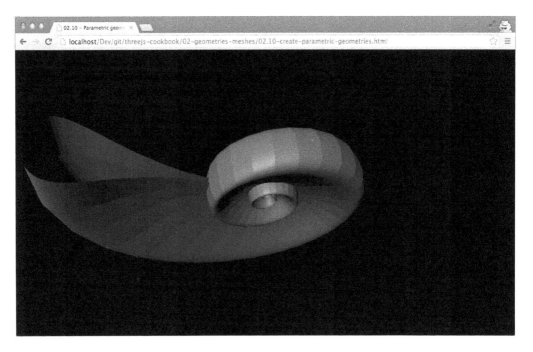

Extending Three.js with a custom geometry object

In the recipes you've seen so far, we create Three.js objects from scratch. We either build a new geometry from scratch with vertices and faces, or we reuse an existing one and configure it for our purpose. While this is good enough for most scenarios, it isn't the best solution when you need to maintain a large code base with lots of different geometries. In Three.js, you create geometries by just instantiating a `THREE.GeometryName` object. In this recipe, we'll show you how you can create a custom geometry object and instantiate it just like the other Three.js objects.

Getting ready

The example that you can use to experiment with this recipe can be found in the provided sources. Open up `02.11-extend-threejs-with-custom-geometry.html` in your browser to see the final result, which will be similar to the following screenshot:

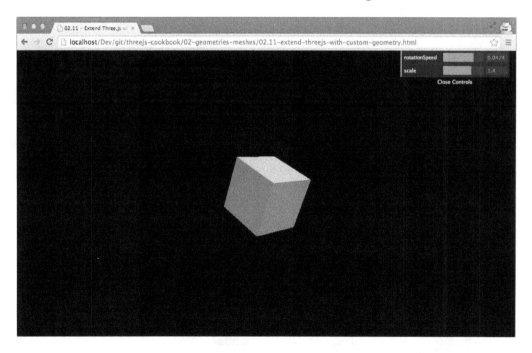

In this screenshot, you see a single rotating cube. This cube is created as a custom geometry and can be instantiated by using new `THREE.FixedBoxGeometry()`. In the upcoming section, we'll explain how to accomplish this.

How to do it...

Extending Three.js with a custom geometry is fairly easy and only takes a couple of simple steps:

1. The first thing we need to do is create a new JavaScript object that contains the logic and properties of our new Three.js geometry. For this recipe, we'll create `FixedBoxGeometry`, which acts exactly like `THREE.BoxGeometry` but uses the same values for its height, width, and depth. For this recipe, we create this new object in the `setupCustomObject` function:

```javascript
function setupCustomObject() {
  // First define the object.
  THREE.FixedBoxGeometry = function ( width, segments) {
    // first call the parent constructor
    THREE.Geometry.call( this );
    this.width = width;
    this.segments = segments;
    // we need to set
    //    - vertices in the parent object
    //    - faces in the parent object
    //    - uv mapping in the parent object
    // normally we'd create them here ourselves
    // in this case, we just reuse the once
    // from the boxgeometry.
    var boxGeometry = new THREE.BoxGeometry(
      this.width,
      this.width,
      this.width, this.segments, this.segments);
    this.vertices = boxGeometry.vertices;
    this.faces = boxGeometry.faces;
    this.faceVertexUvs = boxGeometry.faceVertexUvs;
  }
  // define that FixedBoxGeometry extends from
  // THREE.Geometry
  THREE.FixedBoxGeometry.prototype
    = Object.create( THREE.Geometry.prototype );
}
```

In this function, we define a new JavaScript object using `THREE.FixedBoxGeometry = function ( width, segments) {..}`. In this function, we first call the constructor of the parent object (`THREE.Geometry.call( this )`). This makes sure that all properties are correctly initialized. Next, we wrap an existing `THREE.BoxGeometry` object and use information from that object to set `vertices`, `faces`, and `faceVertexUvs` for our own custom object.

Finally, we need to tell JavaScript that our `THREE.BoxGeometry` object extends from `THREE.Geometry`. This is done by setting a prototype property of `THREE.FixedBoxGeometry` to `Object.create(THREE.Geometry.prototype)`.

2. After `setupCustomObject()` is called, we can now use the same approach to create this object like we do for the other Three.js-provided geometries:

```
var cubeGeometry = new THREE.FixedBoxGeometry(3, 5);
var cubeMaterial = new THREE.MeshNormalMaterial();
var cube = new THREE.Mesh(cubeGeometry, cubeMaterial);
scene.add(cube);
```

At this point, we've created a custom Three.js geometry that you can instantiate just like the standard geometries provided by Three.js.

How it works...

In this recipe, we use one of the standard ways JavaScript provides to create objects that inherit from other objects. We defined the following:

```
THREE.FixedBoxGeometry.prototype
   = Object.create( THREE.Geometry.prototype );
```

This code fragment tells JavaScript that `THREE.FixedBoxGeometry` is created, it inherits all the properties and functions from `THREE.Geometry`, which has its own constructor. This is the reason we also add the following call to our new object:

```
THREE.Geometry.call( this );
```

This calls the constructor of the `THREE.Geometry` object whenever our own custom object is created.

There is more to prototype-based inheritance than what's explained in this short recipe. If you want to know more about prototype-based inheritance, the Mozilla guys have a great explanation on how inheritance using the prototype property works at `https://developer.mozilla.org/en-US/docs/Web/JavaScript/Guide/Inheritance_and_the_prototype_chain`.

There's more...

In this recipe, we've wrapped an existing Three.js object to create our custom object. You can also apply this same approach for objects that are created completely from scratch. For instance, you can create `THREE.TerrainGeometry` from the JavaScript code we used in the *Creating geometries from heightmaps* recipe to create a 3D terrain.

Creating a spline curve between two points

When you create visualizations and, for instance, want to visualize the flight path of an airplane, drawing a curve between the start and end point is a good approach. In this recipe, we'll show you how you can do this using the standard `THREE.TubeGeometry` object.

Getting ready

When you open the example for this recipe, `02.12-create-spline-curve.html`, you can see a tube geometry that curves from start to end:

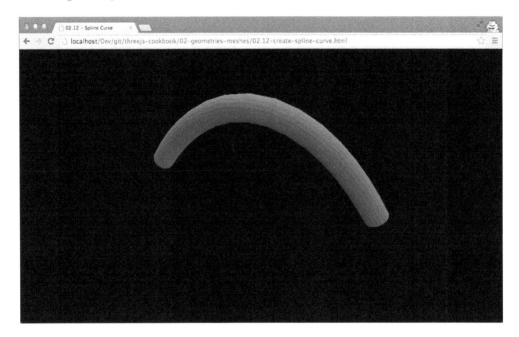

In the upcoming section, we'll explain step by step how to create this curve.

How to do it...

To create a curved spline, like what is shown in the preceding example, we need to take a couple of simple steps:

1. The first thing we need to do is define some constants for this curve:

   ```
   var numPoints = 100;
   var start = new THREE.Vector3(-20, 0, 0);
   var middle = new THREE.Vector3(0, 30, 0);
   var end = new THREE.Vector3(20, 0, 0);
   ```

The `numPoints` object defines how many vertices we'll use to define the curve and the number of segments we use when rendering the tube. The `start` vector defines the position where we want to start the curve, the `end` vector determines the end point of our curve, and finally, the `middle` vector defines the height and center point of our curve. If we, for instance, set `numPoints` to 5, we get a different kind of curve.

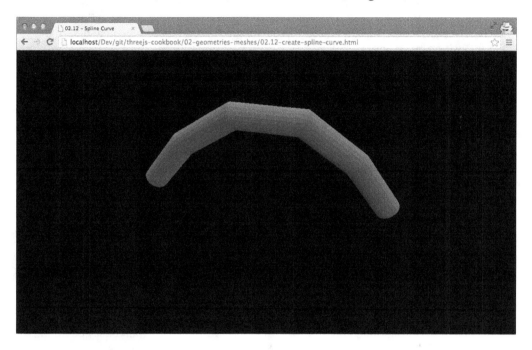

2. Now that we've got the `start`, `end`, and `middle` vectors, we can use them to create a nice curve. For this, we can use an object provided by Three.js, called `THREE.QuadraticBezierCurve3`:

```
var curveQuad = new THREE.QuadraticBezierCurve3(
    start, middle, end);
```

Based on this `curveQuad`, we can now create a simple tube geometry.

3. To create a tube, we use `THREE.TubeGeometry` and pass in `curveQuad`, which we created in the previous step:

```
var tube = new THREE.TubeGeometry(
    curveQuad, numPoints, 2, 20, false);
var mesh = new THREE.Mesh(tube, new
    THREE.MeshNormalMaterial({
    opacity: 0.6,
    transparent: true
}));
scene.add(mesh);
```

How it works...

The `QuadraticBezierCurve3` object we created in this recipe has a number of different functions (`getTangentAt` and `getPointAt`) that determine the location somewhere along the path. These functions return information based on the `start`, `middle`, and `end` vectors passed in to the constructor. When we pass `QuadraticBezierCurve3` into `THREE.TubeGeometry`, `THREE.TubeGeometry` uses the `getTangentAt` function to determine where to position its vertices.

There's more...

In this recipe, we used `THREE.QuadraticBezierCurve3` to create our spline. Three.js also provides a `THREE.CubicBezierCurve3` and `THREE.SplineCurve3` curve, which you can use to define these kinds of splines. You can find more information on the differences between a quadratic Bezier curve and a cubic Bezier curve at `http://stackoverflow.com/questions/18814022/what-is-the-difference-between-cubic-bezier-and-quadratic-bezier-and-their-use-c`.

Creating and exporting a model from Blender

Blender, which you can download from `http://www.blender.org/download/`, is a great tool to create 3D models and has excellent support for Three.js. With the right plugin, Blender can export models directly into Three.js' own JSON format, which can then easily be added to your scene.

Getting ready

Before we can use the JSON exporter in Blender, we first need to install the plugin in Blender. To install the plugin, take the following steps:

1. The first thing you need to do is get the latest version of the plugin. We've added this to the source code of this book. You can find this plugin in the `assets/plugin` folder. In that directory, you'll find a single directory with the `io_mesh_threejs` name. To install the plugin, just copy this complete directory to the plugin location of Blender. As Blender is multiplatform, depending on your OS, this plugin directory might be stored in a different location.

2. For Windows, copy the `io_mesh_threejs` directory to `C:\Users\USERNAME\AppData\Roaming\Blender Foundation\Blender\2.70a\scripts\addons`.

3. For OS X users, it depends on where you installed Blender (extracted the ZIP file). You should copy the `io_mesh_threejs` directory to `/location/of/extracted/zip/blender.app/Contents/MacOS/2.6X/scripts/addons`.

4. Finally, for Linux users, copy the `io_mesh_threejs` directory to `/home/USERNAME/.config/blender/2.70a/scripts/addons`.

5. If you've installed Blender through apt-get, you should copy the `io_mesh_threejs` directory to `/usr/lib/blender/scripts/addons`.

6. The next step is to enable the Three.js plugin. If Blender is already running, restart it and open **User Preferences**. You can find this by navigating to **File | User Preferences**. In the screen that opens, select the **Addons** tab, which lists all the plugins that are available.

7. At this point, the Three.js plugin is enabled. To make sure it stays enabled when you restart Blender, click on the **Save User Settings** button. Now, close this window and if you navigate to **File | Export**, you should see a Three.js export function as shown in the following screenshot:

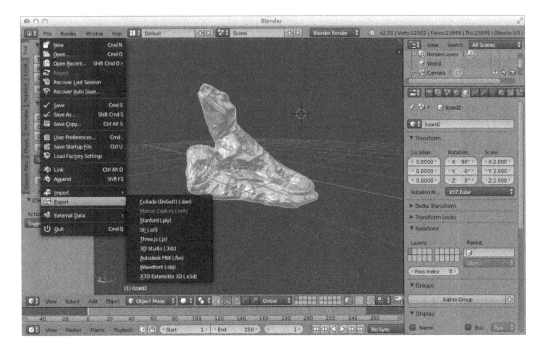

Now, let's look at the rest of this recipe and see how we can export a model from Blender and load it in Three.js.

How to do it...

To export a model from Blender, we first have to create one. Instead of loading an existing one, in this recipe, we'll create one from scratch, export it, and load it in Three.js:

1. To start off, when you open Blender, you'll see a cube. First, we delete this cube. You do this by pressing *x* and clicking on delete in the pop up.

2. Now, we'll create a simple geometry that we can export with the Three.js plugin we installed. For this, click on **Add** in the bottom menu and select **Monkey**, as shown in the following screenshot:

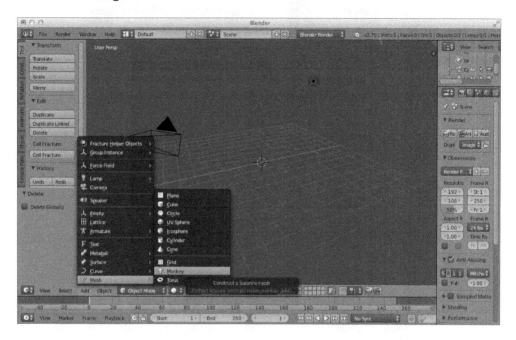

Now, you should have an empty scene in Blender with monkey geometry in the middle:

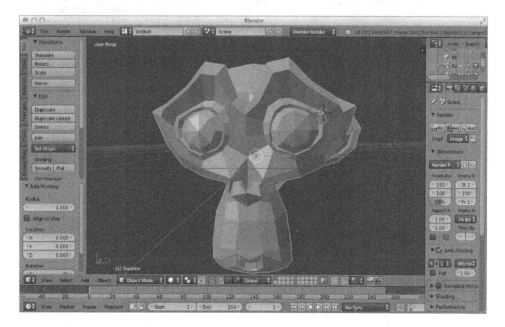

3. We can export this monkey to Three.js using the plugin we installed in the *Getting ready* section of this recipe. To do this, navigate to **Export | Three.js** in the **File** menu. This opens up the export dialog where you can determine the directory to export the model to. In this **Export** dialog, you can also set some additional Three.js-specific export properties, but the default properties usually are okay. For this recipe, we exported the model as `monkey.js`.

4. At this point, we've exported the model and can now load it with Three.js. To load the model, we only have to add the following JavaScript to the *Getting started with the WebGL renderer* recipe we showed in *Chapter 1, Getting Started*:

```
function loadModel() {
  var loader = new THREE.JSONLoader();
  loader.load("../assets/models/monkey.js",
    function(model, material) {
    var mesh = new THREE.Mesh(model, material[0]);
    mesh.scale = new THREE.Vector3(3,3,3);
    scene.add(mesh);
  });
}
```

The result is a rotating monkey, which we created in Blender, rendered by Three.js as shown in the following screenshot:

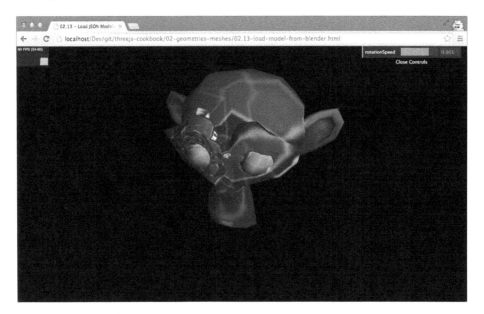

See also

There are a few recipes that you will benefit from reading:

- In the *Using OBJMTLLoader with multiple materials* recipe, we use a different format, which we load into Three.js

- In *Chapter 7*, *Animation and Physics*, where we look at animations, we'll revisit the Three.js exporter plugin when we're working with skeleton-based animations in the *Animating with skeletons* recipe.

Using OBJMTLLoader with multiple materials

Three.js provides a number of standard geometries that you can use to create your 3D scenes. Complex models, however, are more easily created in dedicated 3D modeling applications such as Blender or 3ds Max. Luckily, though, Three.js has great support for a large number of export formats, so you can easily load models created in these kinds of packages. A standard that is widely supported is the OBJ format. With this format, the model is described with two different files: an .obj file that defines the geometries and an .mtl file that defines the material. In this recipe, we'll show you the steps you need to take to successfully load a model using OBJMTLLoader, which is provided by Three.js.

Getting ready

To load models described in the .obj and .mtl format, we need to first include the correct JavaScript file, as these JavaScript objects aren't included in the standard Three.js JavaScript file. So, within the head section, you need to add the following script tags:

```
<script src="../libs/MTLLoader.js"></script>
<script src="../libs/OBJMTLLoader.js"></script>
```

The model we use in this example is a Lego mini figure. In Blender, the original model looks like this:

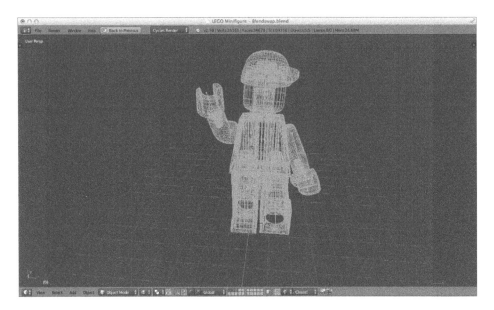

You can see the final model by opening up `02.14-use-objmtlloader-with-multiple-materials.html` in your browser. The following screenshot shows you what the renderer model looks like:

Let's walk you through the steps you need to take to load such a model.

How to do it...

Before we load the model in Three.js, we first need to check whether the correct paths are defined in the .mtl file. So, the first thing we need to do is open the .mtl file in a text editor:

1. When you open the .mtl file for this example, you'll see the following:

```
newmtl Cap
Ns 96.078431
Ka 0.000000 0.000000 0.000000
Kd 0.990000 0.120000 0.120000
Ks 0.500000 0.500000 0.500000
Ni 1.000000
d 1.00000
illum 2
newmtl Minifig
Ns 874.999998
Ka 0.000000 0.000000 0.000000
Kd 0.800000 0.800000 0.800000
Ks 0.200000 0.200000 0.200000
Ni 1.000000
d 1.000000
illum 2
map_Kd ../textures/Mini-tex.png
```

This .mtl file defines two materials: one for the body of the mini figure and one for its cap. What we need to check is the map_Kd property. This property needs to contain the relative path, from where the .obj file is loaded to where Three.js can find the textures. In our example, this path is: .../textures/Mini-tex.png.

2. Now that we've made sure the .mtl file contains the correct references, we can load the model using THREE.OBJMTLLoader:

```
var loader = new THREE.OBJMTLLoader();
// based on model from:
// http://www.blendswap.com/blends/view/69499
loader.load("../assets/models/lego.obj",
"../assets/models/lego.mtl",
function(obj) {
  obj.translateY(-3);
  obj.name='lego';
  scene.add(obj);
});
```

As you can see, we pass both .obj and .mtl files into the load function. The final argument of this load function is a callback function. This callback function will be called when the model is done loading.

3. At this point, you can do everything you want with the loaded model. In this example, we add the scaling and rotation functionality through the menu in the top-right section and apply these properties to the `render` function:

```
function render() {
  renderer.render(scene, camera);
  var lego = scene.getObjectByName('lego');
  if (lego) {
    lego.rotation.y += control.rotationSpeed;
    lego.scale.set(
      control.scale, control.scale, control.scale);
  }
  requestAnimationFrame(render);
}
```

How it works...

The `.obj` and `.mtl` file formats are well-documented formats. `OBJMTLLoader` parses the information from these two files and creates geometries and materials based on that information. It uses the `.obj` file to determine an object's geometry and uses information from the `.mtl` file to determine the material, which is `THREE.MeshLambertMaterial` in this case, to be used for each geometry.

Three.js then combines these together into `THREE.Mesh` objects and returns a single `THREE.Object3D` object that contains all the parts of the `Lego` figure, which you can then add to the scene.

There's more...

In this recipe, we showed you how to load objects defined in the `.obj` and `.mtl` format. Besides this format, Three.js also supports a wide range of other formats. For a good overview of the file formats supported by Three.js, refer to this directory on Three.js' GitHub repository: `https://github.com/mrdoob/three.js/tree/master/examples/js/loaders`.

See also

▶ For this recipe, we assume we have a complete model in the correct format. If you want to create a model from scratch, a good open source 3D modeling tool is Blender. The the *Creating and Exporting a model from a Blender* recipe, explains how to create a new model in Blender and export it so that Three.js can load it.

Applying matrix transformations

In the first couple of recipes in this chapter, we used the `rotation` property and applied translations to get the desired rotational effect. Behind the scenes, Three.js uses matrix transformations to modify the shape and position of the mesh or the geometry. Three.js also provides the functionality to apply custom matrix transformations directly to a geometry or a mesh. In this recipe, we'll show you how you can apply your own custom matrix transformations directly to a Three.js object.

Getting ready

To view this recipe in action and experiment with the various transformations, open the `02.15-apply-matrix-transformations.html` example in your browser. You'll be presented with the following simple Three.js scene:

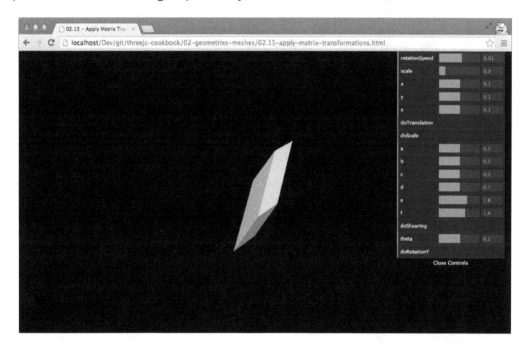

In this scene, you can use the menu on the right-hand side to apply various transformations directly to the spinning cube. In the next section, we'll show you the steps you need to take to create this yourself.

How to do it...

Creating your own matrix transformation is very simple.

1. Firstly, let's look at the code that gets called when you click on the **doTranslation** button:

```
this.doTranslation = function() {
    // you have two options, either use the
    // helper function provided by three.js
    // new THREE.Matrix4().makeTranslation(3,3,3);
    // or do it yourself
    var translationMatrix = new THREE.Matrix4(
        1, 0, 0, control.x,
        0, 1, 0, control.y,
        0, 0, 1, control.z,
        0, 0, 0, 1
    );
    cube.applyMatrix(translationMatrix);
    // or do it on the geometry
    // cube.geometry applyMatrix(translationMatrix);
    // cube.geometry.verticesNeedUpdate = true;
}
```

   As you can see in the code, creating a custom matrix transformation is very easy and requires only the following steps.

2. First, you instantiate a new `THREE.Matrix4` object and pass in the values of the matrix as arguments to the constructor.

3. Next, you use the `applyMatrix` function of either `THREE.Mesh` or `THREE.Geometry` to apply the transformation to that specific object.

4. If you apply this on `THREE.Geometry` you have to set the `verticesNeedUpdate` property to `true`, as vertex changes aren't automatically propagated to the renderer (see the *Informing Three.js about updates* recipe).

How it works

The transformations used in this recipe are based on matrix calculations. Matrix calculations by themselves are a rather complex subject. If you're interested in more information on how matrix calculations work and how they can be used for all different kinds of transformations, a good explanation can be found at `http://www.matrix44.net/cms/notes/opengl-3d-graphics/basic-3d-math-matrices`.

There's more...

In the example for this chapter, you can apply a couple of transformations to the rotating cube. The following code snippet shows you the matrices used for these transformations:

```
this.doScale = function() {
  var scaleMatrix = new THREE.Matrix4(
    control.x, 0, 0, 0,
    0, control.y, 0, 0,
    0, 0, control.z, 0,
    0, 0, 0, 1
  );
  cube.geometry.applyMatrix(scaleMatrix);
  cube.geometry.verticesNeedUpdate = true;
}
this.doShearing = function() {
  var scaleMatrix = new THREE.Matrix4(
    1, this.a, this.b, 0,
    this.c, 1, this.d, 0,
    this.e, this.f, 1, 0,
    0, 0, 0, 1
  );
  cube.geometry.applyMatrix(scaleMatrix);
  cube.geometry.verticesNeedUpdate = true;
}
this.doRotationY = function() {
  var c = Math.cos(this.theta),
  s = Math.sin(this.theta);
  var rotationMatrix = new THREE.Matrix4(
    c, 0, s, 0,
    0, 1, 0, 0, -s, 0, c, 0,
    0, 0, 0, 1
  );
  cube.geometry.applyMatrix(rotationMatrix);
  cube.geometry.verticesNeedUpdate = true;
}
```

In this recipe, we created the matrix transformations from scratch. Three.js, however, also provides some helper functions in the `Three.Matrix4` class that you can use to more easily create these kinds of matrices:

- `makeTranslation(x, y, z)`: This function returns a matrix, which when applied to a geometry or a mesh, translates the object by the specified x, y, and z values

- `makeRotationX(theta)`: This returns a matrix that can be used to rotate a mesh or geometry by a certain amount of radians along the *x* axis

- `makeRotationY(theta)`: This is the same as the previous one—this time around the *y* axis

- `makeRotationZ(theta)`: This is the same as the previous one—this time around the *z* axis

- `makeRotationAxis(axis, angle)`: This returns a rotation matrix based on the provided axis and angle

- `makeScale(x, y, z)`: This function returns a matrix that can be used to scale an object along any of the three axes

See also

We've also used matrix transformations in other recipes in this chapter:

- In the first two recipes, *Rotating an object around its own axis* and *Rotating an object around a point in space*, the actual rotation is applied using a matrix transformation

- In the *Rotating an object around its own axis* recipe, we used the helper functions from the `THREE.Matrix4` object to rotate an object around its axis

3
Working with the Camera

In this chapter, we'll cover the following recipes:

- ▸ Making the camera follow an object
- ▸ Zooming the camera to an object
- ▸ Using a perspective camera
- ▸ Using an orthographic camera
- ▸ Creating a 2D overlay
- ▸ Rotating the camera around a scene
- ▸ Matching the rendered view to a resized browser
- ▸ Converting world coordinates to screen coordinates
- ▸ Selecting an object in the scene

Introduction

One of the most important objects in Three.js is the camera. With the camera, you define what part of the scene will be rendered and how the information will be projected on the screen. In this chapter, we'll show you a number of recipes that will allow you to add more complex camera functionality to your Three.js applications.

Making the camera follow an object

When you are creating games or visualizations with many moving objects, you might want to have the camera follow an object around. Normally, when you create a camera, it points to a single position and shows you the scene that falls within its field of view. In this recipe, we'll explain how you can create a camera that can follow any of your objects around.

Getting ready

This recipe only makes use of core Three.js functions, so there isn't any need to include external JavaScript libraries in your source code. If you want to see the final result of this recipe, you can open `03.01-camera-follow-object.html` in your browser, and you'll see something similar to what is shown in the following screenshot:

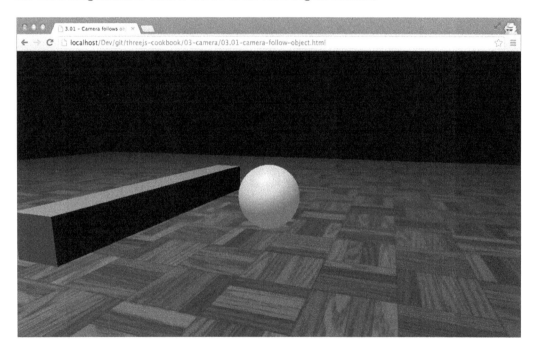

In this example, you can see that the camera is focused on the sphere. As the sphere moves across the scene, the camera moves around to stay focused on the position of the sphere.

How to do it...

For this recipe, we only need to take three simple steps:

1. The first thing we need to do is create the object that we want to follow. For this recipe, we create a simple `THREE.SphereGeometry` object and add it to the scene like this:

```
var sphereGeometry = new THREE.SphereGeometry(1.5,20,
  20);
var matProps = {
  specular: '#a9fcff',
  color: '#00abb1',
  emissive: '#006063',
  shininess: 10
}
var sphereMaterial = new
THREE.MeshPhongMaterial(matProps);
var sphereMesh = new THREE.Mesh(sphereGeometry,
  sphereMaterial);
sphereMesh.name = 'sphere';
scene.add(sphereMesh);
```

As you can see in this short code snippet, we don't need to do anything special with the object we want to follow.

2. The next step is that we need a camera that renders the scene and stays focused on the object we want to follow. The following JavaScript creates and positions this camera:

```
// create a camera, which defines where we're looking at.
camera = new THREE.PerspectiveCamera(45,
  window.innerWidth / window.innerHeight, 0.1, 1000);
// position and point the camera to the center of the
  scene
camera.position.x = 15;
camera.position.y = 6;
camera.position.z = 15;
```

This is a standard `THREE.PerspectiveCamera` object, which we also use in most of the other examples in this chapter. Once again, no special configuration is required.

3. For the final step, we define the render loop that will render the scene and also point the camera in the right direction for this recipe:

```
function render() {
  var sphere = scene.getObjectByName('sphere');
  renderer.render(scene, camera);
  camera.lookAt(sphere.position);
  step += 0.02;
  sphere.position.x = 0 + (10 * (Math.cos(step)));
  sphere.position.y = 0.75 * Math.PI / 2 +
    (6 * Math.abs(Math.sin(step)));
  requestAnimationFrame(render);
}
```

In the `render` function, we use the `camera.lookAt` function to point the camera to the `position` function of the sphere. As we do this in every frame that we render, it will look like camera is exactly following the position of sphere.

How it works...

`THREE.PerspectiveCamera` extends from the `THREE.Object3D` object. `THREE.Object3D` provides the `lookAt` function. When this function is called with the target position to look at, Three.js creates a transformation matrix (`THREE.Matrix4`) that aligns the position of the `THREE.Object3D` object with the target's position. In the case of the camera, the result is that the target object is followed around the scene by the camera and is rendered in the middle of the screen.

There's more...

In this recipe, we use the `lookAt` function to point a camera to a specific object. You can apply this same recipe for all the Three.js objects that extend from Object3D. For instance, you can use this to make sure `THREE.SpotLight` always illuminates a specific object. Or, if you're creating animations, you could use this effect to make sure one character is always looking at the face of a different character.

See also

▶ As the `lookAt` function uses matrix transformations to point one object to another, you could also do this without making use of the `lookAt` function. For this, you'll have to create a transformation matrix yourself. We've explained how to do this in the *Applying matrix transformations* recipe, which you can find in *Chapter 2, Geometries and Meshes*.

Zooming the camera to an object

Usually, when you position a camera in your scene, you might move it around a bit or let it focus on different objects. In this recipe, we'll show you how you can zoom in to an object so that it almost fills the rendered view.

Getting ready

To zoom in, we use the standard functionality from the THREE.PerspectiveCamera object. We've provided an example that demonstrates the result you'll get at the end of this recipe. To experiment with this example, open 03.02-zoom-camera-to-object.html in your browser. You will see something similar to the following screenshot:

Initially, you'll see a small rotating cube in the center of the scene. If you click on the `updateCamera` button in the menu in the top-right section, the camera will update and show you the rotating cube fullscreen like this:

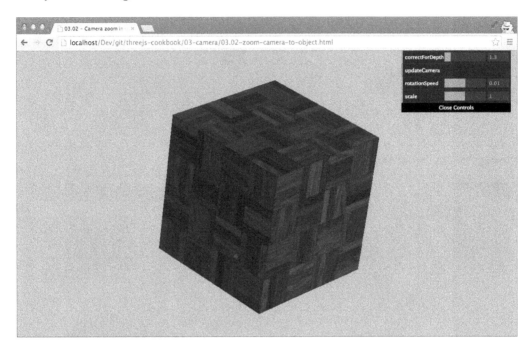

How to do it...

To zoom the camera to an object, we need to take the following steps:

1. The first thing we need to do is create and position the camera that we use to zoom in:

    ```
    camera = new THREE.PerspectiveCamera(45,
      window.innerWidth / window.innerHeight, 0.1, 1000);
    // position and point the camera to the center of the
      scene
    camera.position.x = 15;
    camera.position.y = 15;
    camera.position.z = 15;
    camera.lookAt(scene.position);
    ```

    As you can see, this is a standard `THREE.PerspectiveCamera` object, to which we give a position and add to the scene.

2. To zoom in with the camera, we first need to determine the distance from the camera to the object and its height:

```
// create an helper
var helper = new THREE.BoundingBoxHelper(cube);
helper.update();
// get the bounding sphere
var boundingSphere = helper.box.getBoundingSphere();
// calculate the distance from the center of the sphere
// and subtract the radius to get the real distance.
var center = boundingSphere.center;
var radius = boundingSphere.radius;
var distance = center.distanceTo(camera.position) -
  radius;
var realHeight = Math.abs(helper.box.max.y -
  helper.box.min.y);
```

In the previous code snippet, we used `THREE.BoundingBoxHelper` to determine the `realHeight` function of cube and its distance to the camera.

3. With this information, we can determine the field of view (`fov`) for the camera so that it only shows the cube:

```
var fov = 2 * Math.atan(realHeight *
  control.correctForDepth / (2 * distance))
  * (180 / Math.PI);
```

What you can see in this code fragment is that we use one additional value, which is `control.correctForDepth`, to calculate the field of view. This value, which is set in the menu in the top-right section in the example, increases the resulting field of view slightly. We do this because in this calculation, we assume that the camera is facing the object straight on. If the camera isn't looking straight at the object, we need to compensate for this offset.

4. Now that we've got the field of view for the camera, we can assign this value to the `camera.fov` property:

```
camera.fov = fov;
camera.updateProjectionMatrix();
```

As Three.js caches the `fov` property of the camera, we need to inform Three.js that the camera configuration has some changes. We do this with the `updateProjectionMatrix` function.

At this point, the camera is completely zoomed in on the object.

How it works...

To understand how this works, we need to understand what the field of view property of a `THREE.PerspectiveCamera` object does. The following figure shows you the field of view property:

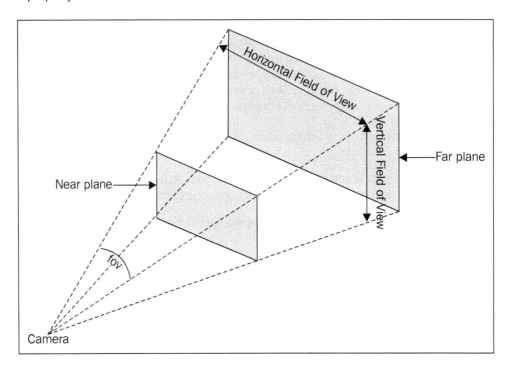

As you can see in this figure, there is a separate horizontal and vertical field of view. Three.js only allows you to set the vertical one, and the horizontal field of view is determined based on the aspect ratio you define on a camera. When you look at this figure, you can also directly see how this recipe works. By changing the field of view, we shrink the near and far planes and limit what is being rendered, and this way, we can zoom in.

There's more...

There is an alternative way of zooming in besides the one shown here. Instead of changing the `fov` property of the camera, we can also move the camera closer to the object. In the latest version of Three.js, a `zoom` property is introduced; you can also use this property to zoom in on a scene, but you can't use it directly to zoom in on a single object.

Using a perspective camera

Three.js provides two cameras: a camera that renders the scene with a perspective projection (as we see images in the real world) and a camera that renders the scene with an orthogonal projection (fake 3D often used in games; for more information on this type of camera, check out the upcoming *Using an orthographic camera* recipe). In this recipe, we'll look at the first of these two cameras and explain how you can use the perspective camera in your own scene.

Getting ready

Working with the properties of a camera can be a bit confusing at times. To help you better understand the steps or this recipe, we've created a simple page that shows you the effect each of the camera properties has. Open up `03.03-use-an-perspective-camera.html` in the browser, and you'll see something like this:

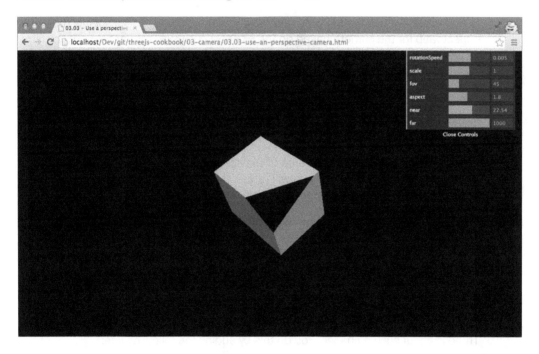

With the last four properties available in the menu in the top-right section, you can set the properties of `THREE.PerspectiveCamera`, which is used to render this scene, and see the effect of each property immediately.

How to do it...

In this recipe, we set up each of the camera properties separately. These properties can also be passed in with the constructor of `THREE.PerspectiveCamera`. In the *There's more...* section of this recipe, we'll show you how to do this.

To set up `THREE.PerspectiveCamera` completely, we need to perform a couple of steps:

1. The first thing we need to do is instantiate the camera:

    ```
    camera = new THREE.PerspectiveCamera();
    ```

    This creates the camera instance, which we configure in the upcoming steps.

2. Now that we've got a camera, we first need to define the aspect ratio between the width of the viewport and the height:

    ```
    camera.aspect = window.innerWidth / window.innerHeight;
    ```

    In our recipe, we use the full width and height of the browser, so we specify the aspect ratio for the camera based on the `window.innerWidth` and `window.innerHeight` properties. If we use a `div` element with a fixed width and height, you should use the ratio between these values as the `aspect` function for the camera.

3. The next two properties we need to define are the `near` and `far` properties:

    ```
    camera.near = 0.1;
    camera.far = 1000;
    ```

    These two properties define the area of the scene that this camera will render. With these two values, the camera will render the scene starting from a distance of `0.1` to a distance of `1000` from the position of the camera.

4. The last of the properties that can be defined is the (vertical) field of view:

    ```
    camera.fov = 45;
    ```

    This property defines, in degrees, the area that the camera sees. For instance, humans have a horizontal field of view of 120 degrees, while in video games, often a field of view of around 90 or 100 degrees is used.

5. Whenever you update one of these four properties of the camera, you have to inform Three.js about such a change. You do this by adding the following line:

    ```
    camera.updateProjectionMatrix();
    ```

6. Now, all that is left to do is position the camera and add it to the scene:

    ```
    camera.position.x = 15;
    camera.position.y = 16;
    camera.position.z = 13;
    scene.add(camera);
    ```

At this point, we can use this camera with any of the available renderers to render a scene like this: `renderer.render(scene, camera)`.

How it works...

The best way to understand how these properties affect what is rendered on screen is by looking at the following figure, which shows you these properties:

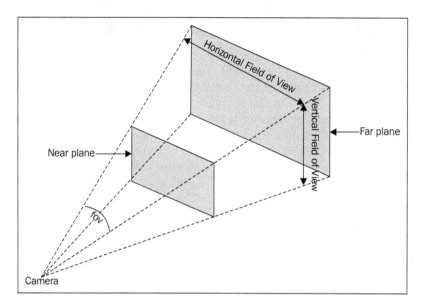

The position of **Near plane** in this figure is based on the `near` property of the camera. **Far plane** is based on the `far` property and the *fov* shown in the figure corresponds to the `fov` property. With the `fov` property, you define the vertical field of view. The horizontal field of view is based on the aspect ratio, which you define with the `aspect` property on the camera.

There's more...

In this recipe, we set each of the properties separately. `THREE.PerspectiveCamera` also provides a constructor that you can use to set all these properties in one statement:

```
camera = new THREE.PerspectiveCamera(45,
    window.innerWidth / window.innerHeight, 0.1, 1000);
```

Also remember that `THREE.PerspectiveCamera` extends from the standard Three.js `THREE.Object3D` object. This means that this camera can be rotated and moved around just like any other object.

See also

▶ In the *Zooming the camera to an object* recipe, we used the `fov` property of the camera to zoom in on an object, and in the *Using an orthographic camera* recipe, we will show you the second of the two cameras provided by Three.js, which is `THREE.OrthographicCamera`.

Using an orthographic camera

In most cases, you'll use `THREE.PerspectiveCamera` to render your scene. With such a camera, the result is a scene with a realistic-looking perspective. Three.js provides an alternative camera with `THREE.OrthographicCamera`. This camera uses an orthographic projection to render the scene. With this type of projection, all objects have the same size regardless of their distance to the camera. This is in contrast to `THREE.PerspectiveCamera`, where objects that are further away from the camera appear smaller. This was used often for fake 3D in games such as the Sims or older versions of SimCity (image taken from `http://glasnost.itcarlow.ie/~powerk/GeneralGraphicsNotes/ projection/projection_images/iosmetric_sim_city.jpg`).

In this recipe, we'll show you how to configure `THREE.OrthographicCamera` so that you can create this fake 3D effect for your own scenes.

Getting ready

For this recipe, the only object from Three.js we use is `THREE.OrthographicCamera`. This camera is available in the standard Three.js distribution, so there is no need to include any external JavaScript files. We've provided an example that shows the Three.Orthographic Camera in action. You can use this camera to better understand the properties you can use to configure the camera. If you open `03.04-use-an-orthographic-camera.html`, you can see a number of cubes that are rendered with `THREE.OrthographicCamera`. With the menu in the top-right section, you can tune the configuration of the camera.

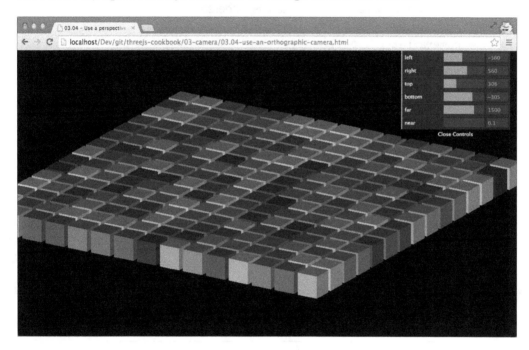

Now, let's look at the steps you need to take to set up this camera.

How to do it...

To set up an orthographic camera in Three.js, we need to perform a couple of very simple steps:

1. The first thing we need to do is create the camera instance:

   ```
   camera = new THREE.OrthographicCamera();
   ```

   This creates `THREE.OrthographicCamera`, which is configured with some default values.

2. The next step is to define the boundaries for this camera:

```
camera.left = window.innerWidth / -2;
camera.right =  window.innerWidth / 2;
camera.top = window.innerHeight / 2;
camera.bottom = window.innerHeight / - 2;
```

This defines the area that is rendered by this camera. In the *There's more...* section of this recipe, we'll explain how this works.

3. Finally, we have to set the `near` and `far` properties of the camera. These properties define which distance from the camera is rendered:

```
camera.near = 0.1;
camera.far = 1500;
```

4. When we don't pass in the arguments in the constructor, we have to inform Three.js that we changed the camera's parameter. For this, we have to add the following line:

```
camera.updateProjectionMatrix();
```

5. The final step is to position and align the camera:

```
camera.position.x = -500;
camera.position.y = 200;
camera.position.z = 300;
camera.lookAt(scene.position);
```

6. Now, we can just use this camera like any other camera and render a scene like this:

```
renderer.render(scene, camera);
```

How it works...

The easiest way to understand how this camera works is by looking at the following figure:

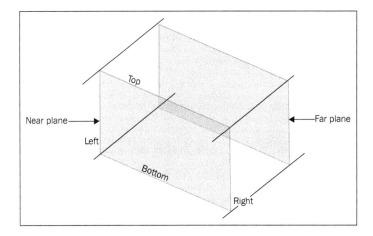

The box you see in this figure is the area an orthographic camera renders. In this figure, you can also see the `left`, `right`, `top`, and `bottom` properties we defined on the camera, which define the boundaries of this box. The final two properties, which are `near` and `far`, are used to define the near plane and the far plane. With these six properties, we can define the complete box that is rendered with `THREE.OrthographicCamera`.

There's more...

We can also configure `THREE.OrthographicCamera` by passing in these arguments in the constructor:

```
camera = new THREE.OrthographicCamera(
    window.innerWidth / -2, window.innerWidth / 2,
    window.innerHeight / 2, window.innerHeight / - 2, 0.1, 1500);
```

An added advantage is that this way, you don't need to explicitly call `camera.updateProjectionMatrix()`.

See also

▶   Three.js provides two types of camera. If you want to use `THREE.PerspectiveCamera` instead, look at the *Using a perspective camera* recipe, where the steps that you need to take to create and configure a perspective camera are explained.

Creating a 2D overlay

In most recipes, we only focus on the 3D aspect of Three.js. We show recipes that explain how 3D objects and scenes are rendered, how they can be viewed with different cameras, and how you can change how they look through materials. When you are creating games, you usually also have a 2D layer on top of your 3D scene. You can use this to show health bars, 2D maps, inventory, and much more. In this recipe, we'll show you how to create a 2D overlay using `THREE.OrthogonalCamera` and `THREE.PerspectiveCamera` together.

Getting ready

For this recipe, we require an image that we will use as an overlay. To demonstrate this recipe, we create a simple image that looks like this:

In this recipe, we'll combine this static image with a 3D scene to create the scene that can be seen by opening the `03.05-create-an-hud-overview.html` example in your browser:

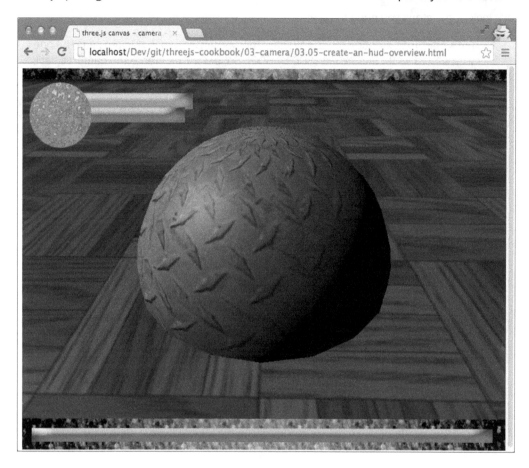

In this example, you can see that we've got a 3D rotating scene with a static 2D overlay on top of it.

How to do it...

Let's look at the steps you need to take:

1. Let's start with creating the 2D overlay. The overlay we use in this recipe is the one with a fixed width and height (800 by 600). So, before we create the cameras, let's first create the `div` variable that serves as container for the rendered scene:

```
container = document.createElement( 'div' );
container.setAttribute(
  "style","width:800px; height:600px");
document.body.appendChild( container );
```

2. Next, let's create the camera that we use to render the overlay. For this, we require `THREE.OrthographicCamera`:

```
orthoCamera = new THREE.OrthographicCamera(
  WIDTH / - 2, WIDTH / 2,      HEIGHT / 2,
  HEIGHT / - 2, - 500, 1000 );
orthoCamera.position.x = 0;
orthoCamera.position.y = 0;
orthoCamera.position.z = 0;
```

The `WIDTH` and `HEIGHT` properties are defined as constants with values of 800 and 600. This code fragment creates and positions a standard `THREE.OrthographicCamera` object.

3. For the 2D overlay, we create a separate scene where we put the 2D elements:

```
orthoScene = new THREE.Scene();
```

4. The only thing we want to add to the 2D scene is the overlay image we showed in the *Getting ready* section of this recipe. As it's a 2D image, we'll use a `THREE.Sprite` object:

```
var spriteMaterial = new THREE.SpriteMaterial({map:
  THREE.ImageUtils.loadTexture(
    "../assets/overlay/overlay.png")});
var sprite = new THREE.Sprite(spriteMaterial);
sprite.position.set(0,0,10);
sprite.scale.set(HEIGHT,WIDTH,1);
orthoScene.add(sprite);
```

`THREE.Sprite` is always rendered in the same size (1 by 1 pixels) regardless of its distance to the camera. To make the sprite fullscreen, we scale the x axis with 800 (`WIDTH`) and the y axis with 600 (`HEIGHT`). With `THREE.SpriteMaterial`, which we used in the previous code fragment, we point to the overlay image so that it is shown when we add `THREE.Sprite` to the scene.

5. At this point, we've got `THREE.OrthogonalCamera` and `THREE.Scene`, which show you the overlay as an 800 by 600 image. The next step is to create the 3D screen on which we want to apply this overlay. You don't have to do anything special here; you can create a 3D scene by defining `THREE.PerspectiveCamera` and `THREE.Scene` and adding some lights and objects. For this recipe, we assume you've got a camera and a scene with the following names:

```
persCamera = new THREE.PerspectiveCamera(60, WIDTH /
  HEIGHT, 1, 2100 );
persScene = new THREE.Scene();
```

6. Before we move to the render loop where we define that we want to render the 2D scene as an overlay, we need to configure an additional property on the renderer:

```
renderer = new THREE.WebGLRenderer();
renderer.setClearColor( 0xf0f0f0 );
renderer.setSize( 800, 600 );
renderer.autoClear = false;
container.appendChild( renderer.domElement );
```

On `THREE.WebGLRenderer`, we set the `autoclear` property to `false`. This means that the screen isn't automatically cleared before renderer renders a scene.

7. The final step is to alter the render loop. We first want to render the 3D scene, and without clearing the 3D-rendered output, render the overlay on the top:

```
function render() {
  renderer.clear();
  renderer.render( persScene, persCamera );
  renderer.clearDepth();
  renderer.render( orthoScene, orthoCamera );
}
```

The first thing we do in the render loop is clear the current output by calling the `clear` function on the renderer. We need to do this, as we disabled `autoclear` on renderer. Now, we render the 3D scene, and before we render the 2D overlay, we call the `clearDepth` function on the renderer. This makes sure the 2D overlay is rendered completely on top and won't intersect at places with the 3D scene. So finally, we render the 2D overlay by passing in `orthoScene` and `orthoCamera`.

How it works...

How this recipe works is actually very simple. We can use the same renderer to render multiple scenes with multiple different cameras in the same render loop. This way, we can position various render results on top of each other. With a `THREE.OrthoGraphic` camera and `THREE.Sprite`, it is easy to position an object at absolute positions on screen. By scaling it to the required size and applying a texture, we can display images using a renderer. This output, combined with a regular 3D result, allows you to create these kinds of overlays.

See also

There are a couple of recipes that use an orthographic camera and more advanced tricks to compose the final rendering:

  ▸ In this chapter, we explored how to set up `THREE.OrthographicCamera` in the *Using an orthographic camera* recipe.

  ▸ In *Chapter 4*, *Materials and Textures*, we'll show how you can use an HTML5 canvas and a HTML5 video as an input to a texture in the *Using HTML canvas as a texture* and *Using an HTML video as a texture* recipes.

  ▸ In *chapter 6*, *Point Clouds and Postprocessing*, we show you how to set up a more complex rendering pipeline in the *Setting up a postprocessing pipeline* recipe.

Rotating the camera around a scene

In *Chapter 2*, *Geometries and Meshes*, we already showed you a number of recipes that explained how to rotate objects. In this recipe, we'll show you how to rotate the camera around a scene while the camera will keep looking at the center of the scene.

Getting ready

For this recipe, we'll use the standard `THREE.PerspectiveCamera` object, which we rotate around a simple scene. To see the final result, open the `03.08-rotate-camera-around-scene-y-axis.html` example in your browser.

On this web page, you can see that the camera rotates around the scene while the floor, box, and lights stay at the same position.

How to do it...

To accomplish this, we only need to perform a couple of very simple steps:

1. The first thing we need to do is create THREE.PerspectiveCamera and position it somewhere in the scene:

```
// create a camera, which defines where we're looking at.
camera = new THREE.PerspectiveCamera(45,
  window.innerWidth / window.innerHeight, 0.1, 1000);
```

```
// position and point the camera to the center of the
  scene
camera.position.x = 15;
camera.position.y = 16;
camera.position.z = 13;
camera.lookAt(scene.position);
```

2. To rotate the camera, we recalculate its position in the render loop as follows:

```
function render() {
  renderer.render(scene, camera);
  var x = camera.position.x;
  var z = camera.position.z;
  camera.position.x = x * Math.cos(control.rotSpeed) +
    z * Math.sin(control.rotSpeed);
  camera.position.z = z * Math.cos(control.rotSpeed) -
    x * Math.sin(control.rotSpeed);
  camera.lookAt(scene.position);
  requestAnimationFrame(render);
}
```

In this render function, we update the `camera.position.x` and `camera.position.z` variables, and by calling `camera.lookAt(scene.position)`, we make sure we keep looking at the center of the scene.

How it works...

What we do here is some basic vector math. We execute a very small rotation of the camera using a rotation matrix. However, instead of the 3D and 4D matrices we used in other recipes, we just use a 2D matrix this time (represented with the two calculations in the **render** loop). After the rotation, we just need to make sure the camera is still looking at the correct position, so we use the `lookAt` function (which once again, internally uses matrix calculations to determine how to align the camera to the scene).

There's more...

In this recipe, we rotated around the scene's *y* axis. This results in a very smooth animation where the camera circles around the scene. We could, of course, also apply this to the other axes. We provided an example that you can view in the sources provided with this book. If you open `03.08-rotate-camera-around-scene-x-axis.html` in your browser, the camera rotates around the *x* axis instead of the *y* axis.

The only change you have to make is change the calculations in the render loop:

```
function render() {
  renderer.render(scene, camera);
  var z = camera.position.z;
  var y = camera.position.y;
  camera.position.y = y * Math.cos(control.rotSpeed) +
    z * Math.sin(control.rotSpeed);
  camera.position.z = z * Math.cos(control.rotSpeed) -
    y * Math.sin(control.rotSpeed);
  camera.lookAt(scene.position);
  requestAnimationFrame(render);
}
```

When you look at this example in your browser, you might notice something strange. At a certain point, it'll look like the camera jumps around. The reason is that the camera tries to stay the right-side up, so it quickly changes orientation when it is at the top or bottom of its rotation.

See also

In *Chapter 2, Geometries and Meshes*, we already discussed some rotation-related recipes. If you want to learn more about rotation or the matrix calculations required for it, look at the following recipes from *Chapter 2, Geometries and Meshes*:

- ▶ *Rotating an object around its own axis*
- ▶ *Rotating an object around a point in space*
- ▶ *Applying matrix transformations*

Matching the rendered view to a resized browser

When you define a camera in Three.js, you need to define the aspect ratio; for a renderer, you need to define its output size. Normally, you do this once when you set up your initial scene. This works great until the user resizes their browser. In this case, the aspect ratio for the camera will probably change, as will the output size for the renderer. In this recipe, we'll show you the steps you need to take to react to changes to the screen size.

Getting ready

As with every recipe, we provide an example that you can use to test and experiment with for this recipe as well. Open `03.06-change-the-camera-on-screen-resize.html` in your browser and make the screen very small.

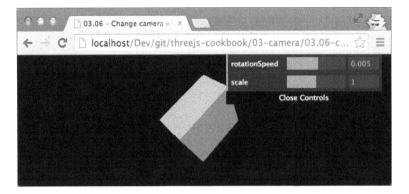

What you see is that the same amount of information is shown in the scene—only rendered smaller. When you now increase the screen size again, you'll see that Three.js always uses the complete available space.

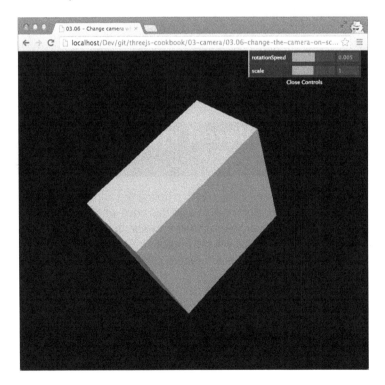

How to do it...

In this recipe, we'll add a resize handler to the web page, which reacts to resize events. Adding this handler only takes a couple of steps:

1. The first thing we need to add is the function that we call when the resize event occurs. The following code fragment shows you the `onResize` function that we will call in the next step:

    ```
    function onResize() {
      camera.aspect = window.innerWidth /
        window.innerHeight;
      camera.updateProjectionMatrix();
      renderer.setSize(window.innerWidth,
        window.innerHeight);
    }
    ```

    In this code snippet, we first recalculate the aspect ratio for the camera based on the new width and height. As Three.js caches certain aspects of the camera, we have to call the `updateProjectionMatrix()` function next to make sure the new aspect ratio is used. We also change the size for the renderer to the new width and height, so the complete screen space is used.

2. Now that we've got our update function, we need to define an event listener:

    ```
    window.addEventListener('resize', onResize, false);
    ```

    As you can see, we add an event listener for the `resize` event. So whenever the screen is resized, the provided function, which is `onResize`, will be called.

How it works...

Whenever something happens within a browser (a button is clicked on, the mouse is moved, the window is resized, and so on), browsers will throw an event. From JavaScript, you can register listeners to these events so that you can respond to them. In this recipe, we use the `resize` event to listen to any change in the window size. For more information on this event, you can look at the excellent documentation Mozilla provides at `https://developer.mozilla.org/en-US/docs/Web/Events/resize`.

Converting world coordinates to screen coordinates

If you are creating a game that provides a 2D interface on top of a 3D world, for instance, as shown in the *Creating a 2D overlay* recipe, you might want to know how the 3D coordinates map to your 2D overlay. If you know the 2D coordinates, you can add all kinds of visual effects to the 2D overlay, such as tracking the code or letting the 2D overlay interact with the objects in the 3D scene.

Getting ready

You don't need to perform any steps to get ready for this recipe. In this recipe, we can use the THREE.Projector object available in Three.js to determine the correct coordinates. You can view the result from this recipe in action by opening 03.07-convert-world-coordintate-to-screen-coordinates.html in your browser as shown in the following screenshot:

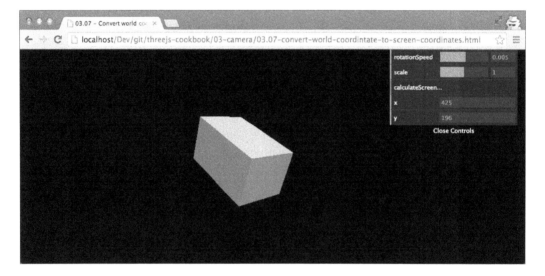

The box appears at random positions when you open this example. When you click on the **calculateScreenCoordinate** button in the menu in the top-right section, the *x* and *y* coordinates of the center of the box will be shown.

How to do it...

To convert world coordinates to screen coordinates, we use a couple of internal Three.js objects:

1. The first object we need is `THREE.Projector`:

   ```
   var projector = new THREE.Projector();
   ```

2. Next, we use this projector to project the position of the cube onto the camera:

   ```
   var vector = new THREE.Vector3();
   projector.projectVector(
     vector.setFromMatrixPosition( object.matrixWorld ),
     camera );
   ```

   The `vector` variable will now contain the position of the object as it is seen by the `camera` object.

3. When you project a vector, as we did in step two, the resulting x and y values range from -1 to 1. So in this final step, we convert these values to the current screen width and height:

   ```
   var width = window.innerWidth;
   var height = window.innerHeight;
   var widthHalf = width / 2;
   var heightHalf = height / 2;
   vector.x = ( vector.x * widthHalf ) + widthHalf;
   vector.y = - ( vector.y * heightHalf ) + heightHalf;
   ```

   At this point, the `vector` variable will contain the screen coordinates of the center of `object`. You can now use these coordinates with standard JavaScript, HTML, and CSS to add effects.

How it works...

In this recipe, we use the same effect that Three.js uses to render the scene. When you render a scene, the objects are projected onto a camera, which determines what area needs to be rendered and where the objects appear. With the projector class, we can perform this projection for a single vector. The result is the position of this vector in two dimensions based on the used camera.

▸ In this recipe, we converted world coordinates to screen coordinates. This is actually rather easy, as we've got all the information (in three dimensions) to correctly determine the coordinates (in two dimensions). In the *Selecting an object in the scene* recipe, we convert a screen coordinate to a world coordinate, which is harder to do, as we don't have any depth information we can use.

Selecting an object in the scene

A common requirement for Three.js applications is to interact with the scene. You might create a shooter where you want to use the mouse for aiming or an RPG where you need to interact with your environment. In this recipe, we'll show you how you can use the mouse to select objects that are rendered on screen.

Getting ready

To apply this effect, we'll need a scene where we can select some objects. For this recipe, we've provided an example, which is `03.10-select-an-object-in-the-scene.html`. If you open this file in your browser, you'll see a number of objects moving around the scene.

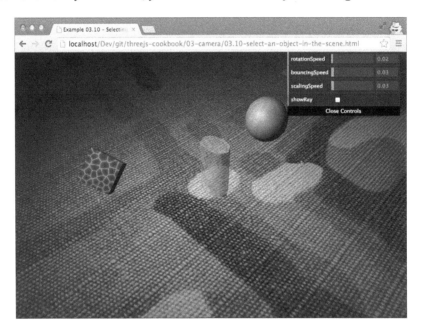

You can use your mouse to select any of the objects on screen. The first time you click on them, they'll become transparent, and the next time, they'll become solid again.

How to do it...

We'll need to work through a couple of steps for this recipe:

1. The first thing we need to do is set up the mouse listener. We want to fire a JavaScript function each time the mouse button is clicked on. To do this, we register the following listener:

```
document.addEventListener('mousedown',
  onDocumentMouseDown, false);
```

This will tell the browser to fire the `onDocumentMouseDown` button whenever a `mousedown` event is detected.

2. Next, we define the `onMouseDown` function as follows:

```
function onDocumentMouseDown(event) { ... }
```

This function will be called when you push the left mouse button. In the upcoming steps, we'll show you what to put into this function to detect which object is selected.

3. The first thing we need to do is convert the *x* and *y* coordinates of the mouse click to a position that `THREE.PerspectiveCamera` can understand:

```
var projector = new THREE.Projector();
var vector = new THREE.Vector3(
  (event.clientX / window.innerWidth) * 2 - 1,
  -(event.clientY / window.innerHeight) * 2 + 1,
  0.5);
projector.unprojectVector(vector, camera);
```

At this point, vector will contain the *x* and *y* coordinates in coordinates the camera and Three.js understands.

4. Now we can use another Three.js object, which is `THREE.Raycaster`, to determine which objects in our scene might be located at the position we clicked on:

```
var raycaster = new THREE.Raycaster(
  camera.position,
  vector.sub(camera.position).normalize());
var intersects = raycaster.intersectObjects(
  [sphere, cylinder, cube]);
```

Here, we first create `THREE.Raycaster` and use the `intersectObjects` function to determine whether `sphere`, `cylinder`, or `cube` are selected. If an object is selected, it will be stored in the `intersects` array.

5. Now we can process the `intersects` array. The first element will be the element closest to the camera, and in this recipe, this is the one we're interested in:

```
if (intersects.length > 0) {
  intersects[0].object.material.transparent = true;
  if (intersects[0].object.material.opacity === 0.5) {
    intersects[0].object.material.opacity = 1;
  } else {
    intersects[0].object.material.opacity = 0.5;
  }
}
```

In this recipe, we just switch the opacity of an object whenever it is clicked on.

That's it. With this setup, you can select objects using your mouse.

How it works...

This recipe works by using `THREE.RayCaster`. With `THREE.RayCaster`, as the name implies, you shoot out a ray into the scene. The path of this ray is based on the properties of the camera, the position of the camera, and the objects provided to the `intersectObjects` function. For each of the provided objects, Three.js determines whether a ray cast using `THREE.RayCaster` can hit the specified object.

There's more

An interesting effect that can be added, and that better visualizes what is happening, is rendering the ray that is cast by `THREE.RayCaster`. You can very easily do this by just adding the following to step 5 of this recipe:

```
var points = [];
points.push(new THREE.Vector3(camera.position.x,
  camera.position.y - 0.2, camera.position.z));
points.push(intersects[0].point);
var mat = new THREE.MeshBasicMaterial({
  color: 0xff0000,
  transparent: true,
  opacity: 0.6
});
var tubeGeometry = new THREE.TubeGeometry( new
  THREE.SplineCurve3(points), 60, 0.001);
var tube = new THREE.Mesh(tubeGeometry, mat);
scene.add(tube);
```

There's nothing too special in this code fragment. We just draw a line from the position of the camera (with a small offset to the *y* axis, or else we don't see anything) to the position where the ray intersects. The result, which you can also see in the example discussed in the *Getting ready* section of this recipe, looks something like this:

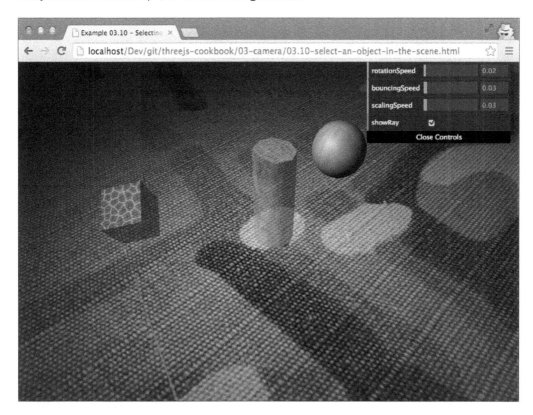

See also

▸   In this recipe, we convert a 2D coordinate into a 3D one. In the *Converting world coordinates to screen coordinates* recipe, we explain how to do the opposite.

4

Materials and Textures

In this chapter, we'll cover the following recipes:

- ► Adding depth to a mesh with a bump map
- ► Adding depth to a mesh with a normal map
- ► Using HTML canvas as a texture
- ► Using HTML video as a texture
- ► Creating a mesh with multiple materials
- ► Using separate materials for faces
- ► Setting up repeating textures
- ► Making part of an object transparent
- ► Using a cubemap to create reflective materials
- ► Using a dynamic cubemap to create reflective materials
- ► Using Blender to create custom UV mapping
- ► Configuring blend modes
- ► Using a shadow map for fixed shadows

Introduction

Three.js offers a large number of different materials and supports many different types of textures. These textures provide a great way to create interesting effects and graphics. In this chapter, we'll show you recipes that allow you to get the most out of these components provided by Three.js.

Adding depth to a mesh with a bump map

For detailed models, you require geometries with a large number of vertices and faces. If a geometry contains a very large number of vertices, loading the geometry and rendering it will take more time than it would take for a simple model. If you've got a scene with a large number of models, it is a good idea to try and minimize the number of vertices for better performance. There are a number of different techniques that you can use for this. In this recipe, we'll show you how you can use a bump map texture to add the illusion of depth to your model.

Getting ready

To get ready for this recipe, we need to get the textures that we want to use on our geometries. For this recipe, we require two textures: a color map, which is a standard texture, and a bump map, which describes the depth associated with the standard texture. The following screenshot shows you the color map that we will use (you can find these textures in the `assets/textures` folder in the sources provided with this book):

As you can see, this is a simple color map of a stone wall. Besides this texture, we also require the bump map. A bump map is a grayscale image, where the intensity of each pixel determines the height:

From the preceding screenshot, you can see that the parts between the stones and the mortar has less height, as it is a dark color, as compared to the stones themselves, which have a lighter color. You can see the result you end up with at the end of this recipe by opening up the `04.01-add-depth-to-mesh-with-bump-map.html` example in your browser.

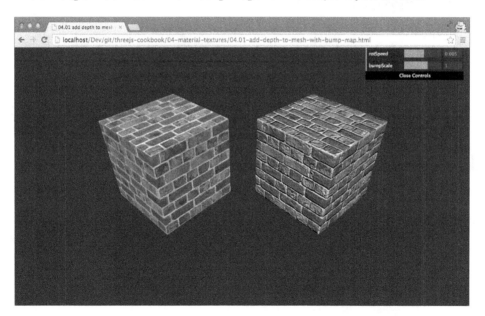

From the preceding screenshot, you can see two cubes. The cube on the left-hand side is rendered without a bump map, and the cube on the right-hand side is rendered with a bump map. As you can see, the right-hand side cube shows much more depth and detail than the cube on the left-hand side.

How to do it...

When you've got textures, using them to add depth to a model is very straightforward:

1. First, create the geometry you want to use together with the bump map:

    ```
    var cubeGeometry = new THREE.BoxGeometry(15, 15, 15);
    ```

    In this recipe, we create `THREE.BoxGeometry`, but you can use a bump map with any kind of geometry.

2. The next step is to create the material on which we define the bump map:

    ```
    var cubeBumpMaterial = new THREE.MeshPhongMaterial();

    cubeBumpMaterial.map = THREE.ImageUtils.loadTexture(
                    "../assets/textures/Brick-2399.jpg");
    cubeBumpMaterial.bumpMap = THREE.ImageUtils.loadTexture(
                "../assets/textures/Brick-2399-bump-map.jpg");
    ```

    Here, we create `THREE.MeshPhongMaterial` and set its `map` and `bumpMap` properties. The `map` property points to the color map texture, and the `bumpMap` property point to the grayscale bump map texture.

3. Now you can just create `THREE.Mesh` and add it to scene:

    ```
    var bumpCube = new THREE.Mesh(cubeGeometry,
                                cubeBumpMaterial);
    scene.add(bumpCube);
    ```

With these three simple steps, you've created a cube that uses a bump map for added depth.

How it works...

The values of each pixel in the bump map determine the height associated with that part of the texture. When rendering the scene, Three.js uses this information to determine how light affects the final color of the pixel it is rendering. The result is that without defining a very detailed model, we can add the illusion of extra depth. If you want to know more details about how bump mapping works, look at this site for a very detailed explanation: http://www.tweak3d.net/articles/bumpmapping/.

There's more...

In this recipe, we showed you the default way to define a bump map. There is, however, one additional property that you can use to tune bump mapping. The material we used in this recipe, `cubeBumpMaterial`, also has a `bumpScale` property. With this property, you can set the amount by which the bump map affects the depth. If this value is very small, you'll see some added depth, and if this value is higher, you'll see a more pronounced depth effect. You can set this property in the example for this cookbook (`04.01-add-depth-to-mesh-with-bump-map.html`).

See also

▸ There is an additional way to add detail and depth to your meshes. In the *Add depth to a mesh with a normal map* recipe, we show how to add depth and detail with a normal map instead of a bump map. In the *Creating geometries from height maps* recipe, of *Chapter 2, Geometries and Meshes*, we showed you a different way to use bump maps by creating `THREE.Geometry` from it.

Adding depth to a mesh with a normal map

With a bump map, we showed in the *Add depth to a mesh with a bump map* recipe, how to add depth and detail to a mesh using a specific texture. In this recipe, we provide another way to add even more depth and details without increasing the vertex count of the geometry. To do this, we will use a normal map. A normal map describes the normal vector for each pixel, which should be used to calculate how light affects the material used in the geometry.

Getting ready

To use normal maps, we first need to get a color map and a normal map. For this recipe, we've used two screenshots. The first is the color map:

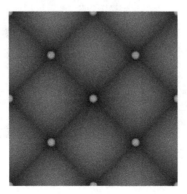

The next screenshot is the normal map:

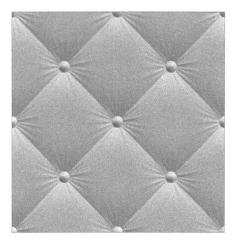

Now that we've got the two images, let's first look at how this would look in practice. To see a normal map in action, open the `04.02-add-depth-to-mesh-with-normal-map.html` example:

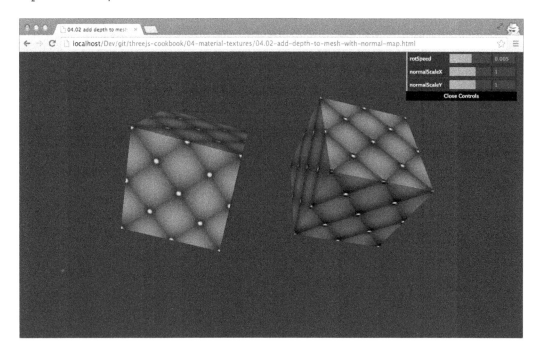

In this example, you can see a standard rendered cube on the left-hand side and one where a normal map is added to on the right-hand side. You can directly see that the face of the right-hand side cube looks much more detailed than the face of the left-hand side cube.

How to do it...

Adding a normal map is actually very easy:

1. First, create the geometry that we want to render:

   ```
   var cubeGeometry = new THREE.BoxGeometry(15, 15, 15);
   ```

   For this recipe, we use a simple THREE.BoxGeometry object, but you can use whichever geometry you want.

2. Now that we've got a geometry, we create the material and configure the properties:

   ```
   var cubeNormalMaterial = new THREE.MeshPhongMaterial();
   cubeNormalMaterial.map = THREE.ImageUtils.loadTexture(
                   "../assets/textures/chesterfield.png");
   cubeNormalMaterial.normalMap = THREE.ImageUtils.loadTexture(
              "../assets/textures/chesterfield-normal.png");
   ```

   The map properties contain the standard texture, and the normalMap properties contain the normal texture, which we showed you in the *Getting ready* section of this recipe.

3. All that is left to do now is to create a THREE.Mesh object and add it to the scene like this:

   ```
   var normalCube = new THREE.Mesh(
                       cubeGeometry, cubeNormalMaterial);
   scene.add(normalCube);
   ```

As you can see from these steps, using a normal map is very simple.

How it works...

In 3D modeling, a couple of mathematical concepts are important to understand. One of these concepts is a **normal** vector. A normal is the vector that stands perpendicular to the surface of the face of a geometry. This is shown in the following screenshot:

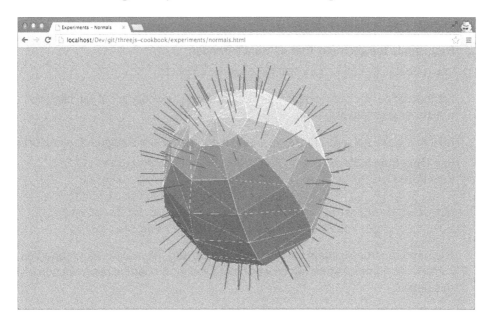

Each blue line represents the normal vector, which is the vector that is perpendicular to the surface of that face. In a normal map, the direction of these vectors are shown as RGB values. When you apply a normal map to a specific face, Three.js uses the information from this normal map and the normal of the face to add depth to that face without adding additional vertices. For more information on how normal maps are used, refer to the site at `http://www.opengl-tutorial.org/intermediate-tutorials/tutorial-13-normal-mapping/`.

There's more...

You can fine-tune the height and direction in which the information from the normal map is applied to the face of geometry. For this, you can use the `normalScale` property like this:

```
normalCube.material.normalScale.x = 1;
normalCube.material.normalScale.y = 1;
```

To see this effect in action, look at the example for this recipe, `04.02-add-depth-to-mesh-with-normal-map.html`, where you can use the menu in the top-right section to change this value.

See also

▶ An alternative for normal maps is bump maps. In the *Add depth to a mesh with a bump map* recipe, we show you how to use such a map instead of a normal map

Using HTML canvas as a texture

Most often when you use textures, you use static images. With Three.js, however, it is also possible to create interactive textures. In this recipe, we will show you how you can use an HTML5 canvas element as an input for your texture. Any change to this canvas is automatically reflected after you inform Three.js about this change in the texture used on the geometry.

Getting ready

For this recipe, we need an HTML5 canvas element that can be displayed as a texture. We can create one ourselves and add some output, but for this recipe, we've chosen something else. We will use a simple JavaScript library, which outputs a clock to a canvas element. The resulting mesh will look like this (see the `04.03-use-html-canvas-as-texture.html` example):

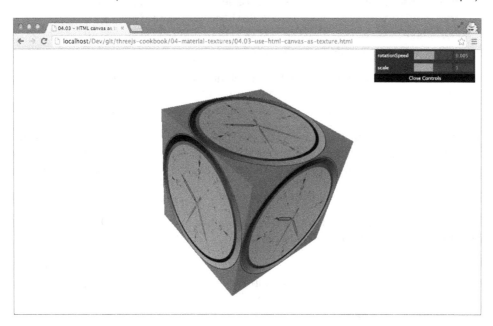

The JavaScript used to render the clock was based on the code from this site: `http://saturnboy.com/2013/10/html5-canvas-clock/`. To include the code that renders the clock in our page, we need to add the following to the `head` element:

```
<script src="../libs/clock.js"></script>
```

How to do it...

To use a canvas as a texture, we need to perform a couple of steps:

1. The first thing we need to do is create the canvas element:

   ```
   var canvas = document.createElement('canvas');
   canvas.width=512;
   canvas.height=512;
   ```

   Here, we create an HTML canvas element programmatically and define a fixed width.

2. Now that we've got a canvas, we need to render the clock that we use as the input for this recipe on it. The library is very easy to use; all you have to do is pass in the canvas element we just created:

   ```
   clock(canvas);
   ```

3. At this point, we've got a canvas that renders and updates an image of a clock. What we need to do now is create a geometry and a material and use this canvas element as a texture for this material:

   ```
   var cubeGeometry = new THREE.BoxGeometry(10, 10, 10);
   var cubeMaterial = new THREE.MeshLambertMaterial();
   cubeMaterial.map = new THREE.Texture(canvas);
   var cube = new THREE.Mesh(cubeGeometry, cubeMaterial);
   ```

   To create a texture from a canvas element, all we need to do is create a new instance of `THREE.Texture` and pass in the `canvas` element we created in step 1. We assign this texture to the `cubeMaterial.map` property, and that's it.

4. If you run the recipe at this step, you might see the clock rendered on the sides of the cubes. However, the clock won't update itself. We need to tell Three.js that the canvas element has been changed. We do this by adding the following to the rendering loop:

   ```
   cubeMaterial.map.needsUpdate = true;
   ```

   This informs Three.js that our canvas texture has changed and needs to be updated the next time the scene is rendered.

With these four simple steps, you can easily create interactive textures and use everything you can create on a canvas element as a texture in Three.js.

How it works...

How this works is actually pretty simple. Three.js uses WebGL to render scenes and apply textures. WebGL has native support for using HTML canvas element as textures, so Three.js just passes on the provided canvas element to WebGL and it is processed as any other texture.

 ▸ Besides using images and canvas elements as textures, we can also use a video element as a texture. In the *Using HTML video as a texture* recipe, we show you how to use a HTML video element as the input for a texture.

Using HTML video as a texture

Modern browsers have great support for playing video without requiring any plugins. With Three.js, we can even use this video as the input for our textures. In this recipe, we'll show you the steps you need to take to output a video on a side of a cube.

Getting ready

For this recipe, we need a video to play, of course. We used the trailer for the Blender-made movie *Sintel* (`http://www.sintel.org/`), which is freely available. To view the result of this recipe, open `04.04-use-html-video-as-texture.html` in your browser.

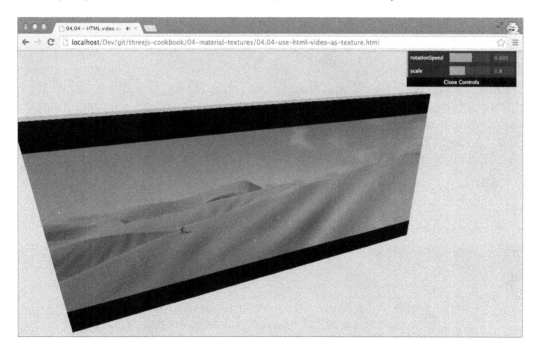

When you run this example, you can see that the video is being played at the side of a cube and keeps updating even when the cube is rotating.

How to do it...

To accomplish this effect, we need to define an HTML video element as the source for a texture. To do this, perform the following steps:

1. The first thing we need is a way to play the video. For this, we add the following HTML element to the `body` element of the page:

```
<video id="video" autoplay loop style="display:none">
    <source src="../assets/video/sintel_trailer-480p.mp4"
            type='video/mp4'>
    <source src="../assets/video/sintel_trailer-480p.webm"
            type='video/webm'>
    <source src="../assets/video/sintel_trailer-480p.ogv"
            type='video/ogg'>
</video>
```

   With this piece of HTML, we'll load the video and play it looped once it is loaded using the `autoplay` and `loop` properties. As we've set `display:none`, this `video` element won't show up on the page.

2. Now that we've got a video playing, we can get a reference to this element and use it to create a texture:

```
var video = document.getElementById( 'video' );

videoTexture = new THREE.Texture( video );
videoTexture.minFilter = THREE.LinearFilter;
videoTexture.magFilter = THREE.LinearFilter;
videoTexture.format = THREE.RGBFormat;
videoTexture.generateMipmaps = false;
```

   The `minFilter`, `magFilter`, `format`, and `generateMipmaps` properties used here provide the best result and performance when using a video as a texture.

3. At this point, we've got a texture that we can use like any other texture:

```
var cubeGeometry = new THREE.BoxGeometry(1,9,20);
var cubeMaterial = new THREE.MeshBasicMaterial({map:videoTextu
re});
```

   Here, we set the `map` property of the material to the video texture. So, any `THREE.Mesh` object we create that uses this material will show the video.

4. To finish the recipe, create `THREE.Mesh` object and add it to the scene:

```
var cube = new THREE.Mesh(cubeGeometry,
                          cubeMaterial);
scene.add(cube);
```

5. Three.js normally caches textures as they usually don't change that often. In this recipe, though, the texture changes continuously. To inform Three.js that the texture has changed, we need to add the following to the render loop:

```
function render() {

    ...

    videoTexture.needsUpdate = true;

    ...

}
```

You can use this approach with any video that can be played in the browser.

How it works...

WebGL, which is used by Three.js to render the scenes, has native support to use video elements as input for the textures. Three.js just passes the video element to WebGL and doesn't need to do any preprocessing. In the WebGL code, the current image shown by the video is converted to a texture. Whenever we set `videoTexture.needsUpdate` to `true`, the texture is updated in WebGL.

There's more...

One thing to remember when working with the video element is that the different browsers have varying support for video formats. A good up-to-date overview of what format is supported by which browser can be found on Wikipedia at `http://en.wikipedia.org/wiki/HTML5_video#Browser_support`.

See also

> ▸ An alternative way to easily create changing textures is explained in the *Using HTML canvas as a texture* recipe. In this recipe, we explain how you can use the HTML `canvas` element as the input for a texture.

Creating a mesh with multiple materials

When you create `THREE.Mesh`, you can only specify a single material that can be used for that mesh. In most scenarios, this will be sufficient. However, there are also cases where you want to combine multiple materials. For instance, you might want to combine `THREE.MeshLambertMaterial` with a material that shows you the wireframe of the geometry. In this recipe, we'll show you the required steps to create a mesh that uses multiple materials.

Getting ready

For this recipe, we don't require additional resources or libraries. If you want to look at the result of this recipe, open up the `04.05-create-a-mesh-with-multiple-materials.html` example in your browser.

In the preceding screenshot, you can see a cylinder. This cylinder is rendered with two materials. In the next section, we'll show you the steps you need to take to create this.

How to do it...

To create a multimaterial mesh, Three.js provides a helper function. You can use
`THREE.SceneUtils` for this, as is shown in the next couple of steps:

1. The first thing you need to do is create the geometry you want to use. For this recipe,
   we use a simple `THREE.CylinderGeometry` object:

   ```
   var cylinderGeometry = new THREE.CylinderGeometry(
                            3, 5, 10,20);
   ```

2. After the geometry, we can create the materials. You can use as many as you want,
   but in this recipe, we'll just use two:

   ```
   var material1 = new THREE.MeshLambertMaterial(
        {color:0xff0000,
         transparent: true,
         opacity: 0.7});
   ```

   ```
   var material2 = new THREE.MeshBasicMaterial(
                            {wireframe:true});
   ```

   As you can see, we create a transparent `THREE.MeshLambertMaterial` object
   and `THREE.MeshBasicMaterial` object, which only renders a wireframe.

3. Now, we can create the object that can be added to the scene. Instead of
   instantiating `THREE.Mesh`, we use the `createMultiMaterialObject` function
   provided by the `THREE.SceneUtils` object:

   ```
   var cylinder = THREE.SceneUtils.createMultiMaterialObject(
                            cylinderGeometry,
                            [material1, material2]);
   ```

   You can add the result from this function to the scene:

   ```
   scene.add(cylinder);
   ```

One thing to take into account is that the object we create here isn't `THREE.Mesh` but
`THREE.Object3D`. Why a different object is created is explained in the next section.

How it works...

What happens when you call the `createMultiMaterialObject` function is that Three.js simply creates multiple meshes and groups them together. If you open the Three.js file and look up this function, you'll see the following code:

```
function createMultiMaterialObject( geometry, materials ) {
var group = new THREE.Object3D();
for ( var i = 0, l = materials.length; i < l; i ++ ) {
group.add( new THREE.Mesh( geometry, materials[ i ] ) );
}
return group;
}
```

In this function, Three.js iterates over the materials that are provided, and for each material, a new `THREE.Mesh` object is created. Because all the created meshes are added to group, the result looks like a single mesh that's created with multiple materials.

See also

▶   When you use the approach from this recipe to create a material that uses multiple materials, the materials are applied to the complete geometry. In the *Using separate materials for faces* recipe, we show you how to use a different material for each specific face of a geometry.

Using separate materials for faces

Each geometry in Three.js consists of a number of vertices and faces. In most cases, when you define a material that can be used together with a geometry, you use a single material. With Three.js, however, it is also possible to define a unique material for each of the faces of your geometry. You could, for instance, use this to apply different textures to each side of a model of a house. In this recipe, we will explain how to set up the materials so that you can use different textures for individual faces.

Getting ready

In this recipe, we won't use any external textures or libraries. It is good, however, to look at the final result that we'll be creating in this recipe. For this, open the `04.06-use-separate-materials-for-faces.html` example in your browser.

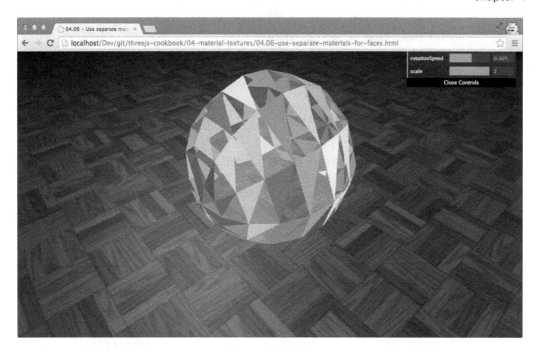

In the preceeding screenshot, you can see a rotating sphere, where each face is rendered with a different color and half of the faces have been made transparent. In the following section, we'll show you the steps you need to take to recreate this.

How to do it...

To define specific materials for each face, we need to perform the following steps:

1. The first thing we need to do is create the geometry. For this recipe, we use `THREE.SphereGeometry`, but these steps can also be applied to other geometries:

```
var sphereGeometry = new THREE.SphereGeometry(3, 10, 10);
```

2. When we create the material in step 3, we provide an array of materials that we want to use. Additionally, we need to specify on each face the material from the array we'll use. You can do this with the following code:

```
var materials = [];
var count = 0;
sphereGeometry.faces.forEach(function(face) {
    face.materialIndex = count++;
    var material = new THREE.MeshBasicMaterial(
```

```
            {color:Math.abs(Math.sin(count/70))*0xff0000});
        material.side = THREE.DoubleSide;
        if (count % 2 == 0) {
            material.transparent = true;
            material.opacity = 0.4;
        }
        materials.push(material);
    });
```

In this code snippet, we traverse all the faces of the geometry we created. For each face, we set the `materialIndex` property to the index of the material we want to use. We also create a unique `material` object for each face in this code snippet, make half of them transparent, and finally, push the materials we create into the materials array.

3. At this point, the materials array contains a unique material for each face of the geometry, and for all the faces, the `materialIndex` property points to one of the materials in that array. Now, we can create `THREE.MeshFaceMaterial` object and together with the geometry, we can create `THREE.Mesh`:

```
var sphere = new THREE.Mesh(
    sphereGeometry, new THREE.MeshFaceMaterial(materials));
scene.add(sphere);
```

That's it. Each face of the geometry will use the material it points to.

How it works...

Because we specify `materialIndex` on each `THREE.Face` object, Three.js knows which material from the provided array it should use when it wants to render a specific face. One thing you need to take into account is that this can affect the performance of your scene, as each of the materials needs to be managed by Three.js; however, the performance is better than using separate meshes but worse than combining the textures into one.

There's more...

Some of the geometries Three.js provides already set a `materialIndex` property when you instantiate them. For instance, when you create `THREE.BoxGeometry`, the first two faces are mapped to `materialIndex` 1, the next two are mapped to `materialIndex` 2, and so on. So, if you want to style the sides of a box, you just have to provide an array with six materials.

Another interesting use of using materials for specific faces is that you can easily create interesting patterns, for instance, when you can very easily create a checked layout like this:

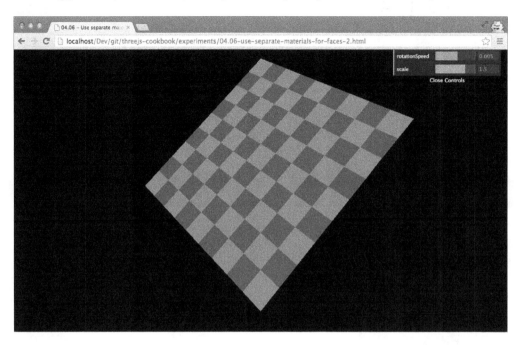

All you need is some small change to how you assign the `materialIndex` properties like this:

```
var plane = new THREE.PlaneGeometry(10, 10, 9, 9);

var materials = [];
var material_1 = new THREE.MeshBasicMaterial(
    {color:Math.random()*0xff0000, side: THREE.DoubleSide});
var material_2 = new THREE.MeshBasicMaterial(
    {color:Math.random()*0xff0000, side: THREE.DoubleSide});

materials.push(material_1);
materials.push(material_2);

var index = 0;
for (var i = 0 ; i < plane.faces.length-1 ; i+=2) {
    var face = plane.faces[i];
    var nextFace = plane.faces[i+1];
    face.materialIndex = index;
    nextFace.materialIndex = index;
```

```
    if (index === 0) {
        index = 1;
    } else {
        index = 0;
    }
}
```

See also

> ▸ If you don't want to style specific faces but apply multiple materials to a complete geometry, you can look at the *Creating a mesh with multiple materials* recipe, where we explain how to do just that

Setting up repeating textures

Sometimes, when you've found a texture you want to apply, you might want to repeat it. For instance, if you've got a large ground plane on which you want to apply a seamless wood texture, you don't want the texture to be applied as a single image for the whole plane. Three.js allows you to define the manner in which a texture is repeated when it is used on a geometry. In this recipe, we'll explain the steps you need to take to accomplish this.

Getting ready

The first thing we need is the image that we'll use for a texture. For the best effect, you should use seamless textures. A seamless texture can be repeated without showing the seam between two textures next to each other. For this recipe, we'll use the `webtreats_metal_6-512px.jpg` texture, which you can find in the `asset/textures` folder that you can find in the sources for this book.

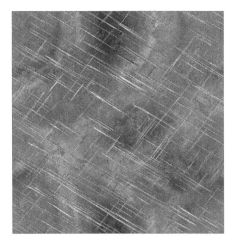

To see the repeat effect in practice, you can open the `04.12-setup-repeating-textures.html` example in your browser.

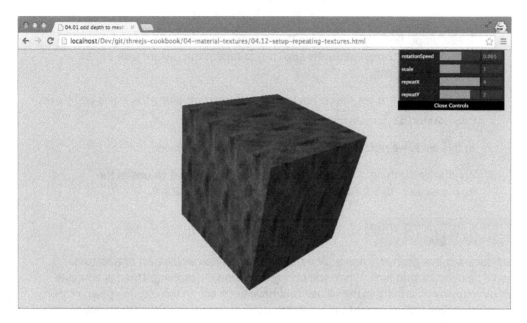

With the menu in the top-right corner, you can define how often the texture is repeated along its *x* axis and *y* axis.

How to do it...

To set up a repeating texture is very simple and only requires a couple of steps:

1. First, create the geometry and the material:

   ```
   var cubeGeometry = new THREE.BoxGeometry(10, 10, 10);
   var cubeMaterial = new THREE.MeshPhongMaterial();
   ```

   In this recipe, we use `THREE.MeshPhongMaterial`, but you can use this recipe for all the materials that allow you use textures.

2. Next, we load the texture and set it on `cubeMaterial`:

   ```
   cubeMaterial.map = THREE.ImageUtils.loadTexture
           ("../assets/textures/webtreats_metal_6-512px.jpg");
   ```

3. The next step is to set the `wrapS` and `wrapT` properties on the texture:

   ```
   cubeMaterial.map.wrapS = cubeMaterial.map.wrapT
                     = THREE.RepeatWrapping;
   ```

   These properties define whether Three.js should stretch the texture to the side (`THREE.ClampToEdgeWrapping`) or repeat the texture with `THREE.RepeatWrapping`.

4. The final step is to set how often to repeat the texture along the x axis and y axis:

   ```
   cubeMaterial.map.repeat.set( 2, 2 );
   ```

   In this case, we repeat the texture along both its axis twice.

5. An interesting thing to know is that by providing negative values to the `map.repeat.set` function, you can also mirror the texture.

How it works...

Each face within a geometry has a UV mapping that defines which part of a texture should be used for that face. When you configure a repeat wrapping, Three.js changes this UV mapping according to the values that have been set on the `map.repeat` property. As we also define that we want to use `THREE.RepeatWrapping`, WebGL knows how to interpret these changed UV values.

See also

▶ Repeating textures works by changing the UV mapping according to the repeat property. You can also configure a UV mapping by hand, as shown in the *Using Blender to create custom UV mapping* recipe.

Making part of an object transparent

You can create a lot of interesting visualizations using the various materials available with Three.js. In this recipe, we'll look at how you can use the materials available with Three.js to make part of an object transparent. This will allow you to create complex-looking geometries with relative ease.

Getting ready

Before we dive into the required steps in Three.js, we first need to have the texture that we will use to make an object partially transparent. For this recipe, we will use the following texture, which was created in Photoshop:

You don't have to use Photoshop; the only thing you need to keep in mind is that you use an image with a transparent background. Using this texture, in this recipe, we'll show you how you can create the following (04.08-make-part-of-object-transparent.html):

As you can see in the preceeding, only part of the sphere is visible, and you can look through the sphere to see the back at the other side of the sphere.

How to do it...

Let's look at the steps you need to take to accomplish this:

1. The first thing we do is create the geometry. For this recipe, we use `THREE.SphereGeometry`:

```
var sphereGeometry = new THREE.SphereGeometry(6, 20, 20);
```

Just like all the other recipes, you can use whatever geometry you want.

2. In the second step, we create the material:

```
var mat = new THREE.MeshPhongMaterial();
mat.map = new THREE.ImageUtils.loadTexture(
        "../assets/textures/partial-transparency.png");
mat.transparent = true;
mat.side = THREE.DoubleSide;
mat.depthWrite = false;
mat.color = new THREE.Color(0xff0000);
```

As you can see in this fragment, we create `THREE.MeshPhongMaterial` and load the texture we saw in the *Getting ready* section of this recipe. To render this correctly, we also need to set the side property to `THREE.DoubleSide` so that the inside of the sphere is also rendered, and we need to set the `depthWrite` property to false. This will tell WebGL that we still want to test our vertices against the WebGL depth buffer, but we don't write to it. Often, you need to set this to false when working with more complex transparent objects or particles.

3. Finally, add the sphere to the scene:

```
var sphere = new THREE.Mesh(sphereGeometry, mat);
scene.add(sphere);
```

With these simple steps, you can create really interesting effects by just experimenting with textures and geometries.

There's more...

With Three.js, it is possible to repeat textures (refer to the *Setup repeating textures* recipe). You can use this to create interesting-looking objects such as this:

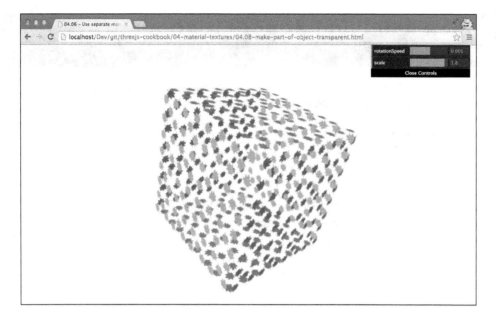

The code required to set a texture to repeat is the following:

```
var mat = new THREE.MeshPhongMaterial();
mat.map = new THREE.ImageUtils.loadTexture(
             "../assets/textures/partial-transparency.png");
mat.transparent = true;
mat.map.wrapS = mat.map.wrapT = THREE.RepeatWrapping;
mat.map.repeat.set( 4, 4 );
mat.depthWrite = false;
mat.color = new THREE.Color(0x00ff00);
```

By changing the `mat.map.repeat.set` values, you define how often the texture is repeated.

See also

- There are two alternative ways of making part of an object transparent. You could divide the object into multiple geometries and group them, or you could make individual faces transparent like we did in the *Using separate materials for faces* recipe.

Using a cubemap to create reflective materials

With the approach Three.js uses to render scenes in real time, it is difficult and very computationally intensive to create reflective materials. Three.js, however, provides a way you can cheat and approximate reflectivity. For this, Three.js uses cubemaps. In this recipe, we'll explain how to create cubemaps and use them to create reflective materials.

Getting ready

A cubemap is a set of six images that can be mapped to the inside of a cube. They can be created from a panorama picture and look something like this:

In Three.js, we map such a map on the inside of a cube or sphere and use that information to calculate reflections. The following screenshot (example `04.10-use-reflections.html`) shows what this looks like when rendered in Three.js:

As you can see in the preceeding screenshot, the objects in the center of the scene reflect the environment they are in. This is something often called a skybox. To get ready, the first thing we need to do is get a cubemap. If you search on the Internet, you can find some ready-to-use cubemaps, but it is also very easy to create one yourself. For this, go to `http://gonchar.me/panorama/`. On this page, you can upload a panoramic picture and it will be converted to a set of pictures you can use as a cubemap. For this, perform the following steps:

1. First, get a 360 degrees panoramic picture. Once you have one, upload it to the `http://gonchar.me/panorama/` website by clicking on the large **OPEN** button:

2. Once uploaded, the tool will convert the panorama picture to a cubemap as shown in the following screenshot:

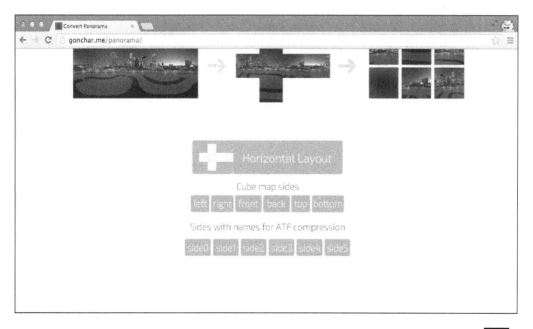

3. When the conversion is done, you can download the various cube map sites. The recipe in this book uses the naming convention provided by **Cube map sides** option, so download them. You'll end up with six images with names such as `right.png`, `left.png`, `top.png`, `bottom.png`, `front.png`, and `back.png`.

Once you've got the sides of the cubemap, you're ready to perform the steps in the recipe.

How to do it...

To use the cubemap we created in the previous section and create reflecting material, we need to perform a fair number of steps, but it isn't that complex:

1. The first thing you need to do is create an array from the cubemap images you downloaded:

```
var urls = [
    '../assets/cubemap/flowers/right.png',
    '../assets/cubemap/flowers/left.png',
    '../assets/cubemap/flowers/top.png',
    '../assets/cubemap/flowers/bottom.png',
    '../assets/cubemap/flowers/front.png',
    '../assets/cubemap/flowers/back.png'
];
```

2. With this array, we can create a cubemap texture like this:

```
var cubemap = THREE.ImageUtils.loadTextureCube(urls);
cubemap.format = THREE.RGBFormat;
```

3. From this cubemap, we can use `THREE.BoxGeometry` and a custom `THREE.ShaderMaterial` object to create a skybox (the environment surrounding our meshes):

```
var shader = THREE.ShaderLib[ "cube" ];
shader.uniforms[ "tCube" ].value = cubemap;

var material = new THREE.ShaderMaterial( {

    fragmentShader: shader.fragmentShader,
    vertexShader: shader.vertexShader,
    uniforms: shader.uniforms,
```

```
        depthWrite: false,
        side: THREE.DoubleSide

    });

    // create the skybox
    var skybox = new THREE.Mesh( new THREE.BoxGeometry( 10000, 10000,
    10000 ), material );
    scene.add(skybox);
```

Three.js provides a custom shader (a piece of WebGL code) that we can use for this. As you can see in the code snippet, to use this WebGL code, we need to define a THREE.ShaderMaterial object. With this material, we create a giant THREE.BoxGeometry object that we add to scene.

4. Now that we've created the skybox, we can define the reflecting objects:

```
    var sphereGeometry = new THREE.SphereGeometry(4,15,15);
    var envMaterial = new THREE.MeshBasicMaterial(
                                    {envMap:cubemap});
    var sphere = new THREE.Mesh(sphereGeometry, envMaterial);
```

As you can see, we also pass in the cubemap we created as a property (envmap) to the material. This informs Three.js that this object is positioned inside a skybox, defined by the images that make up cubemap.

5. The last step is to add the object to the scene, and that's it:

```
    scene.add(sphere);
```

In the example in the beginning of this recipe, you saw three geometries. You can use this approach with all different types of geometries. Three.js will determine how to render the reflective area.

How it works...

Three.js itself doesn't really do that much to render the `cubemap` object. It relies on a standard functionality provided by WebGL. In WebGL, there is a construct called `samplerCube`. With `samplerCube`, you can sample, based on a specific direction, which color matches the `cubemap` object. Three.js uses this to determine the color value for each part of the geometry. The result is that on each mesh, you can see a reflection of the surrounding cubemap using the WebGL `textureCube` function. In Three.js, this results in the following call (taken from the WebGL shader in GLSL):

```
vec4 cubeColor = textureCube( tCube,
                    vec3( -vReflect.x, vReflect.yz ) );
```

A more in-depth explanation on how this works can be found at `http://codeflow.org/entries/2011/apr/18/advanced-webgl-part-3-irradiance-environment-map/#cubemap-lookup`.

There's more...

In this recipe, we created the `cubemap` object by providing six separate images. There is, however, an alternative way to create the `cubemap` object. If you've got a 360 degrees panoramic image, you can use the following code to directly create a `cubemap` object from that image:

```
var texture = THREE.ImageUtils.loadTexture( 360-degrees.png',
                new THREE.UVMapping());
```

Normally when you create a `cubemap` object, you use the code shown in this recipe to map it to a skybox. This usually gives the best results but requires some extra code. You can also use `THREE.SphereGeometry` to create a skybox like this:

```
var mesh = new THREE.Mesh(
        new THREE.SphereGeometry( 500, 60, 40 ),
        new THREE.MeshBasicMaterial( { map: texture }));
mesh.scale.x = -1;
```

This applies the texture to a sphere and with `mesh.scale`, turns this sphere inside out.

Besides reflection, you can also use a `cubemap` object for refraction (think about light bending through water drops or glass objects):

All you have to do to make a refractive material is load the `cubemap` object like this:

```
var cubemap = THREE.ImageUtils.loadTextureCube(urls,
  new THREE.CubeRefractionMapping());
```

And define the material in the following way:

```
var envMaterial = new THREE.MeshBasicMaterial({envMap:cubemap});
envMaterial.refractionRatio = 0.95;
```

See also

> ▶ If you look closely at the example shown at the beginning of this recipe, you might notice that you don't see the reflections of the individual objects on each other. You only see the reflection of the skybox. In the *Using a dynamic cubemap to create reflective materials* recipe, we show you how you can make the `cubemap` object dynamic so that other rendered meshes are reflected.

Using a dynamic cubemap to create reflective materials

In the *Using a cubemap to create reflective materials* recipe, we showed how you can create a material that reflects its environment. The only caveat was that other meshes rendered in the scene didn't show up in the reflection; only the cubemap was shown. In this recipe, we will show you how you can create a dynamic cubemap that also reflects other meshes in the scene.

Getting ready

To get ready for this recipe, you need to follow the steps explained in the *Getting ready* section for the *Using a cubemap to create reflective materials* recipe. For this recipe, we provide a separate example that you can display by opening `04.11-use-reflections-dynamically.html` in your browser.

If you look closely at the central sphere in the preceding, you can see that it not only reflects the environment, but also reflects the cylinder, and if you rotate the scene, you can also see the cube reflection.

How to do it...

To accomplish this, we first need to perform a couple of the same steps, like we did in the *Using a cubemap to create reflective materials* recipe. So, before you start with the steps in this recipe, take the first three steps from that recipe. After these three steps, you can continue with these steps:

1. To create a dynamic cubemap, we need to use `THREE.CubeCamera`:

```
cubeCamera = new THREE.CubeCamera( 0.1, 20000, 256 );
cubeCamera.renderTarget.minFilter =
  THREE.LinearMipMapLinearFilter;
scene.add( cubeCamera );
```

With `THREE.CubeCamera`, we can take a snapshot of the environment and use it as the `cubemap` object in our materials. For the best result, you should position `THREE.CubeCamera` at the same location as the mesh on which you want to use the dynamic `cubemap` object. In this recipe, we use it on the central sphere, which is located at this position: 0, 0, 0. So, we don't need to set the position of `cubeCamera`.

2. For this recipe, we use three geometries:

```
var sphereGeometry = new THREE.SphereGeometry(4,15,15);
var cubeGeometry = new THREE.BoxGeometry(5,5,5);
var cylinderGeometry = new THREE.CylinderGeometry(2,4,10,
  20, false);
```

3. Next, we're going to define the materials. We use the following two materials:

```
var dynamicEnvMaterial = new THREE.MeshBasicMaterial(
  {envMap: cubeCamera.renderTarget });
var envMaterial = new THREE.MeshBasicMaterial(
  {envMap: cubemap });
```

The first one is the material that uses the output from `cubeCamera` as its cubemap, and the second material uses a static `cubemap` object.

4. With these two materials, we can create the meshes and add them to the scene:

```
var sphere = new THREE.Mesh(sphereGeometry, dynamicEnvMaterial);
sphere.name='sphere';
scene.add(sphere);

var cylinder = new THREE.Mesh(cylinderGeometry, envMaterial);
cylinder.name='cylinder';
scene.add(cylinder);
cylinder.position.set(10,0,0);

var cube = new THREE.Mesh(cubeGeometry, envMaterial);
```

```
cube.name='cube';
scene.add(cube);
cube.position.set(-10,0,0);
```

5. The last step we need to take is that in the `render` loop, we update `cubeCamera` like this:

```
function render() {
    sphere.visible = false;
    cubeCamera.updateCubeMap( renderer, scene );
    sphere.visible = true;
    renderer.render(scene, camera);
    ...
    requestAnimationFrame(render);
}
```

When you've taken all these steps, you'll end up with a sphere in the middle of the scene that not only reflects the environment, but also the other objects in the scene.

How it works...

In the *Using a cubemap to create reflective materials* recipe we explained how a cubemap is used to create reflective objects. The same principle also applies to this recipe, so if you haven't read the *How it works...* section from the *Using a cubemap to create reflective materials* recipe, please do that first. The main difference is that for this recipe, we create a cubemap on the fly with `THREE.CubeCamera` instead of using a static one. When you instantiate `THREE.CubeCamera`, you're really creating six `THREE.PerspectiveCamera` objects—one for each side of the cubemap. Whenever you call `updateCubeMap`, as we do in this recipe in the `render` loop, Three.js just renders the scene using these six cameras and uses the render results as the cubemap to be used.

There's more...

In this recipe, we showed you how to make one mesh reflect the complete scene. If you create separate `THREE.CubeCamera` objects for each of the meshes in the scene, you can create a dynamic cubemap for all the objects. Keep in mind, though, that this is a rather computationally-intensive process. Instead of rendering the scene once, you incur six additional render passes for each cube camera you use.

See also

▶ For a static cubemap, you can use the steps explained in the previous recipe, which is the *Using a cubemap to create reflective materials* recipe

Using Blender to create custom UV mapping

If you want to apply a texture (a 2D image) to a geometry, you need to tell Three.js which part of the texture should be used for a specific THREE.face object. The definition of how a texture maps to the individual faces of a geometry is called a UV mapping. A UV mapping, for example, tells Three.js how to map a 2D map of the earth to a 3D sphere geometry. When you're working with simple shapes, or the basic geometries provided with Three.js, the standard UV mapping that's provided is often enough. However, when shapes become more complex or you have some specific texture mapping requirements, you need to change how each face of a geometry is mapped to part of a texture. One option is to do this by hand, but for larger geometries, this is very difficult and time-consuming. In this recipe, we will show you how you can create a custom mapping with Blender.

Getting ready

For this recipe, you need to have Blender installed; if you haven't installed Blender yet, look at the *Getting ready* section of the *Creating and exporting a model from Blender* recipe from *Chapter 2, Geometries and Meshes*. Once you've installed Blender, start it and you're presented with a screen similar to the following screenshot:

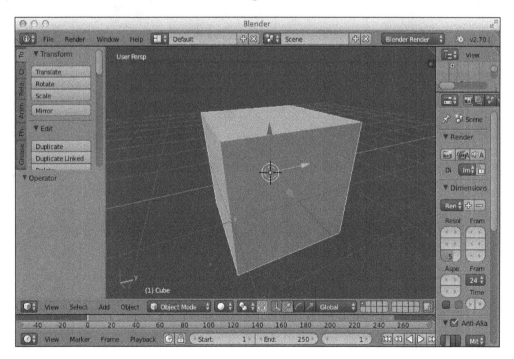

In the following section, we'll show you the steps you need to take to create a custom UV mapping for this cube.

How to do it...

The following steps explain how to create a custom UV mapping in Blender and use it in Three.js:

1. The first thing to do is switch to edit mode. To do this, hover the mouse over the cube and hit **tab**. You should see something like this:

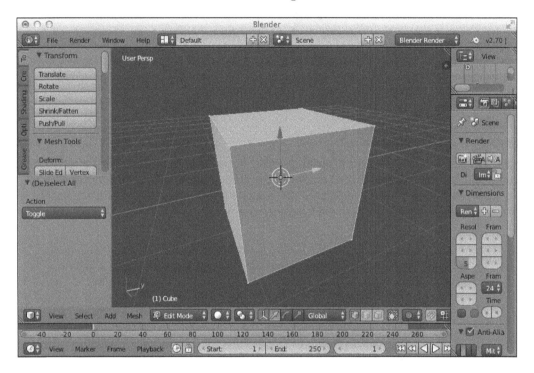

If the cube isn't highlighted, hover over it with the mouse and push a. This will select all the vertices and faces.

2. Now, let's create a standard UV mapping for this cube. To do this, navigate to **Mesh | Uv Unwrap | Unwrap**. Now, split the active view and open the **UV/Image editor** view.

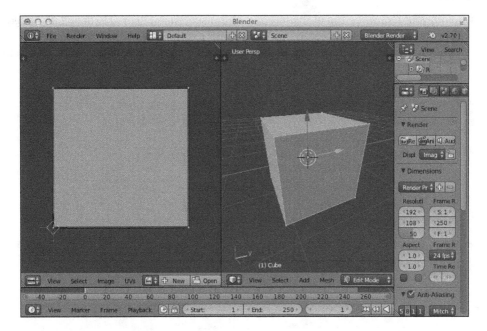

In the left part of the Blender window, we now see how all the selected faces and vertices are mapped to a texture.

3. In the right-hand side view, select the front face, and you can immediately see how that face is mapped to the texture:

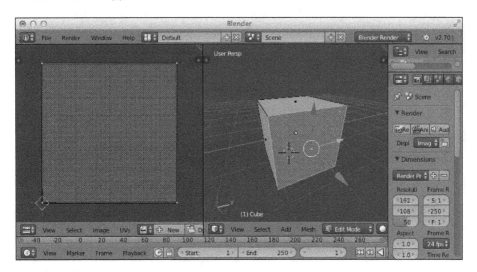

Now, we can change the mapping of this face by moving the vertices on the left-hand side side of the screen. Before we do that, though, we first load a texture image.

4. With your mouse on top of the left part of the screen, hit *Alt + O* to select an image. For this recipe, it is easiest to use the `debug.png` texture you can find in the `assets/textures` directory. Once you open the image, the screen will look like this:

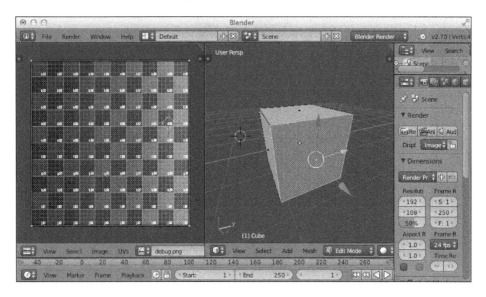

5. By dragging the corners in the left view, we change the UV mapping of the selected face. Move these corners around to create something like this:

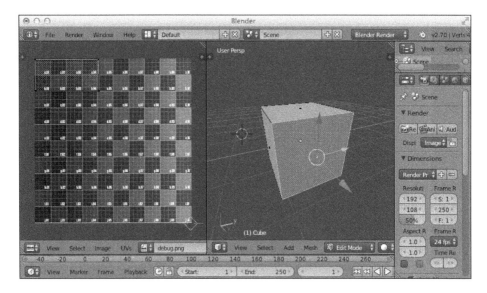

As you can see, we changed the UV mapping for this face from the whole texture to just the top-left corner.

6. The next step is to export this geometry, load it in Three.js, and see whether the mapping has really changed for the face we changed. To export the model, we'll use the OBJ format in this recipe. So, navigate to **File | Export | Wavefront** and save the model.

7. To load the model, we first need to include the OBJLoader JavaScript file on the header of the page:

```
<script src="../libs/OBJLoader.js"></script>
```

8. Now, we can use the loader to load the model and add it to the scene:

```
var loader = new THREE.OBJLoader();
loader.load("../assets/models/blender/uvmap.obj", function(model)
{
    model.children[0].material.map = THREE.ImageUtils
        .loadTexture("../assets/textures/debug.png");
    scene.add(model);
});
```

In this example, we explicitly set the texture we want to use, as we didn't use OBJMTLLoader.

9. As a final step, let's look at the result. We provided an example, 04.14-create-custom-uv-mapping.html, that shows the result of these steps.

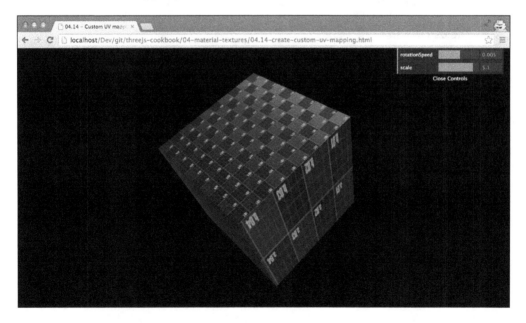

As you can see from the preceding screenshot, the front face for which we changed the UV mapping shows only part of the texture, while the other sides show the complete texture.

There's more...

We've only touched upon a very small part of how Blender can help in creating UV mappings. A good starting point to learn more about UV mapping in Blender are the following two sites:

- ▸ http://en.wikibooks.org/wiki/Blender_3D:_Noob_to_Pro/UV_Map_ Basics

- ▸ http://wiki.blender.org/index.php/Doc:2.6/Manual/Textures/ Mapping/UV

See also

- ▸ For more information on how to integrate Three.js with Blender, you can have a look at the *Creating and exporting a model from Blender* recipe, from *Chapter 2, Geometries and Meshes* where we show how to install the Three.js plugin for Blender and how you can load a model and its material directly in Three.js.

Configuring blend modes

When an object is rendered on top of another object in Three.js, you can configure how to blend in the colors from the objects behind it. In this recipe, we show you the steps you need to take to set a specific blend mode. You can compare this with the way the various blending layers in Photoshop work.

Getting ready

Understanding the results of a specific blend mode is difficult. To help in understanding the different available blend modes, we provide a simple web page that shows you the blend modes and allows you to switch between them. You can see this example by opening 04.13-configuring-blend-modes.html in your browser.

With the menu in the top-right section of the preceding screenshot, you can see what the result of each blend mode is.

How to do it...

Setting a blend mode is easy:

1. First, create a geometry and a material:

```
var cubeGeometry = new THREE.BoxGeometry(10, 4, 10);
var cubeMaterial = new THREE.MeshPhongMaterial(
  {map: THREE.ImageUtils.loadTexture(
    "../assets/textures/debug.png")});
```

2. Next, set the `blending` property to the blend mode you want to use:

```
cubeMaterial.blending = THREE.SubtractiveBlending;
```

3.   Then, set the `transparent` property to `true`:

```
cubeMaterial.transparent = true;
```

You can find an overview of the available, standard blend modes by looking at the Three.js sources:

```
THREE.NoBlending = 0;
THREE.NormalBlending = 1;
THREE.AdditiveBlending = 2;
THREE.SubtractiveBlending = 3;
THREE.MultiplyBlending = 4;
```

How it works...

As we've seen, Three.js uses WebGL to render the scenes. The blend modes you define on the material for Three.js are used internally by WebGL to determine how to blend the background color with the foreground color.

There's more...

Besides the blend modes we've shown in this recipe, it is also possible to define your own custom blend modes. You can do this by setting the `blending` property to `THREE.CustomBlending`. Use these three material properties to define how the foreground is blended with the background: `blendSrc`, `blendDst`, and `blendEquation`. For `blendSrc`, you can use the following values:

```
THREE.DstColorFactor = 208;
THREE.OneMinusDstColorFactor = 209;
THREE.SrcAlphaSaturateFactor = 210;
```

For `blendDst`, you can use these values:

```
THREE.ZeroFactor = 200;
THREE.OneFactor = 201;
THREE.SrcColorFactor = 202;
THREE.OneMinusSrcColorFactor = 203;
THREE.SrcAlphaFactor = 204;
THREE.OneMinusSrcAlphaFactor = 205;
THREE.DstAlphaFactor = 206;
THREE.OneMinusDstAlphaFactor = 207;
```

For the `blendEquation`, WebGL supports the following set:

```
THREE.AddEquation = 100;
THREE.SubtractEquation = 101;
THREE.ReverseSubtractEquation = 102;
```

A very good example that shows many of these settings can be found on the Three.js examples site at `http://threejs.org/examples/#webgl_materials_blending_custom`.

Using a shadow map for fixed shadows

In *Chapter 5, Lights and Custom Shaders* we will show you a number of recipes that deal with lights and shadows. It is, however, also possible to fake shadows using a texture. This kind of texture is called a shadow map or a light map. In this recipe, we explain how you can use such a texture in Three.js.

Getting ready

For this recipe, we first need a shadow map. There are different ways to create shadow maps, but that is outside the scope of this recipe. If you're interested in creating your own shadow maps, you can follow this tutorial from the Blender site: `http://wiki.blender.org/index.php/Doc:2.4/Tutorials/Game_Engine/YoFrankie/Baking_Shadow_Maps`.

In the sources for this book, in the `assets/textures` folder, you can find a `shadow-map.png` file that we'll use in this recipe.

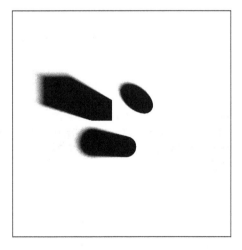

In the preceding figure, you can see what a shadow map looks like. As you can see, a shadow map contains the shadows of a scene prerendered in the target geometry, in this case, a plane. If we use this image as a shadow map, we can easily view the following scene:

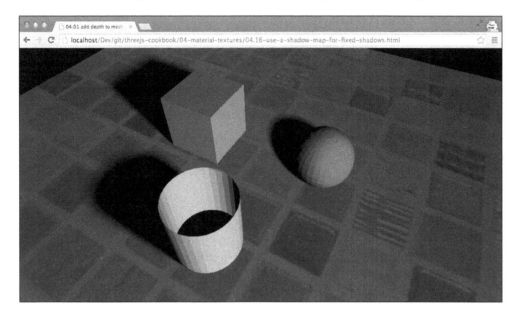

In this scene, we use the shadow map to create shadows for the ground plane.

How to do it...

Using a shadow map is very easy. Before we look at the steps, make sure that you've got a geometry and a material. In the following steps, we have THREE.Mesh with the name floor:

1. A UV mapping defines how a face maps to a specific part of a texture. The UV mapping in a geometry is stored in the faceVertexUvs property of a geometry. The first element of this array contains the UV mappings used for the other kinds of textures, and the second element contains the UV mapping for the shadow map. As this value isn't filled by default, we point it to the first element in the faceVertexUvs array:

    ```
    floor.geometry.faceVertexUvs[1] =
      floor.geometry.faceVertexUvs[0];
    ```

2. Next, you need to set the shadow map to the lightmap property of the material:

    ```
    floor.material.lightMap = THREE.ImageUtils.loadTexture
      ("../assets/textures/shadow-map-soft.png");
    ```

3. Finally, you add the other textures you might want to use:

```
floor.material.map = THREE.ImageUtils.loadTexture
    ("../assets/textures/tiles.jpg");
```

That's all you need to do. This works great, especially when you've got scenes with static meshes and fixed lights, and this is a great boost to performance.

See also

▸   If you require dynamic shadows that update based on animated lighting or objects in the scene, you need something else (or in addition to) than shadow maps. In *Chapter 5, Lights and Custom Shaders* in the *Creating shadows with Three.SpotLight* recipe, we explain how to create dynamic shadows.

5
Lights and Custom Shaders

In this chapter, we'll cover the following recipes:

- ▶ Creating shadows with THREE.SpotLight
- ▶ Creating shadows with THREE.DirectionalLight
- ▶ Softening lights by adding ambient lighting
- ▶ Using THREE.HemisphereLight for natural lighting
- ▶ Adding a moving all-directional light
- ▶ Moving a light source along a path
- ▶ Making a light source follow an object
- ▶ Creating a custom vertex shader
- ▶ Creating a custom fragment shader

Introduction

Three.js provides a large number of light sources out of the box. In this chapter, we'll show you a number of recipes that work on lights and also show you how to get the most out of the lighting options provided by Three.js. We'll also show you two advanced recipes that explain how you can access the raw features of WebGL by creating your own custom vertex and fragment shaders.

Creating shadows with THREE.SpotLight

Three.js offers many different types of lights you can use in your scenes. A couple of these lights also allow you to add shadows to the scene. When you use `THREE.SpotLight` or a `THREE.DirectionalLight` object, you can let Three.js add shadows based on the position of the lights. In this recipe, we'll show you how to do this with `THREE.SpotLight`.

Getting ready

For this recipe, you don't need any external dependencies. Three.js includes all the available lights directly in the main Three.js JavaScript library. We've created a simple example that you can use to see how shadows work in combination with `THREE.SpotLight` in Three.js. You can view this example by opening `05.01-using-shadows-with-a-spotLight.html` in your browser. You will see something similar to the following screenshot:

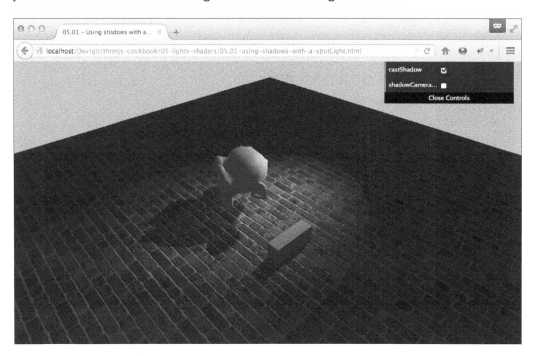

In this scene, you can see that we've added two meshes to the scene, both of which cast a shadow on the floor. From this example, you can also directly see the distinct light shape provided by `THREE.SpotLight`.

How to do it...

To create a shadow with `THREE.SpotLight`, we need to set a couple of properties, which define the area where shadows are created:

1. Before we look at `THREE.SpotLight`, the first thing we need to do is tell the renderer that we want to enable shadows. To do this, set the following property on `THREE.WebGLRenderer`:

   ```
   renderer.shadowMapEnabled = true;
   ```

2. The next step is to inform Three.js which objects cast shadows and which objects receive shadows. If you look back at the screenshot in the *Getting ready* section, you can see that the monkey and the cube both cast a shadow and the floor receives the shadow. To do this, you have to set the following properties on the `THREE.Mesh` objects that should cast shadows:

   ```
   ..monkey.castShadow = true;
     cubeMesh.castShadow = true;
   ```

   For objects that receive shadows, you have to set the following on the `THREE.Mesh` object:

   ```
   floorMesh.receiveShadow = true;
   ```

3. At this point, we're ready to create `THREE.SpotLight`:

   ```
   var spotLight = new THREE.SpotLight();
   spotLight.angle = Math.PI/8; // in radians
   spotLight.exponent = 30;
   spotLight.position = new THREE.Vector3(40,60,-50);
   ```

   These are the standard properties that define how `THREE.SpotLight` adds light to a scene.

4. The next step is to set up the shadow-related properties:

   ```
   spotLight.castShadow = true;
   spotLight.shadowCameraNear = 50;
   spotLight.shadowCameraFar = 200;
   spotLight.shadowCameraFov = 35;
   ```

   The first property, `castShadow`, tells Three.js that this light casts shadows. As casting shadows is an expensive operation, we need to define the area where shadows can appear. This is done with the `shadowCameraNear`, `shadowCameraFar`, and `shadowCameraFov` properties.

5. Three.js uses something called a shadow map to render the shadows. If your shadow looks a bit blocky around its edges, it means the shadow map is too small. To increase the shadow map size, set the following properties:

   ```
   spotLight.shadowMapHeight = 2048;
   spotLight.shadowMapWidth = 2048;
   ```

Alternatively, you can also try to change the `shadowMapType` property of `THREE.WebGLRenderer`. You can set this to `THREE.BasicShadowMap`, `THREE.PCFShadowMap`, or `THREE.PCSSoftShadowMap`.

6. The last step is to add `THREE.SpotLight` to the scene:

   ```
   scene.add(spotLight);
   ```

Determining the correct properties for the various `THREE.SpotLight` properties can be difficult. In the following section, we'll explain a bit more how the various properties affect the area where shadows are rendered.

How it works...

When you want to use `THREE.SpotLight` as a light source that can cast shadows, Three.js needs to know the area that will be affected by these shadows. You can compare this with the arguments you use to configure `THREE.PerspectiveCamera`. So, what you do with the `shadowCameraNear`, `shadowCameraFar`, and `shadowCameraFov` properties is define where Three.js should render shadows. Determining the correct values for these properties can be a bit difficult, but luckily, Three.js can visualize this area. If you set the `shadowCameraVisible` property of `THREE.SpotLight` to `true`, Three.js will show you the affected area, as shown in the following screenshot:

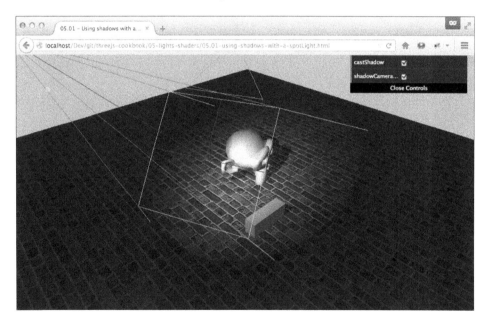

In this screenshot, the size of the area is visualized with orange and red lines. By enabling this `shadowCameraVisible` property and experimenting with the other values, you can quickly determine the correct values.

▶ In Three.js, there are two light sources that can cast shadows: `THREE.SpotLight` and `THREE.DirectionalLight`. In the *Creating shadows with a THREE.DirectionalLight* recipe, we explain how to cast shadows using `THREE.DirectionalLight`. A more performant but static way to create shadows is explained in the *Using a shadow map for fixed shadows* recipe in *Chapter 4, Materials and Textures*.

Creating shadows with THREE. DirectionalLight

With `THREE.DirectionalLight`, you can simulate a light source from far away whose rays run parallel to each other. A good example of this is light received from the sun. In this recipe, we'll show you how to create `THREE.DirectionalLight` and use it to create shadows.

Getting ready

For this recipe, we've created an example that shows you what the shadows cast by a `THREE.DirectionalLight` object look like. Open up the `05.02-using-shadows-with-a-directionalLight.html` example in your browser, and you'll see something like what is shown in the following screenshot:

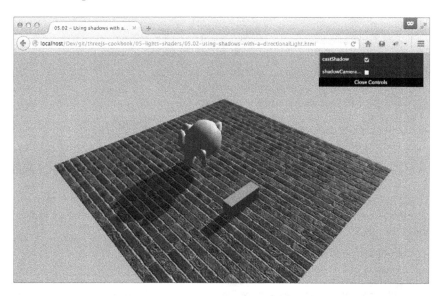

In this screenshot, a single `THREE.DirectionalLight` object provides the shadows and lighting.

How to do it...

Using `THREE.DirectionLight` as a shadow only takes a couple of steps:

1. The first thing we need to do to enable any kind of shadow is set `shadowMapEnabled` on `THREE.WebGLRenderer` to `true`:

    ```
    renderer.shadowMapEnabled = true;
    ```

2. Next, we inform Three.js which of our objects should receive shadows and which should cast shadows. So, for the objects that should cast a shadow, set the `castShadow` property on `THREE.Mesh` to `true`:

    ```
    monkey.castShadow = true;
    cubeMesh.castShadow = true;
    ```

    For the objects that should receive a shadow, the floor in this case, set the following property on `THREE.Mesh` to `true`:

    ```
    floorMesh.receiveShadow = true;
    ```

3. Now, we can create `THREE.DirectionalLight` and configure this light source. Add the following code to create `THREE.DirectionalLight`:

    ```
    var directionalLight = new THREE.DirectionalLight();
    directionalLight.position = new THREE.Vector3(70,40,-50);
    directionalLight.castShadow = true;
    ```

4. This will create and position `THREE.DirectionalLight` and together with the `castShadow` property, this light source will be used by Three.js to render shadows.

5. The next step is to configure the area where shadows should be rendered:

    ```
    directionalLight.shadowCameraNear = 25;
    directionalLight.shadowCameraFar = 200;
    directionalLight.shadowCameraLeft = -50;
    directionalLight.shadowCameraRight = 50;
    directionalLight.shadowCameraTop = 50;
    directionalLight.shadowCameraBottom = -50;
    ```

    With these properties, we create a box-like area where Three.js will render shadows.

6. Three.js uses two additional properties to determine the detail of the rendered shadow: `shadowMapWidth` and `shadowMapHeight`. If your shadows look a bit rough or blocky, you should increase the values like this:

    ```
    directionalLight.shadowMapWidth = 2048;
    directionalLight.shadowMapHeight = 2048;
    ```

7. After all these properties have been set, you can add the light source to the scene:

    ```
    scene.add(directionalLight);
    ```

As you can see from these steps it is a little complicated to correctly configure
THREE.DirectionalLight. Determining the correct values can be difficult. In the next
section, we'll explain a bit more what these properties do and how you can determine their
optimal values for your scene.

How it works...

If you look back to the *Using an orthographic camera* recipe in *Chapter 3, Working
with the Camera*, you'll notice that the camera uses the same properties as THREE.
DirectionalLight. Both these objects define a bounding box that is rendered in
the case of THREE.OrthographicCamera and is used to determine where to render
shadows in the case of THREE.DirectionalLight. With shadowCameraNear,
shadowCameraFar, shadowCameraLeft, shadowCameraRight, shadowCameraTop,
and shadowCameraBottom, you define this area. You can set an additional property on
THREE.DirectionalLight to visualize the affected area. If you set directionalLight.
shadowCameraVisible to true, Three.js will draw the box defined by the
shadowCameraXXX properties. The following screenshot shows you the result of enabling the
shadowCameraVisible property:

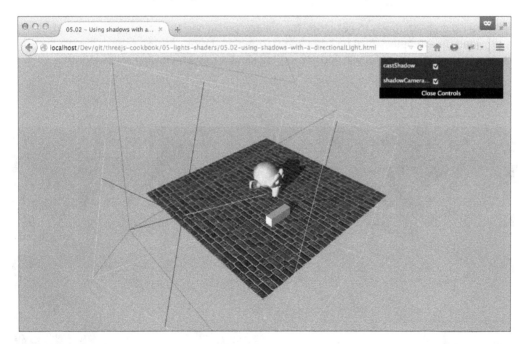

Shadows will only be rendered in the area contained by the orange box.

See also

> ▸ In Three.js, there are two light sources that can cast shadows: `THREE.SpotLight` and `THREE.DirectionalLight`. In the *Creating shadows with THREE.SpotLight* recipe, we explain how to cast shadows using `THREE.SpotLight`. An alternative way to create shadows is explained in the *Using a shadow map for fixed shadows* recipe in *Chapter 4, Materials and Textures*.

Softening lights by adding ambient lighting

When you add lights to a scene, the result might look a bit harsh. You can see a strong contrast between the areas that receive lights and those that don't. When you look at real-life lighting, everything is a bit softer and almost every surface will receive some light, most often reflected from other surfaces. In this recipe, we'll show you how you can soften the light usage in your scene using `THREE.AmbientLight`.

Getting ready

There are no steps required to get ready for this recipe. To see the final result in action, we provided an example, which you can see by opening the `05.03-soften-lights.html` example in your browser. You will find something similar to the following screenshot:

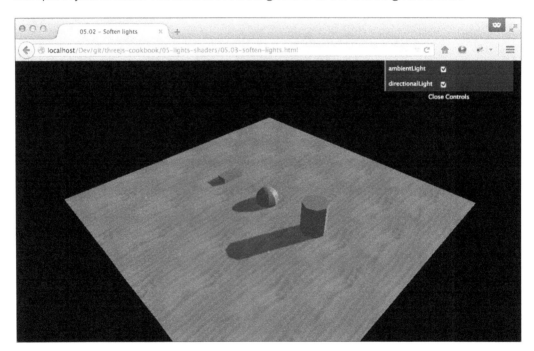

With the menu in the top-right section, you can enable or disable THREE.AmbientLight to see the effect THREE.AmbientLight object has.

How to do it...

THREE.AmbientLight is the simplest of lights to use. As it applies light to the complete scene, there is no need to position the light source. All you have to do is create an instance of THREE.AmbientLight and add it to the scene:

1. First, create the instance of THREE.AmbientLight:

   ```
   var ambientLight = new THREE.AmbientLight(0x332222);
   ```

   This will create the light source. When you create the ambient light, you can specify its color as a hex value. Don't specify it too high; if you do, your whole scene will be very bright.

2. The only thing left to do is add this light to the scene:

   ```
   scene.add(ambientLight);
   ```

With these two very simple steps, you've created THREE.AmbientLight.

How it works...

THREE.AmbientLight works in a very simple way. When you create THREE.AmbientLight, you pass in a color (in hex) into its constructor. When the scene is rendered, Three.js just blends in the specified color to the color of any of your meshes.

See also

▶ Even though THREE.AmbientLight can be used to soften the lighting in a scene, it's hard to create natural-looking lighting. In the *Using THREE.HemisphereLight for natural lighting* recipe, we show you how to use a different light source for natural outside lighting.

Using THREE.HemisphereLight for natural lighting

If you look at the lighting outside, you'll see that the lights don't really come from a single direction. Part of the sunlight is reflected by Earth, and other parts are scattered by the atmosphere. The result is a very soft light coming from lots of directions. In Three.js, we can create something similar using `THREE.HemisphereLight`.

Getting ready

Just like the other lights provided by Three.js, there is no need to include any additional JavaScript file to work with `THREE.HemisphereLight`. All you need is a scene with some objects, and you can add this light. To see the effect `THREE.HemisphereLight` object has, we've provided a simple example. Open up `05.04-create-a-sun-like-light.html` in your browser. You will see something similar to the following screenshot:

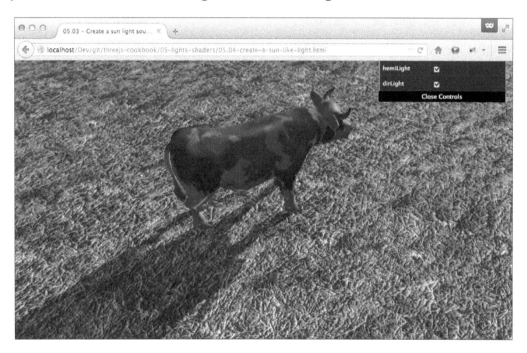

With the controls in the top-right section, you can enable and disable `THREE.HemisphereLight` and `THREE.DirectionalLight`, which are used in this scene.

How to do it...

Creating `THREE.HemisphereLight` works in pretty much the same way as creating the other lights:

1. You first need to instantiate a `THREE.HemisphereLight` instance:

   ```
   var hemiLight = new THREE.HemisphereLight(
     0xffffff, 0xffffff, 0.6 );
   ```

   The first parameter sets the color of the sky, and the second color sets the color reflected from the floor. In both these cases, we just set a white light. With the last property, you can control the intensity of `THREE.HemisphereLight` object. In this case, we dampen the light by setting it to `0.6`.

2. Next, we need to position the light:

   ```
   hemiLight.position.set( 0, 500, 0 );
   ```

   When you position `THREE.HemisphereLight`, it's best to position it directly above the scene for the best effect.

3. Finally, with the position set, the last step is to add the light to the scene:

   ```
   scene.add( hemiLight );
   ```

You could use `THREE.HemisphereLight` as the main light source of your scene, but most often, this light source is used together with a different light source. For the best outdoor effect, use it with `THREE.DirectionalLight`, which can cast shadows.

How it works...

`THREE.HemisphereLight` pretty much acts as two `THREE.DirectionalLight` objects: one positioned at the specified position and another one in exactly the opposite position. So, when a scene is rendered, `THREE.HemisphereLight` lights an object from the top and from the opposite direction to create a natural-looking effect.

There's more...

You can, of course, also use two `THREE.DirectionalLight` objects instead of `THREE.HemisphereLight`. With careful tuning, you can reach the exact same effect as you would get with `THREE.HemisphereLight`. The added advantage is that you could also make very faint shadows with this approach, as `THREE.DirectionalLight` supports casting shadows whereas `THREE.HemisphereLight` does not.

See also

▸ In the *Softening lights by adding ambient lighting* recipe, we showed you a more simple approach of supporting the main light sources in your scene. We showed you how you can use `THREE.AmbientLight` as an extra light source to soften the lights and the shadows.

Adding a moving all-directional light

In a lot of cases, you don't need a light source that casts shadows but just a light source that illuminates your scene. In the *Creating shadows with THREE.SpotLight* and *Creating shadows with THREE.DirectionalLight* recipes, we already showed you how you can use `THREE.SpotLight` and `THREE.DirectionalLight`. In this recipe, we'll show you a third kind of light, which is `THREE.PointLight`; this kind of light emits light to all directions and in this recipe, we will show you how to create one and move it through the scene.

Getting ready

As the Three.js standard comes with the `THREE.PointLight` object, there is no need to include any additional JavaScript. The same is the case with all the recipes where we've included an example where you can see the result of this recipe in action. For this recipe, open the `05.05-use-a-point-light.html` example in your browser, and you'll see the following result:

In this example, there are four `THREE.PointLight` objects that move from the top to the bottom in between three models of a shark. You can use your mouse to move around this scene and see how `THREE.PointLight` illuminates the models.

How to do it...

Creating a moving `THREE.PointLight` object is very easy and only takes a couple of steps:

1. The first thing to do is create a `THREE.PointLight` instance:

```
var pointLight = new THREE.PointLight();
pointLight.color = new THREE.Color(0xff0000);
pointLight.intensity = 3;
pointLight.distance = 60;
pointLight.name = 'pointLight';
```

   With the `color` property, we set the color `THREE.PointLight` object emits, and the intensity allows us to set how much light is emitted. Finally, the `distance` property is used to calculate how much the intensity decreases the farther away the lit object is from the light. In this case, the intensity will be 0 when the distance to the light is 60.

2. `THREE.PointLight` emits lights in all directions, so we need to set the `position` property and then we can add the light to the scene:

```
pointLight.position = new THREE.Vector3(-30,0,0);
scene.add(pointLight);
```

3. The last thing we need to do for this recipe is move `THREE.PointLight` through the scene. Like all animations, we do this in the render loop by adding the following to the `render` function:

```
var light = scene.getObjectByName('pointLight');
light.position.y = 15 * Math.sin(count+=0.005);
```

   In this small code snippet, we first get a reference to our `THREE.PointLight` object and then update its `position.y` property. For this to work, we also need to define a global `count` property at the top of our JavaScript like this:

```
var count = 0;
```

With these simple steps, you've created `THREE.PointLight`, which moves up and down through the scene.

How it works...

THREE.PointLight emits light in all directions; you can compare this a bit with THREE.SpotLight but with a 360 degree field of view in all directions. This is also the main reason that THREE.PointLight can't be used to cast shadows. As there is so much light being emitted by THREE.PointLight, it is very difficult and resource-intensive to calculate the resulting shadows.

So, if you want shadows and also use THREE.PointLight, you could use a shadow map if you have a static THREE.PointLight object or an extra THREE.SpotLight object and set it to only cast shadows with the onlyShadow property.

See also

There are a couple of recipes that you can look at in relation to this recipe:

▸ In the *Creating shadows with a THREE.SpotLight* recipe, we showed you how you can use THREE.SpotLight to create shadows. You can use this together with THREE.PointLight.

▸ In the *Creating shadows with a THREE.DirectionalLight* recipe, we show you how to set up and configure THREE.DirectionalLight. This light casts shadows and can be used together with THREE.PointLight.

▸ In *Chapter 4, Materials and Textures*, we showed you the *Using a shadow map for fixed shadows* recipe. This recipe explained how to use shadow maps to fake shadows. If you use that recipe together with this one, you can use it to fake the shadows cast by THREE.PointLight.

Moving a light source along a path

In the *Add an moving all-directional light* recipe, we moved a light source up and down. While these simple kinds of paths are often enough, there are cases where you want more control over how your light source moves through a scene. In this recipe, we'll show you how you can move a light source along a predefined path.

Getting ready

To create this recipe, we'll use a THREE.SplineCurve3D and THREE.SpotLight object. As both of these objects are included with Three.js, we don't need to take any steps to get ready. A good thing to do, however, is look at the provided example for this recipe, which will show you what you'll get when you execute the steps from this recipe when you run the 05.06-move-a-light-through-the-scene.html example:

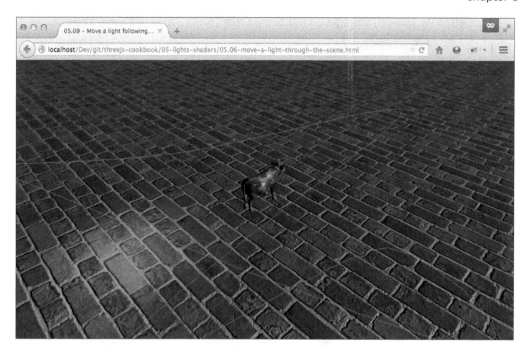

In the screenshot, you can see a light that moves slowly along the purple line. In the next section, we'll show you how you can create this yourself.

How to do it...

For this recipe, we first need to create the path that we'll follow:

1. For this path, we'll create `THREE.SplineCurve3`:

    ```
    var spline = new THREE.SplineCurve3([
      new THREE.Vector3(-100, 20, 100),
      new THREE.Vector3(-40, 20, 20),
      new THREE.Vector3(0, 20, -100),
      new THREE.Vector3(20, 20, -100),
      new THREE.Vector3(40, 20, 100),
      new THREE.Vector3(70, 20, 10),
      new THREE.Vector3(100, 20, 30),
      new THREE.Vector3(-100, 20, 100)]);
    ```

    This will result in a curved path that moves through the points added in the constructor of the `THREE.SplineCurve3` object.

2. Before we position our light on the path of this `THREE.SplineCurve3` object, let's create the light:

```
var pointLight = new THREE.PointLight();
pointLight.color = new THREE.Color(0xff0000);
pointLight.intensity = 3;
pointLight.distance = 60;
pointlight.name = 'pointLight';
```

3. Now, we can use this `SplineCurve3` object to determine the position of our light. For this, we create a helper function called `positionLight`:

```
var pos = 0;
function positionLight() {
    light = scene.getObjectByName('pointLight');
    if (pos <= 1) {
        light.position = spline.getPointAt(pos);
        pos += 0.001
    } else {
        pos = 0;
    }
}
```

In this function, we use `spline.getPointAt(pos)` to determine where on the `THREE.SplineCurve3` path we need to position our light. With `pos` at `0`, we're at the beginning of spline and with `pos` at `1`, we're at the end. This way, we slowly (in steps of `0.001`) move the light along the spline.

4. All that is left to do is call the `positionLight` function from the render function:

```
function render() {
    renderer.render(scene, camera);
    positionLight();
    orbit.update();
    requestAnimationFrame(render);
}
```

As the render function is called approximately 60 times per second and we take 1000 steps for our complete path, the light will move along the complete path in about 17 seconds.

How it works...

When you instantiate a THREE.SplineCurve3 object, you pass in an array of THREE.Vector3 objects. Three.js internally interpolates these points to create a fluid curve that moves through all these points. Once the curve is created, you have two ways to get positions. You can use the getPointAt function, as we did in this recipe, to get a relative position based on the provided parameter, from 0 to 1, and the length of the curve. Alternatively, you can also use the getPoints function, where you specify, as the parameter, in how many points the line should be divided.

There's more...

In the *Getting ready* part of this recipe, we showed you an example where a light moved through a scene. What you could see was that we also showed the path along which the light moved. To do this for yourself, you can use the getPoints function from the created THREE.SplineCurve3 object to create a THREE.Line object:

```
var geometry = new THREE.Geometry();
var splinePoints = spline.getPoints(50);
var material = new THREE.LineBasicMaterial({
  color: 0xff00f0
});
geometry.vertices = splinePoints;
var line = new THREE.Line(geometry, material);
scene.add(line);
```

In this recipe, we moved a light along a specific path. However, as a light is also just an object with a specific position, we can apply this same principle to all the other objects in the scene, such as THREE.Mesh, THREE.PerspectiveCamera, or THREE.OrthographicCamera.

Making a light source follow an object

If you've got a moving object in the scene that you want to highlight with a spotlight, you need to be able to change the direction a light is pointed at. In this recipe, we will show you how to do just that. We will show you how you can keep THREE.SpotLight pointed at a moving object in the scene.

Getting ready

There are no steps that you need to take to run this recipe. You can see the final result of this recipe by opening up the `05.07-make-a-light-follow-object.html` example in your browser. You will see something similar to the following screenshot:

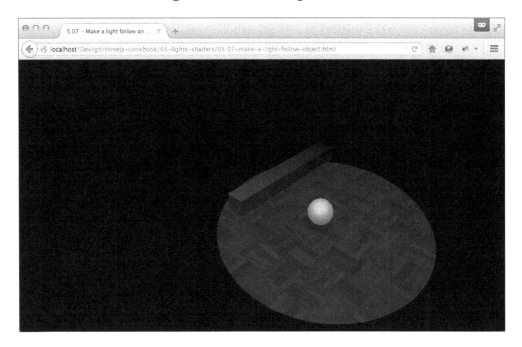

In this example, you can see a sphere that moves from left to right and back again. `THREE.SpotLight` in this scene follows the position of this sphere so that it is always pointed directly at the center of that object.

How to do it...

Following an object in Three.js is very easy and only takes a couple of easy steps:

1. The fist thing we need to do is create the object that we want to follow. For this recipe, this is `THREE.SpotLight`:

```
var sphereGeometry = new THREE.SphereGeometry(1.5, 20,
  20);
var matProps = {
  specular: 0xa9fcff,
  color: 0x00abb1,
  emissive: 0x006063,
  shininess: 10
}
```

```
var sphereMaterial = new
  THREE.MeshPhongMaterial(matProps);
var sphereMesh = new THREE.Mesh(
  sphereGeometry, sphereMaterial);sphereMesh.name =
  'sphere'; scene.add(sphereMesh);
```

2. Next, we create and add `THREE.SpotLight` to the scene:

```
spotLight = new THREE.SpotLight();
spotLight.position.set(20, 80, 30);
spotLight.castShadow = true;
spotLight.angle = 0.15;
spotLight.distance = 160;
scene.add(spotLight);
```

Note that at this step, we don't point the created light to the sphere. We'll do this in the next step in the render loop.

3. To keep the light pointed at the sphere, we need to set the `target` property to the correct value. We do this in the `render` function of the scene:

```
var step = 0;
function render() {
  step += 0.02;
  renderer.render(scene, camera);
  var sphere = scene.getObjectByName('sphere');
  sphere.position.x = 0 + (10 * (Math.cos(step)));
  sphere.position.y = 0.75 * Math.PI / 2 +
    (6 * Math.abs(Math.sin(step)));
  spotLight.target = sphere;
  requestAnimationFrame(render);
}
```

One thing to notice in the last step is that we set the target property of `spotLight` to the `THREE.Mesh` object and not to the position property of `THREE.Mesh`.

There's more...

To point `THREE.SpotLight` at a certain position, we set its `target` property. As you've seen in the recipe steps, we target `THREE.Object3D`, from which `THREE.Mesh` extends, instead of a position. If we want to point `THREE.SpotLight` to an arbitrary position, we need to first create an empty `THREE.Object3D` object:

```
var target = new THREE.Object3D();
target.position = new THREE.Vector3(20,10,-10);
scene.add(target);
spotLight.target = target;
```

This way, you can point `THREE.SpotLight` not just to an existing object in the scene but to any position you want.

See also

▶ In this recipe, we pointed a light at a specific target, and we can also make a camera follow an object around the scene, as we showed in the *Making the camera follow an object* recipe from *Chapter 3*, *working with the Camera* and point one object to another, as shown in the *Pointing an object to another object* recipe in *Chapter 2*, *Geometries and Meshes*.

Creating a custom vertex shader

When you want to create advanced 3D effects with great performance, you can choose to write your own shaders. **Shaders** are programs that directly affect what your results look like and which colors are used to represent them. A shader always comes as a pair. A vertex shader determines what a geometry will look like, and a fragment shader will determine the resulting color. In this recipe, we'll show you how you can use your own custom vertex shader in Three.js.

Getting ready

WebGL and GLSL, which is the language in which you write shaders, are supported by most modern browsers. So, for this recipe, there aren't any additional steps you need to take before you can walk through this recipe. A good resource on GLSL is always the khronos website (`http://www.khronos.org`); they have a great tutorial (`http://www.khronos.org/webgl/wiki/Tutorial`) on WebGL that can help you better understand what we're doing in this recipe. For this specific recipe, we've provided two examples. The first one is the one we'll use in this recipe, and you can view this one by opening `05.09-custom-vertex-shader.html` in your browser.

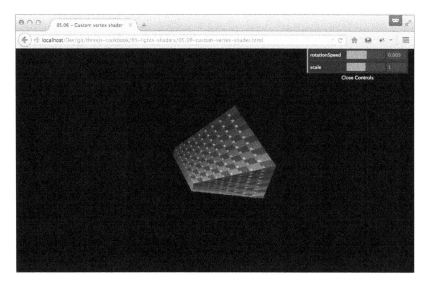

This example, as you can see in the previous screenshot, shows you THREE.BoxGeometry, where the position of its individual vertices have been replaced using a vertex shader. A more advanced example can be found in 05.09-custom-vertex-shader-2.html.

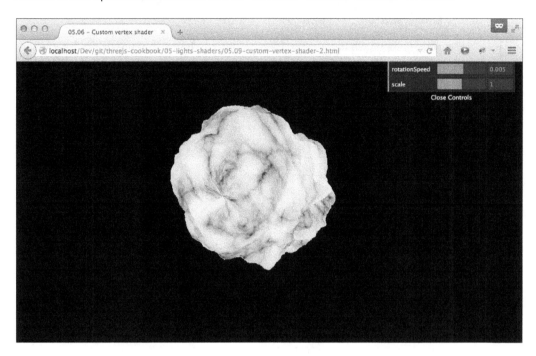

In this example, we once again change the position of individual vertices, but this time, we use THREE.SphereGeometry as the source and combine it with a perlin noise generator.

How to do it...

To create a custom vertex shader, you need to follow these steps:

1. As we just want to write a vertex shader, we'll use a standard fragment shader, which is the one also used by THREE.MeshBasicMaterial from Three.js. You can get a reference to this shader by selecting the correct one from THREE.ShaderLib:

   ```
   var basicShader = THREE.ShaderLib['basic'];
   ```

2. The next step is to define the Uniforms object. Uniforms are parameters that are passed into the shaders as arguments:

   ```
   Var uniforms = {}
   uniforms = THREE.UniformsUtils
     .merge([basicShader.uniforms]);
   ```

```
var texture = THREE.ImageUtils
  .loadTexture('../assets/textures/debug.png');
uniforms['map'].value = texture;
uniforms.delta = {type: 'f', value: 0.0};
uniforms.scale = {type: 'f', value: 1.0};
```

In this code snippet, we first `merge` the standard uniforms that are by the fragment shader we reuse, we set a texture, and the last two uniforms are the ones we access in our own custom vertex shader, as we'll see later on.

3. Now, we can define `THREE.ShaderMaterial` and tell Three.js the shaders that we want to use:

```
var defines = {};
defines[ "USE_MAP" ] = "";
var material = new THREE.ShaderMaterial({
  defines: defines,
  uniforms: uniforms,
  vertexShader: document
    getElementById('sinusVertexShader').text,
  fragmentShader: basicShader.fragmentShader
});
```

In this code snippet, you can see that we reference the uniform value we saw in step 2, as `fragmentShader` we use `basicShader` from step 1, and for the `vertexShader` parameter, we reference our custom shader, which we'll define in the next step. Note that we also provide a `defines` element; this is needed to make sure Three.js shows our texture.

4. At this point, we can define our own custom vertex shader. We do this directly in the HTML as follows:

```
<script id="sinusVertexShader" type="x-shader/x-vertex">
  varying vec2 vUv;
  uniform float delta;
  uniform float scale;
  void main() {
    vUv = uv;
    vec3 p = position;
    p.z += sin(2.0 * p.y + delta) * 5.0;
    p.z += cos(2.0 * p.z + delta / 2.0) * 5.0;
    p.z += cos(2.0 * p.x + delta) * 5.0;
    p.x += sin(p.y + delta / 2.0) * 10.0;
    vec4 mvPosition =
      modelViewMatrix * vec4(scale * p, 1.0 );
    gl_Position = projectionMatrix * mvPosition;
  }
</script>
```

With this shader, we change the location of the vertices by changing the `p.z` and the `p.x` part of its position.

5. At this point, we can just create a geometry and use the material we created in step 3:

```
var cubeGeometry = new THREE.BoxGeometry(5, 5, 5);
var cube = new THREE.Mesh(cubeGeometry, material);
scene.add(cube);
```

6. If you look in the shader code in step 4, you can see that the position is influenced by the delta uniform value. We use the `render` function to pass in a new value for this uniform:

```
function render() {
  renderer.render(scene, camera);
  uniforms.delta.value += 0.01;
  requestAnimationFrame(render);
}
```

These are all the steps you need to take to create and use a custom vertex shader combined with a simple fragment shader from Three.js.

How it works...

Let's look a bit closer at what is happening in the vertex shader used in this recipe. Before we start, we'll give you a very short introduction to the types of qualifiers that you can use with the variables in your shader code:

▸ The `uniform` qualifier: This is a global variable that can be passed in from JavaScript to the shaders. You can change this value in each rendering loop but can't change the value in the shader itself.

▸ The `attribute` qualifier: This is a value that can be specified for each individual vertex. The `attributes` qualifier are passed on into the vertex shader.

▸ The `varying` qualifier: This is used to pass data between the vertex shader and the fragment shader. It can be written into the vertex shader but can only be read in the fragment shader.

▸ The `const` qualifier: This is a constant value and is defined directly in your shader code. This value can't change during the execution of your shaders.

The first thing we do is define some parameters:

```
varying vec2 vUv;
uniform float delta;
uniform float scale;
```

The vUv vector is a varying variable and is a value that is passed into the fragment shader and is required for the basic shader to work in Three.js. The other two parameters are passed in as uniforms from the JavaScript you saw in the previous section. Let's look at the main function, which is the function that is exectured for each vertex:

```
void main() {
  vUv = uv;
  vec3 p = position;
  p.z += sin(2.0 * p.y + delta) * 5.0;
  p.z += cos(2.0 * p.z + delta / 2.0) * 5.0;
  p.z += cos(2.0 * p.x + delta) * 5.0;
  p.x += sin(p.y + delta / 2.0) * 10.0;
  vec4 mvPosition =
    modelViewMatrix * vec4(scale * p, 1.0 );
  gl_Position = projectionMatrix * mvPosition;
}
```

The main thing that happens here is that we change the position of the vertex based on the passed-in delta and some sin and cos functions. The result is that each vertex of our model is displaced in some manner. Finally, we need to set the gl_Position variable with the new position of our vertex.

There's more...

When you look for information on custom shaders, you'll most often see examples of fragment shaders. In many use cases, a vertex shader doesn't need to change the positions of the vertices. When it does, it is often for effects such as smoke or fire. There aren't that many good vertex shaders examples out there. The following two sites, however, provide a good starting point if you want to learn more about vertex shaders:

▸ A good resource to learn more about vertex shaders is the shader tutorial from lighthouse3d at http://www.lighthouse3d.com/tutorials/glsl-tutorial/shader-examples/

▸ There is also an online vertex shader editor available at kickjs.org, which you can find at http://www.kickjs.org/example/shader_editor/shader_editor.html

See also

▸ As a vertex shader is always accompanied with a fragment shader, it is good to also understand how they work. In the *Creating a custom fragment shader* recipe, we explain the steps you need to take to set up a custom fragment shader.

Creating a custom fragment shader

A WebGL shader always consists of two parts: the vertex shader that can be used to reposition the individual vertices of the model and a fragment shader that can be used to add color to the model. In this recipe, we'll show you the steps you need to take to use a custom fragment shader.

Getting ready

Before we start with the fragment shader, there is one thing you need to know. Just like with a vertex shader, you don't write the fragment shader code in JavaScript. These shaders are written in the GLSL language. So, if you want to learn more about the functions and notations used in this example, look at the WebGL specification, which can be found at `https://www.khronos.org/registry/webgl/specs/1.0/`. If you want to experiment with the provided shader code, you can just open up `05.10-custom-fragment-shader.html` in your browser.

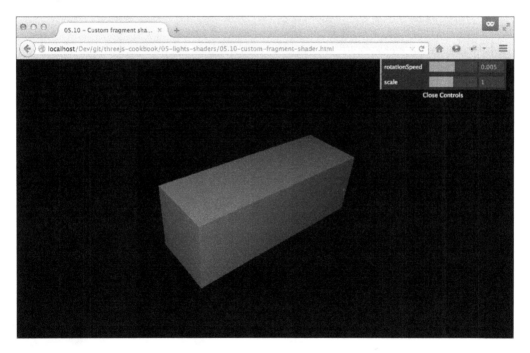

This shader colors an object based on the normal vector and on the distance from the camera. In the following sections, we will explain how you can do this.

How to do it...

Let's start with the JavaScript part of this recipe:

1. A shader always consists of a vertex shader and a fragment shader. In this recipe, we'll use the standard vertex shader provided by Three.js and provide our own custom fragment shader. Three.js keeps all its shaders in `THREE.ShaderLib`:

```
var basicShader = THREE.ShaderLib['normal'];
```

In step 3, we'll reference this `basicShader` object to get the standard vertex shader.

2. For our custom shader, we have some configuration options. These options are passed into a shader using uniforms:

```
var uniforms = {};
uniforms.delta = {type: 'f', value: 0.0};
uniforms.mNear = { type: "f", value: 1.0 };
uniforms.mFar = { type: "f", value: 60.0 };
```

This means that in our shader code, we can access the `delta`, `mNear`, and `mFar` values, all of which are floating point values, and we can use them to calculate the colors we want to render.

3. Next, we can create the shader material:

```
var material = new THREE.ShaderMaterial({
  uniforms: uniforms,
  vertexShader: basicShader.vertexShader,
  fragmentShader: document
    .getElementById('simple-fragment').text,
});
```

In the configuration of `THREE.ShaderMaterial`, we reference our uniform variable, the standard vertex shader, `basicShader.vertexShader` provided by Three.js, and our own custom fragment shader. We'll show you the definition of our custom shader in step 5.

4. The last thing we need to do is create `THREE.BoxGeometry` and add it to the scene using the material created in the previous step:

```
var boxGeometry = new THREE.BoxGeometry(5, 15, 5);
var box = new THREE.Mesh(boxGeometry, material);
scene.add(box);
```

5. In step 3, we referenced a DOM element with the simple-fragment name. In your HTML page, you should define it like this:

```
<script id="simple-fragment" type="x-shader/x-fragment">
  varying vec3 vNormal;
  uniform float delta;
  uniform float mNear;
  uniform float mFar;
  const float PI = 3.1415926535897932384626;
  void main()
  {
    float depth = gl_FragCoord.z / gl_FragCoord.w;
    float depthColor = smoothstep( mNear, mFar
      , depth );
    gl_FragColor = vec4(abs(sin(delta + 0.7*PI) +
      cos(normalize(vNormal).x)/2.0) - depthColor
      ,abs(sin(delta + 1.0*PI) +
      cos(normalize(vNormal).y)/2.0) - depthColor
      ,abs(sin(delta + 1.2*PI) +
      cos(normalize(vNormal).z)/2.0) - depthColor, 1.0);
  }
</script>
```

If you want to know more about how this fragment shader works, look at the explanation in the *How it works...* section of this recipe.

6. If you've looked at the example from the *Getting ready* section, you can see that the colors change constantly. This happens because we update the delta property, which is passed into our custom shader, in the render loop of this page:

```
function render() {
  renderer.render(scene, camera);
  uniforms.delta.value += 0.005;
  requestAnimationFrame(render);
}
```

How it works...

To understand how this shader works, let's look through the code step by step. Let's start by looking at the variables used in this shader:

```
varying vec3 vNormal;
uniform float delta;
uniform float mNear;
uniform float mFar;
float PI = 3.1415926535897932384626;
```

The vNormal object is a variable that is passed in from the standard Three.js vertex shader and contains the value of the normal vector applicable to this fragment. The three uniform values are passed in from the JavaScript, as we've seen in the previous section. The PI variable is a constant that doesn't change over time. Each fragment shader should set the gl_fragColor vector, which determines the color and opacity of each fragment. For this shader, we set the vector as follows:

```
void main()
{
  float depth = gl_FragCoord.z / gl_FragCoord.w;
  float depthColor = smoothstep( mNear, mFar, depth );
  gl_FragColor = vec4(
    abs(sin(delta + 0.7*PI)
    + cos(normalize(vNormal).x)/2.0) - depthColor
    ,abs(sin(delta + 1.0*PI)
    + cos(normalize(vNormal).y)/2.0) - depthColor,
    abs(sin(delta + 1.2*PI)
    + cos(normalize(vNormal).z)/2.0) - depthColor,
    1.0);
}
```

Without going into too many GLSL details, roughly the following steps are taken:

1. First, we determine the depth of this fragment. You can see this as the distance of this fragment from the camera.

2. As depth is an absolute value, we convert it to a scale of 0 to 1 using the smoothstep function. As this function also takes the mNear and mFar uniforms as its parameters, we can control how much the depth affects the color of a fragment from JavaScript.

3. Finally, we define the color of the fragment by setting gl_FragColor. The gl_FragColor variable is of type vec4, where the first three values determine the RGB value of the color and the last one defines the opacity. This is all on a scale of 0 to 1. For each part of the color, we use a function that includes the vNormal vector and calculated depthColor variable to generate a color.

This is just the tip of the iceberg of what you can do with custom fragment shaders. In the upcoming section, you can find some resources to learn more about this.

There's more...

Creating custom fragment shaders is rather difficult. It'll take a lot of experimenting, a good grasp of math, and a lot of patience. There are, however, a number of resources available that can help you understand fragment shaders and learn from the work of others:

- ▸ Lots of fragment shaders can be found at `http://glslsandbox.com/`
- ▸ On the Shadertoy site, you can experiment fragment shaders using different kinds of input: `https://www.shadertoy.com/`
- ▸ A simple online shader editor can be found at `http://shdr.bkcore.com/`

Another great help can be the latest version of Firefox Dev Tools. This is a special version of Firefox, which provides great debugging support and even includes a shader editor that you can use to edit a shader program and directly see the results. You can download this version from `https://www.mozilla.org/en-US/firefox/developer/`.

There is, of course, the khronos website (`http://www.khronos.org`), which is a great resource to find out what a specific function actually does.

See also

- ▸ As a fragment shader is always accompanied with a vertex shader, it is good to also understand how they work. In the *Creating a custom vertex shader* recipe, we explained the steps you need to take to set up a custom vertex shader.

6
Point Clouds and Postprocessing

In this chapter, we'll cover the following recipes:

- ▶ Creating a point cloud based on a geometry
- ▶ Creating a point cloud from scratch
- ▶ Coloring individual points in a point cloud
- ▶ Styling individual points
- ▶ Moving individual points of a point cloud
- ▶ Exploding a point cloud
- ▶ Setting up the basic postprocessing pipeline
- ▶ Creating custom postprocessing steps
- ▶ Saving WebGL output to disk

Introduction

Three.js has support for many different types of geometries and objects. In this chapter, we'll show you a number of recipes that use the THREE.PointCloud object. With this object, you can create a point cloud where the individual vertices are rendered instead of the complete mesh. You have all kinds of different styling options available for the points, and you can even move the individual points around to create very interesting-looking (and realistic) animations and simulations.

Creating a point cloud based on a geometry

An interesting feature of Three.js is that it also allows you to create point clouds. A point cloud isn't rendered as a solid geometry, but all the individual vertices are rendered as single points. In this recipe, we'll show you how to create such a point cloud based on an already existing geometry.

Getting ready

There are no additional steps required to start with this recipe. For the example we use in this recipe, however, we use an external model as the basis for our point cloud. We also use a camera control object, THREE.OrbitControls, to make navigation around the example easier. If you want to use the camera control object yourself, you need to add the following JavaScript libraries to the scene (besides the standard Three.js one):

```
<script src="../libs/OrbitControls.js"></script>
<script src="../libs/OBJLoader.js"></script>
```

The external model we use is also provided with the sources in this book and can be found in the assets/models/cow folder. To see what the result of this recipe can look like, we provided an example that shows you a point cloud that was created based on an existing geometry (06.01-create-point-cloud-from-geometry.html).You will see something similar to the following screenshot:

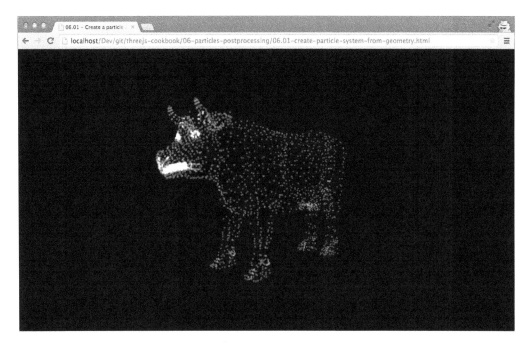

As you can see in this screenshot, we've loaded a cow geometry and created a point cloud based on it. You can, of course, use any geometry you want, but especially complex models look really great when rendered as a point cloud.

How to do it...

Creating a point cloud isn't that different from creating a simple `THREE.Mesh` object. The following section explains the steps you should take:

1. The first thing you need in this approach is `THREE.Geometry`. You can use either one of the standard geometries or load an external one. For this recipe, we'll load an external one (the cow we mentioned in the *Getting ready* section of this recipe):

```
var loader = new THREE.OBJLoader();
loader.load(
    "../assets/models/cow/cow.obj",
    function(cow) {
        // get the main cow geometry from the
        // loaded object hierarchy
        var cowGeometry = cow.children[1].geometry;
    }
);
```

In this code snippet, we load the external model, so we have geometry on which we can base the point cloud.

2. Before we create the point cloud, we first have to tell Three.js what we want the point cloud to look like. For this, we create `THREE.PointCloudMaterial`:

```
var pcMat = new THREE.PointCloudMaterial();
pcMat.map = THREE.ImageUtils.loadTexture
    ("../assets/textures/ps_smoke.png");
pcMat.color = new THREE.Color(0x5555ff);
pcMat.transparent = true;
pcMat.size = 0.2;
pcMat.blending = THREE.AdditiveBlending;
```

This material defines what each point will look like. Most of the properties are pretty self-explanatory. The interesting one here is the `blending` property. By setting the `blending` property to `THREE.AdditiveBlending`, you get the nice glow effect you can see in the screenshot at the beginning of this recipe.

3. At this point, we have `THREE.Geometry` and `THREE.PointCloudMaterial`; with these two objects, we can create the point cloud:

```
pc = new THREE.PointCloud(geometry, pcMat);
pc.sizeAttenuation = true;
pc.sortPoints = true;
```

As you can see, we pass in `THREE.Geometry` and `THREE.PointCloudMaterial` to create `THREE.PointCloud`. On the created point cloud, we set two additional properties to `true`. The `sizeAttenuation` property makes sure that the size of a point also depends on the distance from the camera. So, points farther away look smaller. The `sortPoints` property makes sure that when you use transparent points, as we do in this recipe, they are rendered correctly.

4. The last step to perform is to add the created `THREE.PointCloud` object to the scene:

```
scene.add(pc);
```

Now, Three.js will render the point cloud just like it does any other 3D object.

How it works...

When you create `THREE.PointCloud`, Three.js creates a point for each vertex of the provided `THREE.Geometry` object. No other information in `THREE.Geometry` is used. Internally, for `THREE.WebGLRenderer`, it directly uses `GL_POINTS`, which is a WebGL primitive, to render the individual points (refer to `https://www.khronos.org/opengles/sdk/docs/man/xhtml/glDrawElements.xml` for more information). Then, using a custom fragment shader, it styles these points. The result is that when you use `THREE.WebGLRenderer`, you can easily render millions of points while maintaining great performance.

There's more...

Points are a great way to represent all kinds of different effects. For some interesting applications of points, you can look at the following examples:

▶ One million points rendered on WebGL: `http://soulwire.github.io/WebGL-GPU-Particles/`

▶ Morphing from one geometry to another using a point cloud: `http://oos.moxiecode.com/js_webgl/particles_morph/index.html`

See also

In this chapter, we have a number of recipes that deal with points that are closely related to this one:

▶ In the *Creating a point cloud from scratch* recipe, we create a point cloud from a custom-created geometry

▶ In the *Styling individual points* recipe, we show you how you can style the individual points of a point cloud

▶ In the *Moving individual points of a point cloud* and *Exploding a point cloud* recipes, we show you how you can move the points around

Creating a point cloud from scratch

When you want to create a point cloud, you can pass in an existing geometry and base the point cloud on it. In this recipe, we'll show you how you can create THREE.Geometry from scratch and create a point cloud from it.

Getting ready

For this recipe, we don't require any additional JavaScript libraries and we don't need to load external models, as we create our geometry from scratch. You can look at the geometry we created by opening 06.02-create-point-system-from-scratch.html in your browser. You will see something similar to the following screenshot:

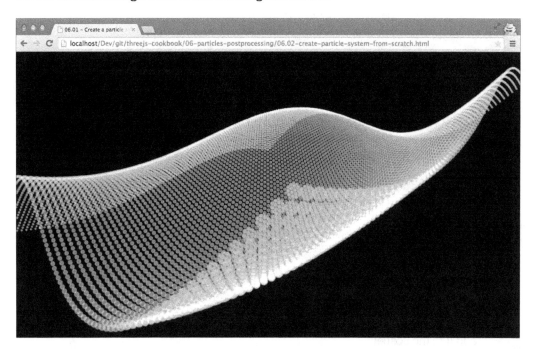

In the next section, we'll explain how to create this custom geometry and use it together with THREE.PointCloud.

How to do it...

The steps are pretty much the same as shown in the *Creating a point cloud based on a geometry* recipe, except that first, we need to create our own custom geometry:

1. Creating a custom geometry is fairly easy:

```
var x = 100;
var y = 100;
var geometry = new THREE.Geometry();
for (var i = 0 ; i < x ; i++) {
  for (var j = 0 ; j < y ; j++) {
    var v = new THREE.Vector3();
    v.x = i / 10;
    v.y = Math.sin(i/100 * Math.PI*2)
      + Math.cos(j/100 * Math.PI) * 2;
    v.z = j / 10;
    geometry.vertices.push(v);
  }
}
```

As you can see from this code snippet, you first need to instantiate `THREE.Geometry` and then create `THREE.Vector3` instances and push them to the vertices property of geometry.

2. Now that we've got a geometry, we just need `THREE.PointCloudMaterial`:

```
var pcMat = new THREE.PointCloudMaterial(geometry);
pcMat.map = THREE.ImageUtils.loadTexture
  ("../assets/textures/ps_smoke.png");
pcMat.color = new THREE.Color(0x55ff55);
pcMat.transparent = true;
pcMat.size = 0.2;
pcMat.blending = THREE.AdditiveBlending;
```

3. Use this material together with the geometry to create `THREE.PointCloud` and add it to the scene:

```
pc = new THREE.PointCloud(geometry, pcMat);
pc.sizeAttenuation = true;
pc.sortPoints = true;
scene.add(pc);
```

If you've already looked at the *Creating a point cloud based on a geometry* recipe, you'll notice that most of the steps are the same. The only difference between these two recipes is how you create the geometry.

How it works...

For an explanation on how this works, look at the *How it works...* section from the *Creating a point cloud based on a geometry* recipe.

There's more...

In *Chapter 2, Geometries and Meshes*, we showed how you could render 3D formulas with Three.js. With the setup from this recipe, you can also create 3D formulas that are visualized as point clouds. For instance, the following screenshot shows you a 3D formula from *Chapter 2, Geometries and Meshes*, rendered as a point cloud:

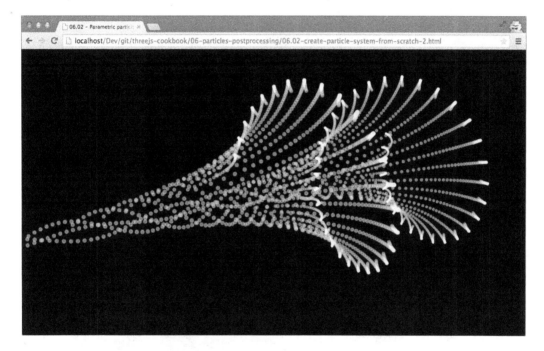

As you can see, you can very easily create great-looking point clouds this way.

See also

There are a couple of recipes in this chapter that are related to this recipe:

▸ In the *Creating a point cloud based on a geometry* recipe, we use an existing geometry to create a point cloud

> ▶ In the *Styling individual points* recipe, we show you how you can style the individual points of a point cloud

> ▶ In the *Moving individual points of a point cloud* and *Exploding a point cloud* recipes, we show you how you can move the points around

Coloring the individual points in a point cloud

When you create a point cloud, every point has the same color and style, as every point uses the same `THREE.PointCloudMaterial` object. There is, however, a way to add color to the individual points.

Getting ready

There is no need for any additional steps to run this recipe. We'll create a custom geometry, just like we did in the *Creating a point cloud from scratch* recipe, and this time, we color each individual point. The result of this recipe can be seen by opening `06.03-color-individual-points-in-point-system.html` in your browser. You will see something similar to the following screenshot:

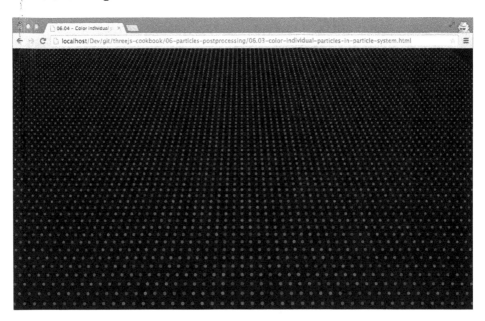

As you can see, we've colored the individual points in various shades of red.

How to do it...

To accomplish individual colored points, we need to set one additional property when we create `THREE.Geometry`. The following steps show you how to do this:

1. We start by creating the geometry. When we create the individual vertices, we can also inform Three.js about the color that we want to use for it:

```
var x = 100;
var y = 100;
var geometry = new THREE.Geometry();
for (var i = 0 ; i < x ; i++) {
  for (var j = 0 ; j < y ; j++) {
    var v = new THREE.Vector3(i,0,j);
    var rnd = Math.random()/2 + 0.5;
    geometry.colors.push(
      new THREE.Color(rnd, rnd/4, 0));
    geometry.vertices.push(v);
  }
}
```

   In this code snippet, we create a random color and push it to the `geometry.colors` array. At the end of these two loops, we will have 10000 vertices in the `vertices` array and 10000 colors in the `colors` array.

2. Now, we can create `THREE.PointCloudMaterial` and use it together with the geometry to create `THREE.PointCloud`:

```
var pcMat = new THREE.PointCloudMaterial(geometry);
pcMat.vertexColors = true;
pcMat.map = THREE.ImageUtils
  .loadTexture("../assets/textures/ps_smoke.png");
pcMat.transparent = true;
pc = new THREE.PointCloud(geometry, pcMat);
scene.add(pc);
```

   To use the colors we created in step 1, we need to set the `vertexColors` property of `THREE.PointCloudMaterial` to `true`. In this code snippet, we also load a texture and assign it to the `map` property. We use individual colors, so there is no need to set the `color` property on the material we need to set color on `THREE.Geometry`, which we show in the next step.

3. If you've already looked at the example shown in the *Getting ready* section of this recipe, you'll notice that the colors of the points change. We can easily do this by just changing the color in the `colors` array of the geometry in the render loop:

```
for (var i = 0 ; i < pc.geometry.colors.length ; i++) {
  var rnd = Math.random()/2 + 0.5;
  pc.geometry.colors[i] = new THREE.Color(rnd, rnd/4, 0);
}
pc.geometry.colorsNeedUpdate = true;
```

When you change the colors, you need to set the `colorsNeedUpdate` property to `true` so that Three.js knows that the colors of the points need to be updated.

How it works...

Three.js uses WebGL to render individual points. For this, Three.js uses vertex shaders and fragment shaders (see the previous chapter for more recipes on this). To color the individual points, Three.js passes the information into the fragment shader used to determine the output color. The corresponding piece of shader code looks like this:

```
gl_FragColor = vec4( psColor, opacity );
```

The `psColor` variable is the one that is passed from the colors array of `THREE.Geometry` to the shader used to color the points.

See also

▶ Coloring an individual point in Three.js is very simple and straightforward. However, if you want to change more properties of the points, such as the opacity or the size, you can't do that with standard Three.js. In the *Styling individual points* recipe, we'll show you how you can create a custom shader to also change these properties of the points within a point cloud.

▶ If you're interested in adding animation to the points in the point cloud, you can look at the *Moving individual points of a point cloud* and *Exploding a point cloud* recipes.

Styling individual points

With the standard Three.js functionality, you can't style the individual points of a point cloud. You can change their color, as we've shown in the *Coloring the individual points in a point cloud* recipe, but it isn't possible to change a point's size or opacity. In this recipe, we'll show you how to create a custom vertex and fragment shader, which allow you to change the color, opacity, and size of the individual points of a point cloud and that you can also easily extend to add more properties.

Getting ready

There are no external libraries used in this recipe. We'll just extend the basic Three.js functionality by creating our own custom shaders. To see the shaders in action, open the `06.04-style-individual-points-in-point-system-with-custom-shader.html` example in your browser. You will see something similar to the following recipe:

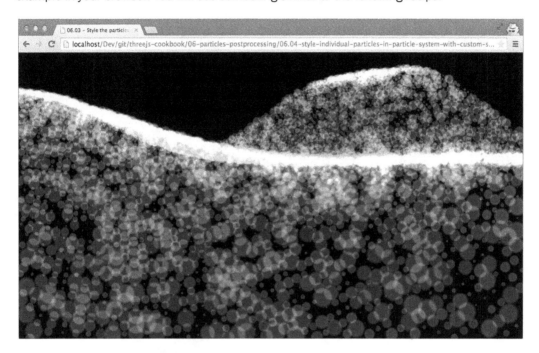

As you can see in this screenshot, the size, color, and opacity of the individual points differ.

How to do it...

Let's look at the steps that you need to take to accomplish this:

1. Let's start simple and first create the geometry from which we'll create the point cloud:

    ```
    var geometry = new THREE.Geometry();
    var pSize = [];
    var pOpacity = [];
    var width= 100;
    var height = 100;
    ```

```
// create the geometry and set custom values
for (var i = 0 ; i < width ; i++) {
  for (var j = 0 ; height < y ; j++) {
    var v = new THREE.Vector3();
    v.x = i / 10;
    v.y = (Math.sin(i/200 * Math.PI*2)
      + Math.cos(j/50 * Math.PI)
      + Math.sin((j+i)/40 * Math.PI))/2;
    v.z = j / 10;
    // add the vertex
    geometry.vertices.push(v);
    // add vertex specific color, size and opacity
    geometry.colors.push(new
      THREE.Color(v.y,0.5,0.7));
    pSize.push(Math.random());
    pOpacity.push(Math.random()/4+0.5);
  }
}
```

As you can see, we create `THREE.Geometry` from scratch and generate 10,000 vertices. As we want to change the color, size, and opacity of the individual vertices, we also generate values for these properties for each of the 10,000 vertices. The colors are stored in the `geometry.colors` array as this is the standard Three.js functionality. We store the size in the `pSize` array and the opacity in the `pOpacity` array.

2. Now that we've got a geometry and a couple of arrays containing the expected size and opacity for the individual vertices, let's define the material for the point cloud:

```
var attributes = ...; // filled in next steps
var uniforms = ...;   // filled in next steps
var psMat2 = new THREE.ShaderMaterial({
  attributes: attributes,
  uniforms: uniforms,
  transparent : true,
  blending : THREE.AdditiveBlending,
  vertexShader: document
    getElementById('pointVertexShader').text,
  fragmentShader: document
    getElementById('pointFragmentShader').text
});
```

Instead of using the standard `THREE.PointCloudMaterial` object, we use `THREE.ShaderMaterial`. The `transparent` and `blending` are properties standard material properties and behave as you'd expect. We'll explain the other properties in the upcoming steps.

3. In step 2, the material referenced the attributes variable. In this step, we'll configure this variable:

```
var attributes = {
  pSize:    { type: 'f', value: pSize },
  pOpacity: { type: 'f', value: pOpacity }
};
```

Our `attributes` object contains two properties. The first one points to the array that contains the sizes of the vertices and the second one points to the array that contains the opacity values. The `f` value for type means that it is an array of floats. As we reference this attribute from our shader material, we can access the individual values in our shaders.

4. In step 2, we also defined some uniforms. The `uniforms` object are also passed into the shader but are the same for all vertices:

```
var basicShader = THREE.ShaderLib['point_basic'];
var uniforms = THREE.UniformsUtils
  .merge([basicShader.uniforms]);
uniforms['map'].value = THREE.ImageUtils.loadTexture(
  "../assets/textures/ps_smoke.png");
uniforms['size'].value = 100;
uniforms['opacity'].value = 0.5;
uniforms['psColor'].value = new THREE.Color(0xffffff);
```

Here, we reuse the standard uniforms Three.js uses in its shaders and use it to further configure the shaders.

5. Looking back at step 2, the only two properties we need to define are the actual shaders: `document.getElementById('pointVertexShader').text` and `document.getElementById('pointFragmentShader').text`. Let's start with the vertex shader:

```
<script id="pointVertexShader"
  type="x-shader/x-vertex">
  precision highp float;
  precision highp int;
  attribute vec3 color;
  attribute float pSize;
  attribute float pOpacity;
  uniform float size;
  uniform float scale;
  varying vec3 vColor;
  varying float vOpacity;
  void main() {
    vColor = color;
```

```
        vOpacity = pOpacity;
        vec4 mvPosition = modelViewMatrix
          * vec4( position, 1.0 );
        gl_PointSize = 2.0 * pSize * size
          * ( scale / length( mvPosition.xyz ) );
        gl_Position = projectionMatrix * mvPosition;
      }
    </script>
```

A vertex shader is used to determine the position and the size of a vertex. In this shader, we set the size of the vertex and the point and use the pSize attribute in the calculation. This way, we can control the size of the individual pixel. We also copy the value of color and pOpacity to a varying value so that we can access it from our fragment shader in the next step.

6. So far, the size of the point could be configured directly from Three.js. Now, let's look at the fragment shader and do the same for the color and opacity:

```
    <script id="pointFragmentShader"
      type="x-shader/x-fragment">
      precision highp float;
      precision highp int;
      uniform vec3 psColor;
      uniform float opacity;
      varying vec3 vColor;
      varying float vOpacity;
      uniform sampler2D map;
      void main() {
        gl_FragColor = vec4( psColor, vOpacity );
        gl_FragColor = gl_FragColor * texture2D( map,
          vec2( gl_PointCoord.x, 1.0 - gl_PointCoord.y ) );
        gl_FragColor = gl_FragColor * vec4( vColor, 1.0 );
      }
    </script>
```

The fragment shader is only a small program. What we do here is the following:

1. We first set the color of the fragment (the point) to the color defined on the material (psColor), and the opacity is set to the point-specific opacity (vOpacity).

2. Next, we apply the provided texture (map).

3. Finally, we multiply the color value(gl_Fragcolor) with the point specific color(vcolor).

7. At this point, we've configured the material and created the specific shaders. Now, we can just create the point cloud and add it to the scene:

```
ps = new THREE.PointCloud(geometry, psMat2);
ps.sortPoints = true;
scene.add(ps);
```

With this last step, you're done.

As you can see, as this isn't a standard Three.js functionality, we need to take some additional steps to accomplish our goals.

How it works...

In the previous section, we've already explained a bit how the styling of individual points works. The main thing to remember here is that under the hood, Three.js creates vertex and fragment shaders for rendering. If there is a functionality you want that can't be configured in the standard shaders, you can use `THREE.ShaderMaterial` to create your own custom implementations. You can still use Three.js to create your geometries and handle all the WebGL initialization stuff but use your own shader implementations.

There's more...

With this setup, you've got a basic skeleton to create your own custom shader based on point clouds. You can now easily add more functionalities, other configuration options, and more by just adding to this setup.

See also

*   If you just want to color an individual point, you can refer to the *Coloring the individual points in a point cloud* recipe, and if you're interested in adding animation to the points in the point cloud, you can refer to the *Moving individual points of a point cloud* and *Exploding a point cloud* recipes.

*   There are also a couple of other recipes that use vertex and fragment shaders. In this chapter, you can find the *Creating custom postprocessing steps* recipe, which uses a shader as a postprocessing effect. In *Chapter 5, Light and Custom Shaders*, we have the *Creating a custom vertex shader* recipe, which uses a custom vertex shader to alter the shape of a geometry, and the *Creating a custom fragment shader* recipe, which colors 3D objects using a custom fragment shader implementation.

Moving individual points of a point cloud

When you create a point cloud from a geometry, the position of the points is based on the vertices from the provided geometry. The result is a point cloud where the individual points don't move. In this recipe, we show you how you can move the individual points of a point cloud.

Getting ready

For this recipe, we require a point cloud that contains some points. You can create your own one (as we explained in the *Creating a point cloud from scratch* and *Creating a point cloud from an existing geometry* recipes). We will use the point cloud we created in the *Styling individual points* recipe. As always, we've provided an example where you can see the final result of this recipe. Open `06.05-move-individual-points.html` in your browser, and you'll see the following screenshot:

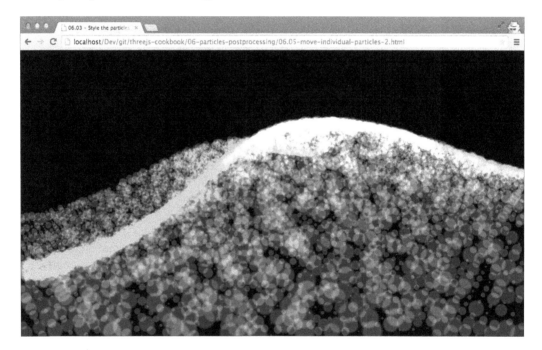

If you open this in your browser, you'll see all the points being moved around the screen. In the following section, we'll explain how you can do that.

How to do it...

To create moving points, we need to perform the following steps:

1. Make sure you've got a point cloud with a geometry. Look at the *Creating a point cloud from scratch* and *Creating a point cloud based on a geometry* recipes to learn how to create such a point cloud. In this recipe, we assume the point cloud can be referenced through the `ps` variable.

2. The next step is to update the position of the individual points of the point cloud. We do that by updating the `render` loop:

```
var step = 0;
function render() {
  renderer.render(scene, camera);
  requestAnimationFrame(render);
  step=0.005;
  var count = 0;
  var geometry = ps.geometry;
  geometry.vertices.forEach(function(v){
    // calculate new value for the y value
    v.y =  ( Math.sin((v.x/20+step) * Math.PI*2)
      + Math.cos((v.z/5+step*2) * Math.PI)
      + Math.sin((v.x + v.y + step*2)/4
      * Math.PI))/2;
    // and calculate new colors
    geometry.colors[count++]=
      new THREE.Color(v.y,0.5,0.7);
  });
  geometry.verticesNeedUpdate = true;
  geometry.colorsNeedUpdate = true;
}
```

In the `render` loop, we access geometry through the `ps` variable. Next, we change the `y` position (`v.y`) of each point based on the value of the step variable. By increasing the step value in each render loop, we create the animation you can see when you look at the example for this recipe. Finally, we need to tell Three.js that the positions of the vertices in the geometry have changed by setting `geometry.verticesNeedUpdate` to `true`.

In this recipe, we also change the colors of each point, so to inform Three.js about these changes, we also set `geometry.colorsNeedUpdate` to `true`.

How it works...

This recipe works in a very simple way. A point cloud is created based on the position of the vertices of `THREE.Geometry` by simply changing the position of the vertices around which we can move the points.

▸ In this recipe, we changed the position of the vertices in a very simple way. We just changed the *y* value of the vertex. In the *Exploding a point cloud* recipe, we show you an approach where the position of a vertex is changed based on its normal vector.

Exploding a point cloud

You can create many interesting effects with point clouds. You can, for instance, create water, smoke, and cloud effects. In this recipe, we show you another interesting effect you can create with points. We'll show you how you can explode a point cloud where each point's path is based on its normal vector.

Getting ready

For this recipe, there aren't any steps that need to be taken before we start looking at the recipe. We've provided an example where you can see the resulting explosion in action. Open the `06.06-explode-geometry.html` example in your browser and you'll see a screen that looks like the following screenshot:

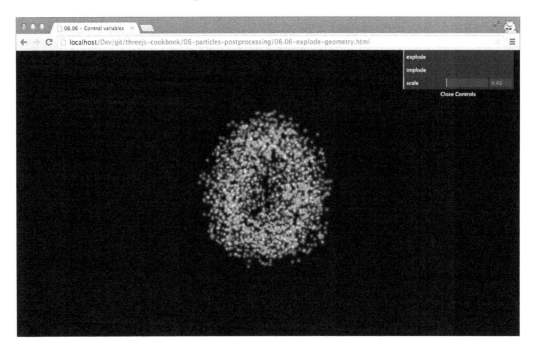

If you click on the **implode** button, the points will move to the middle of the screen; if you click on **explode**, they'll move outwards. With the **speed** property, you can set the speed at which the points will move.

How to do it...

To accomplish this effect, you only need to perform a couple of small steps:

1. The first thing we need to do is create the geometry. For the best effect, we use a geometry with lots of vertices:

   ```
   cube = new THREE.CubeGeometry(4,6,4,20,20,20);
   cube.vertices.forEach(function(v) {
     v.velocity = Math.random();
   });
   createPointSystemFromGeometry(cube);
   ```

   As you can see, we don't just create the geometry; we also add a `velocity` parameter to each of the vertices, which we set to a random value. We do this to make sure not all the points explode at the same speed (which would have the same effect as just scaling the geometry).

2. Now, we can create the point cloud:

   ```
   var psMat = new THREE.PointCloudMaterial();
   psMat.map = THREE.ImageUtils.loadTexture(
     "../assets/textures/ps_ball.png");
   psMat.blending = THREE.AdditiveBlending;
   psMat.transparent = true;
   psMat.opacity = 0.6;
   var ps = new THREE.PointCloud(cube, psMat);
   ps.sortPoints = true;
   scene.add(ps);
   ```

   This is just a standard point cloud based on the geometry we created in step 1.

3. In the introduction to the recipe, we mentioned that we wanted to explode the points based on their normal vector. So, before we start rendering the scene and updating the position of the individual points, we first need to calculate the normal of each vector:

   ```
   var avgVertexNormals = [];
   var avgVertexCount = [];
   for (var i = 0 ; i < cube.vertices.length ; i++) {
     avgVertexNormals.push(new THREE.Vector3(0,0,0));
     avgVertexCount.push(0);
   ```

```
    }
    // first add all the normals
    cube.faces.forEach(function (f) {
      var vA = f.vertexNormals[0];
      var vB = f.vertexNormals[1];
      var vC = f.vertexNormals[2];
      // update the count
      avgVertexCount[f.a]+=1;
      avgVertexCount[f.b]+=1;
      avgVertexCount[f.c]+=1;
      // add the vector
      avgVertexNormals[f.a].add(vA);
      avgVertexNormals[f.b].add(vB);
      avgVertexNormals[f.c].add(vC);
    });
    // then calculate the average
    for (var i = 0 ; i < avgVertexNormals.length ; i++) {
      avgVertexNormals[i].divideScalar(avgVertexCount[i]);
    }
```

We won't explain this code snippet in detail, but what we do here is that we calculate the normal vector of each vertex based on the normal vectors of the faces the particular vector is part of. The final normal vector is stored in the `avgVertexNormals` array.

4. Next, we look at a helper function that we'll call from the `render` loop in the next step. This function determines the new position of each vertex based on the velocity function we defined in step 1 and the normal vector we calculated in step 3:

```
function explode(outwards) {
  var dir = outwards === true ? 1 : -1;
  var count = 0;
  cube.vertices.forEach(function(v){
    v.x+=(avgVertexNormals[count].x
      * v.velocity * control.scale)*dir;
    v.y+=(avgVertexNormals[count].y
      * v.velocity * control.scale)*dir;
    v.z+=(avgVertexNormals[count].z
      * v.velocity * control.scale)*dir;
    count++;
  });
  cube.verticesNeedUpdate = true;
}
```

The `control.scale` variable is set through GUI and determines the speed at which our geometry expands, and the `dir` property is based on whether we want to move the points outwards or inwards. The `verticesNeedUpdate` property is required to inform Three.js about these changes.

5. Now all that is left to do is call the explode function from the `render` loop:

```
function render() {
  renderer.render(scene, camera);
  explode(true); // or explode(false)
  requestAnimationFrame(render);
}
```

There's more

In this example, we've used a standard geometry; you can, of course, also use an externally loaded model.

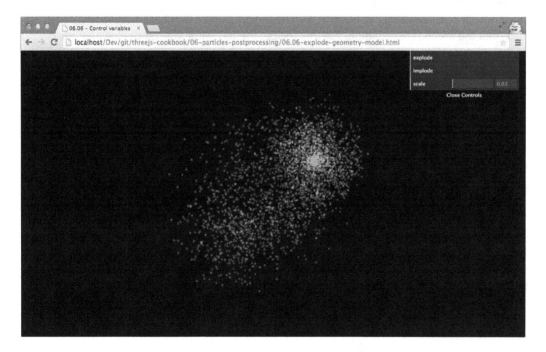

This screenshot, for instance, shows you an exploding model of a cow.

See also

▸ Another recipe that deals with animation and moving individual points around can be found in the *Moving individual points of a point cloud* recipe.

Setting up the basic postprocessing pipeline

Besides rendering a scene in 3D, Three.js also allows you to add postprocessing effects to the final output. With postprocessing, you can take the final rendered 2D image and apply all different kinds of filters to it. You could, for instance, add specific blurring effects, sharpen specific colors, and much more. In this recipe, we'll show you how to set up a postprocessing pipeline in Three.js, which you can use to add effects to the final rendered scene.

Getting ready

To work with postprocessing in Three.js, you need to include a number of additional JavaScript files from the Three.js distribution. For this recipe, the following JavaScript files should be added to your HTML page:

```
<script src="../libs/postprocessing/CopyShader.js"></script>
<script src="../libs/postprocessing/EffectComposer.js"></script>
<script src="../libs/postprocessing/RenderPass.js"></script>
<script src="../libs/postprocessing/ShaderPass.js"></script>
<script src="../libs/postprocessing/MaskPass.js"></script>
```

To demonstrate how postprocessing works, we'll apply the dot-screen effect to a Three.js scene. For this effect, we require one additional JavaScript file:

```
<script src="../libs/postprocessing/DotScreenShader.js">
</script>
```

We've also provided an example that shows you the final result of this recipe. You can view this by opening `06.07-setup-basic-post-processing-pipeline.html` in your browser. You will see something similar to the following screenshot:

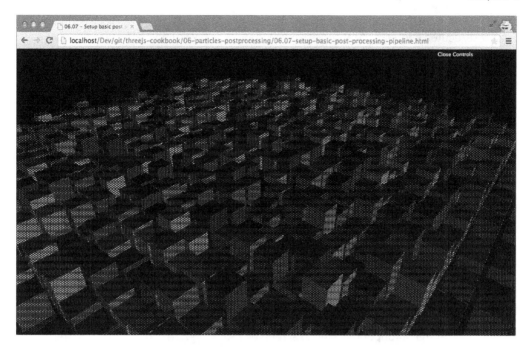

In this screenshot, you can see that we've rendered a scene with a large number of cubes and applied an effect to render it as a series of dots.

How to do it...

Setting up a postprocessing pipeline only takes a couple of small steps:

1. To set up a postprocessing pipeline, we need something called a composer. We'll use this composer in the `render` loop to create the final output. The first thing we need for that is a new global variable:

    ```
    var composer;
    ```

2. Next, we need to instantiate a composer as a new instance of `THREE.EffectComposer`:

    ```
    composer = new THREE.EffectComposer( renderer );
    ```

    We pass in `THREE.WebGLRenderer`, which we would normally use to render the scene.

3. Now, we need to define the steps that the composer will execute. These steps are executed sequentially and we can use them to apply multiple effects to the scene. The first step we always need to take is to render the scene. For this, we use `THREE.RenderPass`:

```
var renderPass = new THREE.RenderPass( scene, camera );
composer.addPass( renderPass );
```

A render pass renders a scene object using the provided camera and renderer we configured in step 2.

4. Now that we've rendered the scene, we can apply a postprocessing effect. For this recipe, we use `THREE.DotScreenShader`:

```
var effect = new THREE.ShaderPass( THREE.DotScreenShader
 );
effect.uniforms[ 'scale' ].value = 4;
effect.renderToScreen = true;
composer.addPass( effect );
```

In this code snippet, we create a postprocessing step (`THREE.ShaderPass`), add it to the composer (`composer.addPass(effect)`), and tell the effect composer to render the output of this step to screen by setting `renderToScreen` to `true`.

5. The final step we need to take is to alter the render loop:

```
function render() {
  composer.render();
  requestAnimationFrame(render);
}
```

As you can see, we now use the `composer` object we created in step 2 to render the final output instead of `THREE.WebGLRenderer`.

In this recipe, we've only used a single postprocessing step, but you can use as many steps as you want. You just have to remember that in the final step, you set the `renderToScreen` property to `true`.

How it works...

In a couple of recipes, we've already explained that Three.js uses WebGL shaders to render the 3D scenes. `THREE.EffectComposer` uses the same approach. Each of the steps you add run a simple vertex and fragment shader on the output from the previous step. In the *Creating custom postprocessing steps* recipe, we'll dive into more detail and create a custom postprocessing step ourselves.

There's more

Three.js provides a large number of standard shaders and steps you can use in `THREE.EffectComposer`. For a complete overview of the possible shaders and standard steps, look at the following directories:

- ▶ `https://github.com/mrdoob/three.js/tree/master/examples/js/postprocessing`: This directory contains all the standard postprocessing steps you can use with `THREE.EffectComposer`.

- ▶ `https://github.com/mrdoob/three.js/tree/master/examples/js/shaders`: Three.js provides the `THREE.ShaderPass` postprocessing step, which allows you to directly use WebGL shaders. On this page, you can find a large number of shaders that can be used with the `THREE.ShaderPass` object.

See also

- ▶ Even though Three.js provides a large number of standard shaders and postprocessing steps, you can also easily create your own. In the *Creating custom postprocessing steps* recipe, we show you how to create a custom vertex and fragment shader that works with `THREE.EffectComposer`.

Creating custom postprocessing steps

In the *Setting up the basic postprocessing pipeline* recipe, we showed you how you can use `THREE.EffectComposer` to add postprocessing effects to a rendered Three.js scene. In this recipe, we'll explain how you can create custom processing steps that you can use with `THREE.EffectComposer`.

Getting ready

This recipe uses `THREE.EffectComposer`, so we need to load some additional JavaScript files with the correct objects. For this, you need to add the following at the top of your HTML page:

```html
<script src="../libs/postprocessing/CopyShader.js"></script>
<script src="../libs/postprocessing/EffectComposer.js"></script>
<script src="../libs/postprocessing/RenderPass.js"></script>
<script src="../libs/postprocessing/ShaderPass.js"></script>
<script src="../libs/postprocessing/MaskPass.js"></script>
```

In this recipe, we'll create a postprocessing effect that converts the output using a mosaic effect. You can look at the final result by opening `06.08-create-custom-post-processing-step.html` in your browser. You will see something similar to the following screenshot:

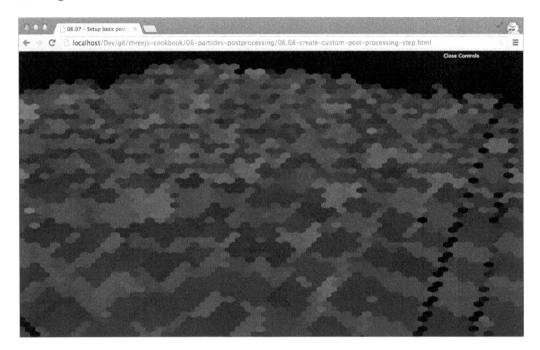

You might not recognize this, but what you're seeing is a large number of cubes that are rotating.

How to do it...

We create this effect by using a custom fragment shader. The following steps explain how to set this up:

1. We first need to create `THREE.EffectComposer` and configure the steps:

```
var composer = new THREE.EffectComposer( renderer );
var renderPass = new THREE.RenderPass( scene, camera );
composer.addPass( renderPass  );
```

So far, we have only added the render step (`THREE.RenderPass`), which renders the scene and allows us to add additional postprocessing effects.

2. To use custom shaders, we'll need to use the `THREE.ShaderPass` object:

```
var customShader = {
  uniforms: {
    "tDiffuse": { type: "t", value: null},
    "scale":    { type: "f", value: 1.0 },
    "texSize":  { type: "v2", value:
      new THREE.Vector2( 50, 50 ) },
    "center":   { type: "v2", value:
      new THREE.Vector2( 0.5, 0.5 ) },
  },
  vertexShader: document.
    getElementById('hexagonVertexShader').text,
  fragmentShader: document.
    getElementById('hexagonFragmentShader').text
};
var effect = new THREE.ShaderPass( customShader );
effect.renderToScreen = true;
composer.addPass( effect );
```

We pass in `customShader` as an argument to `THREE.ShaderPass`. This `customShader` object contains the configuration of our custom shader. The `uniforms` objects are the variables we pass into our custom shader, and `vertexShader` and `fragmentShader` point to our shader programs.

3. Let's first look at `vertexShader` from step 2:

```
<script id="hexagonVertexShader"
  type="x-shader/x-vertex">
  varying vec2 texCoord;
  void main() {
    texCoord = uv;
    gl_Position = projectionMatrix * modelViewMatrix
      * vec4( position, 1.0 );
  }
</script>
```

This is a simple vertex shader that doesn't change anything related to the output. The only thing to notice in this shader code is that we pass the coordinate that we're working on (uv, which is automatically passed in by Three.js) to the fragment shader as a `varying` value with the `texCoord` name.

4. The final step is to look at the fragment shader from step 2:

```
<script id="hexagonFragmentShader"
  type="x-shader/x-fragment">
  uniform sampler2D tDiffuse;
  uniform vec2 center;
```

```
uniform float scale;
uniform vec2 texSize;
varying vec2 texCoord;
void main() {
  vec2 tex = (texCoord * texSize - center) / scale;
  tex.y /= 0.866025404;
  tex.x -= tex.y * 0.5;
  vec2 a;
  if (tex.x + tex.y - floor(tex.x) - floor(tex.y)
    < 1.0)
  a = vec2(floor(tex.x), floor(tex.y));
  else a = vec2(ceil(tex.x), ceil(tex.y));
  vec2 b = vec2(ceil(tex.x), floor(tex.y));
  vec2 c = vec2(floor(tex.x), ceil(tex.y));
  vec3 TEX = vec3(tex.x, tex.y, 1.0 - tex.x - tex.y);
  vec3 A = vec3(a.x, a.y, 1.0 - a.x - a.y);
  vec3 B = vec3(b.x, b.y, 1.0 - b.x - b.y);
  vec3 C = vec3(c.x, c.y, 1.0 - c.x - c.y);
  float alen = length(TEX - A);
  float blen = length(TEX - B);
  float clen = length(TEX - C);
  vec2 choice;
  if (alen < blen) {
    if (alen < clen) choice = a;
    else choice = c;
  } else {
    if (blen < clen) choice = b;
    else choice = c;
  }
  choice.x += choice.y * 0.5;
  choice.y *= 0.866025404;
  choice *= scale / texSize;
  gl_FragColor = texture2D(tDiffuse, choice
    + center / texSize);
  }
</script>
```

This is a rather large shader program and explaining the details is a bit out of scope for this recipe. In short, what happens is that this shader looks at the color of the surrounding pixels and based on that, it determines how to draw this pixel. The important item to notice here is `uniform sampler2D tDiffuse` at the top of the code. This is the output of the previous render step passed into the shader as a 2D texture. Using `tDiffuse` in the calculations, we can change the output that is rendered on screen. If we don't want to apply an effect, we would just use `vec4 color = texture2D(tDiffuse, texCoord)` to set the output color.

5. The last step is to update the `render` loop to use composer instead of renderer:

```
function render() {
  composer.render();
  requestAnimationFrame(render);
}
```

Writing shaders is difficult work; a setup like this, however, makes it a lot easier to create your own custom shaders. Just replace the fragment shader from step 4 with your own implementation and you can start experimenting.

How it works...

In this recipe, we've used `THREE.EffectComposer` together with `THREE.RenderPass` to render the scene. If we add more steps to `THREE.EffectComposer`, we can access the current rendering directly from our shader by accessing the `tDiffuse` texture. This way, we can easily add all kinds of effects by just writing a shader that uses the `tDiffuse` texture as its input.

There's more...

When you write shaders, you can pretty much create whatever you want. Getting started with shaders, however, can be rather difficult. A good example of some shaders that apply a specific effect can be found at `https://github.com/evanw/glfx.js`. The shader we used in this recipe was also adopted from the `hexagonpixalte.js` shader that you can find in the `src/filters/fun/hexagonalpixelate.js` folder in the mentioned GitHub repository.

You can also look at the sources of the effects that are provided by Three.js. You can access them directly from GitHub at `https://github.com/mrdoob/three.js/tree/master/examples/js/shaders`.

See also

In *Chapter 5, Lights and Custom Shaders*, we've also created two custom shaders:

▶ In the *Creating a custom vertex shader* recipe, we explain the steps you need to take to set up a custom vertex shader

▶ In the *Creating a custom fragment shader* recipe, we explain the steps you need to take to set up a custom fragment shader

Saving WebGL output to disk

In this book we've created some very beautiful visualizations so far. The trouble with this, however, is that it's difficult to save the output of your rendering as an image. In this recipe, we'll show you how you can create a normal image from a WebGL-rendered scene, which can be saved to the disk.

Getting ready

There isn't much to do in order to get ready for this recipe. We'll be using standard HTML5 features, which you can apply not just to Three.js-based outputs, but to any HTML5 canvas element. We've prepared a very simple example page, where you test the result of this recipe. For this, open the `06.09-save-webgl-output.html` example in your browser. You will see something similar to the following screenshot:

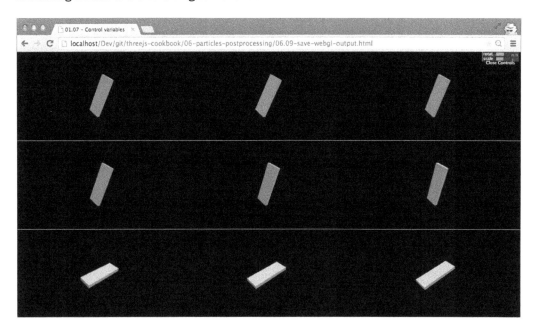

On this page, you'll see a single Three.js scene. If you hit the *p* key, the current state will be saved as a new image, which you can then download normally. Note that in the preceding screenshot, we've zoomed out of the page.

How to do it...

For this recipe, we only need to take a couple of simple steps:

1. The first thing we do is register an event listener for key presses:

   ```
   window.addEventListener("keyup", copyCanvas);
   ```

   Whenever a key is pressed, the copyCanvas function will be called.

2. Now let's look at the copyCanvas function:

   ```
   function copyCanvas(e) {
     var imgData, imgNode;
     if (e.which !== 80) {
       return;
     } else {
       imgData = renderer.domElement.toDataURL();
     }
     // create a new image and add to the document
     imgNode = document.createElement("img");
     imgNode.src = imgData;
     document.body.appendChild(imgNode);
   }
   ```

   The first thing we do here is check which key was pressed. If the *p* key was pressed, we'll continue. Next, we take the image data from the canvas with the toDataURL() function. The final step we need to take is to create a new img element, assign the data (imgData), and add it to the document.

3. This would work for non-WebGL canvas elements. However, if you work with WebGL, we need to take one additional step. We need to instantiate THREE.WebGLRenderer like this:

   ```
   renderer = new THREE.WebGLRenderer(
     {preserveDrawingBuffer: true});
   ```

   If we don't do this, you'll only see a black screen in the output and not the actual WebGL output. Note, though, that this does have an adverse impact on performance.

How it works...

In HTML5, it is possible to describe a file or any other resource using a URL starting with data. So, instead of fetching resources in multiple HTTP requests, these resources could be included directly in the HTML document. The canvas element allows you to copy its contents as a URL that complies with this scheme. In this recipe, we use this data URL to create a new `img` element, which can be saved like a normal image.

If you want to dive into the details of the data URL scheme, you can look at the RFC (Request For Comments) that describes this scheme at `http://tools.ietf.org/html/rfc2397`.

There's more

In the most recent version of Chrome and Firefox, you can also save the output of an HTML canvas element by right-clicking and selecting **Save Image As**. Besides using the standard browser functionality, it is also possible to directly start the download of the image. If you use the following piece of code instead of creating and adding a new image, the browser will automatically download the canvas as an image:

```
var link = document.createElement("a");
link.download = 'capture.png';
link.href = imgData;
link.click();
```

Finally, If you've got an animation that you want to save as a movie, you can do that as well. You can find instructions on how to do this at: `http://www.smartjava.org/content/capture-canvas-and-webgl-output-video-using-websockets`

7

Animation and Physics

In this chapter, we'll cover the following recipes:

- ▶ Creating animations with Tween.js
- ▶ Animation using morph targets
- ▶ Animation with skeletons
- ▶ Using morph animations created in Blender
- ▶ Using skeleton animations created in Blender
- ▶ Adding a simple collision detection
- ▶ Saving a movie of an animation in Chrome
- ▶ Dragging and dropping objects around a scene
- ▶ Adding a physics engine

Introduction

In the chapters so far, we've mostly dealt with static scenes or scenes with limited animation. In this chapter, we show you a number of recipes that you can use to make your scenes more dynamic. We show you recipes that talk about how to add advanced animations, how to drag and drop objects around your scene, and even how to add physics to your scene, such as gravity and collision detection.

Creating animations with Tween.js

In *Chapter 1*, *Getting Started*, we've already showed you how to set up an animation loop, and in *Chapter 2*, *Geometries and Meshes*, we showed you how to create simple animations by changing properties of `THREE.Mesh`. When you have many or complex animations, the code can quickly become complex to maintain or understand. In this recipe, we'll show you how you can use an external JavaScript library that makes the creation of animations easier and more maintainable. We'll use the **Tween.js** library for this.

Getting ready

For this recipe, we use a library from `https://github.com/sole/tween.js/`. As this is an external library, we first need to make sure it is included in our HTML page. For this, first add the following within the head element of your page:

```
<script src="../libs/tween.js"></script>
```

For this recipe, we'll create a simple animation using this library. If you open the `07.01-animation-with-tweenjs.html` example in your browser, you can view the final result, which is similar to what is shown in the following screenshot:

If you open this example in your browser, you'll see a small red cube that moves to a different position and rotates while it is moving. This animation is configured using the `Tween.js` library.

How to do it...

Once you've added the required library to your HTML page, creating the animation only takes a couple of simple steps:

1. To use this library, we need to first create an instance of a `TWEEN.Tween` object:

   ```
   var tween = new TWEEN.Tween({x:0 , y:1.25, z:0, rot: 0});
   ```

   This creates a `TWEEN.Tween` instance. We can use this instance to move the provided properties from the start value (the value we added in this step) to an end value.

2. The next step is to define the target values for the properties. We do this by using the `to` function:

   ```
   tween.to({x:5, y:15, z:-10, rot: 2*Math.PI}, 5000);
   ```

   With this function, we tell the `tween` object that we want to slowly change the provided values in the constructor to these values. So, we change the `x` property from `0` to `5`. The second parameter, which is `5000`, defines how many milliseconds this change should take.

3. We can also choose how the value changes over time. You can for instance use a linear easing function, which changes the values at a constant rate, a quadratic one, which starts with small changes and quickly increases, or even use an easing function that bounces (overshoots) at the end. There are many more easing functions that are predefined in `TWEEN` (see the *There's more...* section for more information). You do this by calling the easing function:

   ```
   tween.easing(TWEEN.Easing.Elastic.InOut);
   ```

4. So far, we have changed the values of these properties from one value to another, but we don't really do anything when a value changes. In this recipe, we want to change the position and the rotation of the cube. You do this by calling the `onUpdate` function and passing in the function that should be called on each change:

   ```
   tween.onUpdate(function() {
     cube.position.set(this.x, this.y, this.z);
     cube.rotation.set(this.rot, this.rot, this.rot);
   });
   ```

   As you can see in this code snippet, we use the provided properties to set the rotation and position properties of cube.

5. There are a number of other settings you can use on the `tween` object to control how the animation behaves. For this recipe, we tell the `tween` object to repeat its animation indefinitely and use a yo-yo effect that reverses the animation each time it is repeated:

```
tween.repeat(Infinity);
tween.yoyo(true);
```

6. Finally, we can start the `tween` object by calling the start function:

```
tween.start();
```

7. At this point, you won't see anything happening. There is one last step you need to add to the `render` loop to inform the `tween` object how much time has passed so that it can calculate the correct values for the properties you provided in step 1:

```
TWEEN.update();
```

This will update all the `TWEEN.Tween` objects you've defined and call the `onUpdate` functions with the `updated` values.

You define the start value, the end value, and how the start value should transition to the end value.

How it works...

Whenever you call `TWEEN.update()`, the `TWEEN` library will determine how much time has passed from the previous call to `TWEEN.update` for each `TWEEN.Tween` object (or in the case of the first time, the time from calling `start()` on the `TWEEN.Tween` object). Based on this difference, the start time of `tween`, and the configured `easing` property, this library calculates new values for the passed-in properties. Finally, it will call the function passed into `onUpdate()` so that you can take action on the changed values.

There's more...

In this recipe, we didn't show all the configuration you can pass into the `TWEEN.Tween` object. For a complete overview of all the different easing options and other properties of the `TWEEN.Tween` object, refer to the GitHub project site at `https://github.com/sole/tween.js/`.

Before we move on to the next recipe, there is one additional interesting aspect of the Tween.js library. In our recipe, we configured the `TWEEN.Tween` object step by step. You can also configure the object in one call like this:

```
var tween = new TWEEN.Tween({x:0 , y:1.25, z:0, rot: 0})
    .to({x:5, y:15, z:-10, rot: 2*Math.PI}, 5000)
    .easing(TWEEN.Easing.Elastic.InOut)
    .onUpdate(function() {
    cube.position.set(this.x, this.y, this.z);
    cube.rotation.set(this.rot, this.rot, this.rot);
})
.repeat(Infinity)
.yoyo(true)
.start();
```

This works because Tween.js offers a fluent API. So for each function call, this library returns the original `TWEEN.Tween` object. This means that you can easily chain calls together like we did in the previous code fragment.

See also

▸   You can use the Tween.js library in pretty much every case where we used an animation in this book. For instance, in *Chapter 2, Geometries and Meshes*, we showed you the Rotating an object around its own axis recipe. The rotation could be easily managed using a `TWEEN.Tween` object. In *Chapter 3, Working with the Camera*, we showed you how to zoom in on an object in the *Zooming the camera to an object* recipe. With the Tween.js library, we can easily animate this zoom functionality.

Animating using morph targets

When modeling 3D objects and characters, there are generally two different ways of creating animations. You can animate using morph targets, or you can use skeleton-and-bones-based animations. Three.js facilitates both of these approaches. In this recipe, we'll look at the morph-based animation. With morph-based animations, like the name implies, you morph one geometry shape into another. This works great for facial expressions and other very detailed animations.

Getting ready

For this recipe, we don't require any additional libraries as morph-based animations are supported by the standard Three.js distribution. To make this recipe more understandable, we use an existing 3D model to demonstrate how morphing works. You can see the model and the available morphs when you open the `07.02-animation-with-morphing.html` example in your browser. You will see something similar to what is shown in the following screenshot:

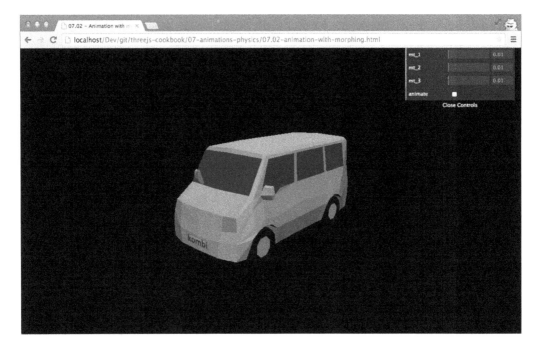

In this example, you can see a simple model of a car. Using the sliders in the top-right section, you can slowly morph this car into a different model, as shown in the following screenshot:

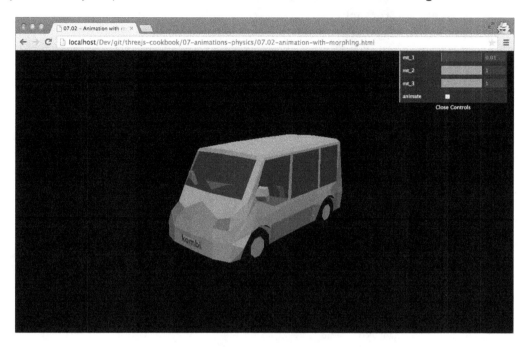

If you check the **animate** box, an animation that automatically morphs this car will start.

How to do it...

To use morphing animations, we need to take the following steps:

1. The first thing we need to do is load the model that contains morph targets. For this recipe, we've got a JSON-based model, which we load like this:

    ```
    var jsonLoader = new THREE.JSONLoader();
    jsonLoader.load("../assets/models/morph/car.js",
    function(model, materials) {
        ...
    });
    ```

    Here, we use `THREE.JSONLoader` to load a model, and once it is loaded, we call the provided function.

2. Before we create `THREE.Mesh`, there is one additional step we need to take. We need to set the `morphTargets` property on the materials that are set to `true`:

```
materials.forEach(function(mat) {
  mat.morphTargets = true;
});
```

3. Next, we need to create `THREE.Mesh` and add it to the scene:

```
car = new THREE.Mesh(model,
  new THREE.MeshFaceMaterial( materials ));
scene.add(car);
```

As you can see, we follow the standard way of creating `THREE.Mesh` and add it to the scene just like any other object.

4. Now that we've got an object in the scene that can be morphed, we can use the `morphTargetInfluences` property to set how much the object is morphed into a specific direction. In the example for this recipe, we used the UI to control this setting as follows:

```
gui.add(control, 'mt_1', 0,
  1).step(0.01).listen().onChange(function(a){
  car.morphTargetInfluences[1] = a;
});
gui.add(control, 'mt_2', 0,
  1).step(0.01).listen().onChange(function(a){
  car.morphTargetInfluences[2] = a;
});;
gui.add(control, 'mt_3', 0,
  1).step(0.01).listen().onChange(function(a){
  car.morphTargetInfluences[3] = a;
});
```

The model we used in this recipe has four morph targets (with names `mt_0`, `mt_1`, `mt_2`, and `mt_3`), its base state and three other car models. By increasing the `morphTargetInfluence` object of one of those other models, we can morph the model into that direction.

As you can see in this recipe, by simply changing the value of a specific `morphTargetInfluences` value, you can change the way your model looks.

How it works...

In models that support multiple morph targets, an additional set of vertices is stored to represent that position for each of the targets. So, if you've got a face model that has a morph target for a smile, one for a frown, and one for a smirk, you effectively store four times as many vertex positions. With the `morphTargetInfluences` property, you can tell Three.js how far the base state (the `geometry.vertices` property) should be morphed toward that specific morph target. Three.js will then calculate the average position of each individual vertex and render the updated model. A very interesting thing is that you can combine morph targets. So if you've got separate morph targets for eye movement and mouth movement, you can easily create very animated and lifelike animations.

There's more...

In this recipe, we loaded an external model that contained the morph targets. If you've already got a simple geometry that you want to use for morph-based animations, you can also easily do that. For instance, if you've got a geometry, you can add `morphTargets` using the following code:

```
cubeGeometry.morphTargets[0] = {name: 't1', vertices:
cubeTarget2.vertices};
cubeGeometry.morphTargets[1] = {name: 't2', vertices:
  cubeTarget1.vertices};
```

The important aspect here is to make sure you provide the same amount of vertices to the `vertices` property as there are in the `initial` geometry. You can now control the morph between the various targets using the `morphTargetInfluences` properties on `THREE.Mesh`:

```
cube.morphTargetInfluences[0] = 0.4;
cube.morphTargetInfluences[1] = 0.6;
```

See also

- ▶ An alternative way to animate models can be done using skeleton and bones. We explain how to do this in the *Animation with skeletons* recipe. We also provide two recipes in this chapter where we define morph-and-skeleton-based animations in an external tool (Blender, in our case) and play the animation in Three.js. See the *Using morph animations created in Blender* and *Using skeleton animations created in Blender* recipes for more information about these approaches.

Animating with skeletons

A common way to animate complex models is using bones and skinning. In this approach, we define a geometry, add a skeleton, and tie the geometry to that skeleton. Whenever we move or rotate one of the bones of the skeleton, the geometry is deformed accordingly. In this recipe, we will show you how you can use the Three.js functionality to move and rotate bones directly from JavaScript.

Getting ready

For this recipe, we use an external model that already contains a skeleton we can move around. To load this model, we use THREE.JSONLoader, which is available in the standard distribution of Three.js. So, we don't need to import any additional JavaScript files to get this recipe to work. Of course, we've provided an example of this recipe in action, which you can view by opening the 07.03-animation-with-skeleton.html example in your browser. You will see something similar to what is shown in the following screenshot:

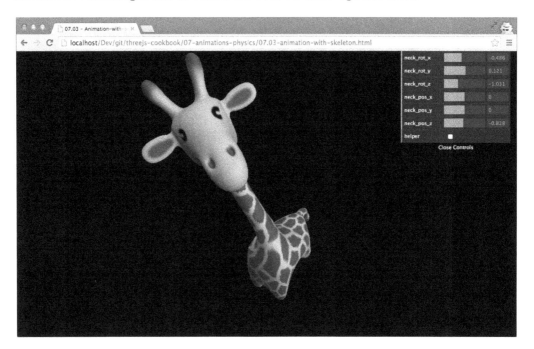

This example shows you a model of a giraffe and provides an interface that you can use to move the neck bone. You can change the rotation of the neck bone and even its position. When you do this, you'll see that part of the mesh responds to the movement of this bone. In this recipe, we'll show you how to accomplish this for yourself.

How to do it...

Working directly with bones isn't that difficult and only takes a couple of small steps:

1. The first thing we need to do is load a model that contains bones. For this recipe, we once again use `THREE.JSONLoader`:

```
var jsonLoader = new THREE.JSONLoader();
jsonLoader.load("../assets/models/bones/giraffe.js",
   function(model, materials) {
      ...
   });
```

2. Once the model from step 1 has been loaded, we can set up the materials and create the mesh. Let's first look at the materials:

```
materials.forEach(function(mat) {
   mat.skinning = true;
});
```

Here, we set the `skinning` property of the material to `true`. This tells Three.js that this object contains bones and the geometry should deform when the bones move.

3. Next, we create the mesh and add it to the scene:

```
var giraffe = new THREE.SkinnedMesh(model, materials[0]);
scene.add(giraffe);
```

As you can see, we've used a different kind of mesh for this object. Instead of the `THREE.Mesh` object, we've used a `THREE.SkinnedMesh` object.

4. To access the bones, we access the children elements of `THREE.SkinnedMesh`. Getting the correct bone to animate might take some experimenting if the bones aren't clearly named. The easiest way to determine which bone to use is to look through the output of the JavaScript console and browse the children of the mesh.

5. In this case, we want to rotate the tail bone and rotate and position the neck. For this, we add the following to the `render` loop:

```
// the neck bone
giraffe.children[0].children[1].children[0].children[0]
   .rotation.x = control.neck_rot_x;
giraffe.children[0].children[1].children[0].children[0]
   .rotation.y = control.neck_rot_y;
giraffe.children[0].children[1].children[0].children[0]
   .rotation.z = control.neck_rot_z;
giraffe.children[0].children[1].children[0].children[0]
   .position.x = control.neck_pos_x;
giraffe.children[0].children[1].children[0].children[0]
   .position.y = control.neck_pos_y;
giraffe.children[0].children[1].children[0].children[0]
   .position.z = control.neck_pos_z;
// the tail bone
giraffe.children[0].children[0].children[0]
   .rotation.z -= 0.1
```

That's it! Whenever we now change the position of the rotation of the bones we used in the previous code snippet, the geometry will deform accordingly.

Working with bones isn't that difficult, but selecting the correct bone to change and move around can take some experimentation.

How it works...

When you enable the `skinning` property on the material, Three.js passes all the information about the relevant bones and positions into its vertex shader. The vertex shader will use this information to position the vertices to their new position based on the position and rotation of the relevant bones. More information and a good introduction on how to execute skeletal animations from a vertex shader can be found on the OpenGL website at `https://www.opengl.org/wiki/Skeletal_Animation`.

There's more...

If you want to get a quick overview of how the bones are organized in a model, you can use a specific helper class that is provided by Three.js. The following code snippet shows you how to create `THREE.SkeletonHelper` for the model we used in this recipe:

```
var helper = new THREE.SkeletonHelper(giraffe);
scene.add(helper);
```

This will visualize the bones of a model, as shown in the following screenshot:

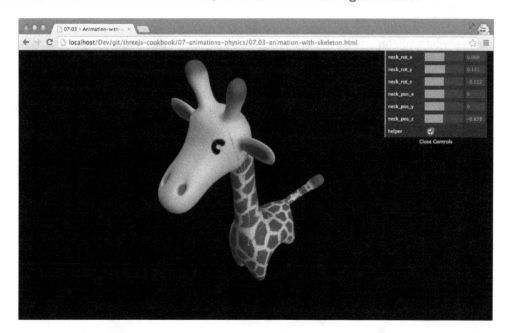

If you move bones around, which we do in our recipe, you also need to add the following line to your `render` loop:

```
helper.update();
```

This way, `THREE.SkeletonHelper` will always reflect the latest state of the model.

See also

▶ A simpler way to animate models is using morph targets. We explain how to do this in the *Animation using morph targets* recipe. We also provide two recipes in this chapter where we define morph-and-skeleton-based animations in an external tool (Blender, in our case) and play the animation in Three.js. Refer to the *Using morph animations created in Blender* and *Using skeleton animations created in Blender* recipes for more information on these approaches.

Using morph animations created in Blender

Creating morph animations by hand is difficult to do in Three.js. Simple transformations can probably be handled, but creating advanced animations programmatically is very difficult. Luckily, there are a large number of external 3D programs that you can use to create the models and animations. In this recipe, we'll use Blender, which we already used in *Chapter 2, Geometries and Meshes*, to create a morph-based animation and play it back using Three.js.

Getting ready

To use this recipe, you have to have Blender installed and enable the Three.js exporter plugin. We've already explained how to do this in the *Creating and exporting a model from Blender* recipe, in *Chapter 2, Geometries and Meshes*. So if you haven't already done so, you should first install Blender and then the Three.js export plugin. Once you've installed Blender, you should create an animation that uses shape keys to define various formats. Doing this is out of the scope of this book, but to make sure, you can test the steps explained in this recipe—we've included a Blender file, which has a minimal shape-keys-based animation. So before we get started with the recipe, we'll load the example Blender model.

For this, take the following steps:

1. Open **Blender** and navigate to **File | Open**.

2. In the window that opens, navigate to the sources provided with the book and open the `simplemorph.blend` file, which can be found in the `assets/models/blender` directory.

3. Once this file is opened, you'll see a cube in the center of an empty scene like this:

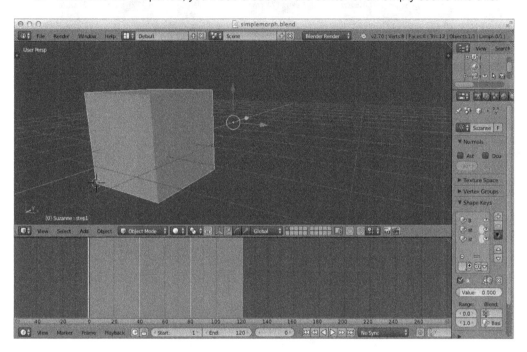

This is the starting point from where we start the recipe.

4. If you want to preview the (very simple) animation we've created here, just click on the **play** button or use the *Alt + A* key combination.

5. We will load this file in Three.js and play the animation we created in Blender. To see the final result, open the `07.04-create-morph-in-blender.html` example in your browser. You will see something similar to what is shown in the following screenshot:

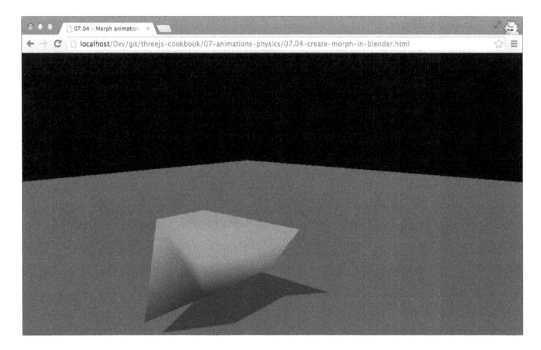

You'll see an animating cube that uses morph targets (defined as shape keys in Blender) to morph a cube into different shapes.

How to do it...

If you've followed the steps explained in the *Getting ready* section of this recipe, you'll be looking at a simple Blender workspace with a single cube and an animation that slowly morphs the cube using a set of shape keys. To export this animation from Blender and use it in Three.js, we need to take a couple of steps:

1. The first thing we need to do is export the model and the animation to which we can load it in Three.js. To do this, navigate to **File | Export | Three.js**.

2. In the window that opens, we can select a destination and a filename. For this recipe, name the file `simplemorph.js` and set the destination to the `assets/models/morph` folder.

3. Before we hit the **Export** button, we need to configure some Three.js-specific properties. You can do this in the panel on the left-hand side in the **Export Three.js** section. In that section, make sure that the **Morph animation** checkbox is selected. Once you've checked the box, click on the **Export** button.

4. Now we're done with our work in Blender and can load the exported model in Three.js. For this, we use `THREE.JSONLoader` like this:

```
var loader = new THREE.JSONLoader();
loader.load("../assets/models/morph/simplemorph.js"
  ,function(model){
  ...
});
```

   In this code snippet, we load the model using `THREE.JSONLoader`.

5. Once the model is loaded, we need to create a material where we need to set the `morphTargets` property to `true`:

```
var mat = new THREE.MeshLambertMaterial(
  {color: 0xff3333, morphTargets:true})
```

6. With this material, we can create the mesh to be added to the scene. This time, as we want to use the animation provided from Blender, we create `THREE.MorphAnimMesh`, which we add to the scene:

```
mesh = new THREE.MorphAnimMesh(model, mat);
mesh.castShadow = true;
scene.add(mesh);
```

7. We need to take a final step before we can play the animation:

```
mesh.parseAnimations();
mesh.playAnimation('animation', 20);
mesh.duration = 10;
render();
```

   With the `parseAnimation()` function, Three.js will parse the names of the provided morph target elements from the model and use it to create an animation. When you export using the Three.js plugin from Blender, the name of the animation is `animation`. To play the animation, we call `playAnimation` with the name of the animation and the frame rate, and finally, we set the duration (in seconds) of the animation. Note that you don't always have to set the duration of an animation. In some cases, the model itself provides the duration.

8. The final change we need to make is in the `render` function itself:

```
var t = new THREE.Clock();
function render() {
  renderer.render(scene, camera);
  mesh.updateAnimation(t.getDelta());
  requestAnimationFrame(render);
}
```

Here, we create a global `THREE.Clock()` instance, which we use to determine how much time is passed between sequential calls to the `render` function. This is passed into the `updateAnimation` function of `THREE.MorphAnimMesh` so that it can calculate which frame to show.

As you've seen from the recipe, getting an animation to play in Three.js from Blender isn't that difficult. One thing to take into account here, though, is that this can result in huge files when you've got models with a high vertex count. This happens because the Blender export plugin creates a new morph target for each frame of the animation.

There's more...

In this recipe, we've used the Three.js export function of Blender to save the model in a format `THREE.JSONLoader` can load. There are a large number of other 3D formats available, which can be used to store 3D scenes and animations that are supported by Three.js. An overview of the file formats that are available in Three.js can be found on the Three.js GitHub site at `https://github.com/mrdoob/three.js/tree/master/examples/js/loaders`.

See also

In this chapter, we've got some other recipes that deal with animations:

▸ *Animation using morph targets*

▸ *Animation with skeletons*

▸ *Using skeleton animations created in Blender*

Using skeleton animations created in Blender

In the *Animation with skeletons* recipe, we animated a model by directly changing the position and rotation of its bones. This works great in an interactive scenery but isn't a practical way to create animations. With Blender and other 3D tools, you've got a large set of tools to create animations based on a specific skeleton and a set of bones. In this recipe, we'll show you how you can play back a skeleton-based animation that was created in Blender.

To use this recipe, you need to have Blender installed and enable the Three.js exporter plugin. If you haven't done so, follow the steps from the *Creating and exporting a model from Blender* recipe, in *Chapter 2, Geometries and Meshes*. Once Blender and the Three.js export plugin have been installed, we need to create a skeleton-based animation. Creating this in Blender is out of the scope of this book, so we've provided an existing model to demonstrate this recipe. To get started, perform the following steps:

1. Open **Blender** and navigate to **File | Open**.

2. In the window that opens, navigate to the sources provided with the book and open the `crow-skeleton.blend` file, which can be found in the `assets/models/blender` directory.

3. Once this file is open, you'll see a crow in the center of an empty scene like this:

This is the starting point of this recipe.

4. If you want to preview the crow animation, click on the **play** button or use the *Alt + A* key combination.

We have also provided an example that you can open in your browser to see the same animation in a Three.js scene. When you open the `07.05-create-skeleton-animation-in-blender.html` example in your browser, you should see something like this:

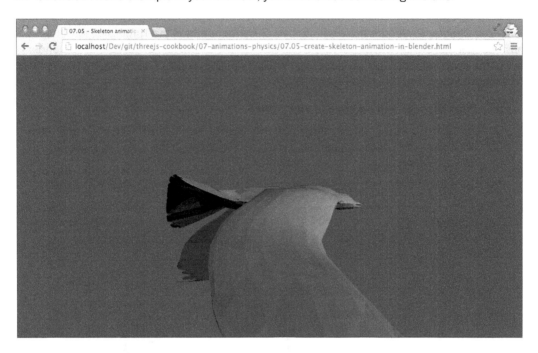

How to do it...

Before we can use the model in Three.js, we first have to export it from Blender:

1. To start the export, first navigate to **File** | **Export** | **Three.js**.

2. In the window that opens, we can select a destination and a filename. For this recipe, name the file `crow.js` and set the destination to the `assets/models/bones` folder.

3. Before we hit the **Export** button, we need to configure some Three.js-specific properties. You can do this in the panel on the left-hand side in the **Export Three.js** section. In that section, make sure that the **Bones**, **Skinning**, and **Skeletal** animation checkboxes are selected. If the **Morph Animation** checkbox is selected, disable it. Once you've checked the box, click on the **Export** button.

4. Now that we've exported the model, the first thing we need to do in Three.js is load the model using `THREE.JSONLoader`:

```
var loader = new THREE.JSONLoader();
loader.load("../assets/models/bones/crow.js"
   ,function(model){
   ...
});
```

5. Once the model is loaded in Three.js. we can process it. The first thing we do in the callback from the `loader.load` function is to set up the material:

```
var mat = new THREE.MeshLambertMaterial({color: 0xf33f33,
   shading: THREE.FlatShading, skinning:true})
```

This is just a standard `THREE.MeshLambertMaterial` object. The only thing you need to make sure is to set the `skinning` property of the material to `true`.

6. Now that we've got the model and the material, we can create a mesh. As we're working with skeletons, we need to create `THREE.SkinnedMesh`:

```
mesh = new THREE.SkinnedMesh(model, mat);
```

7. Next, we need to select the animation we want to play. For this, you use the following code snippet:

```
model.animation = "Crow.ArmatureAction";
THREE.AnimationHandler.add(model.animations[0]);
var animation = new THREE.Animation(
   mesh, model.animation );
animation.play();
```

You need to make sure the `animation` property contains the name of an animation from the `model.animations` array. In this case, we've only got one animation with the `Crow.ArmatureAction` name. Skeleton-based animations are handled using `THREE.AnimationHandler`. So, we add the animation from our model to the handler. Next, we need to create a `THREE.Animation` instance. This object combines our model with the animation we want to play. When we have this object we can call the `play()` function to tell Three.js to play the animation.

8. The final step we need to take before the animation will play is to update the `render` loop:

```
var t = new THREE.Clock();
function render() {
   renderer.render(scene, camera);
   THREE.AnimationHandler.update( t.getDelta() );
   requestAnimationFrame(render);
}
```

Here, we use `THREE.Clock()` to determine how much time has passed (`t.getDelta()`) between this frame and the previous one. This is passed into `THREE.AnimationHandler` to update all the registered animations and move the mesh in the correct position.

How it works...

When exporting the animation, the Three.js exporter will write out the position and rotation of the bones at the times we specified in Blender. This information can then be used directly in Three.js to determine the position and rotation of the bones when we're playing back the animation. This way, we can create fairly complex animations without having to create huge model files.

There's more...

Working with skeletons in Blender and creating animations from them is a subject on which much is written. If you're interested in learning more about rigging models and creating skeleton-based animations, a couple of good resources to start with are the following:

- Blender Tutorial: Basics of Character Rigging at `http://www.youtube.com/watch?v=cGvalWG8HBU`
- Blender manual: rigging at `http://wiki.blender.org/index.php/Doc:2.6/Manual/Rigging`
- Blender Guru: introduction to rigging at `http://www.blenderguru.com/tutorials/introduction-to-rigging`
- Building A Basic Low Poly Character Rig In Blender at `http://cgi.tutsplus.com/tutorials/building-a-basic-low-poly-character-rig-in-blender--cg-16955`

See also

In this chapter, we have some other recipes that deal with animations:

- *Animation using morph targets*
- *Animation with skeletons*
- *Using morph animations created in Blender*

Adding a simple collision detection

When you're creating games or interactive environments, a common requirement is the option to detect collisions between objects. In the *Adding a physics engine* recipe, we use an external library to handle collisions (and other physics). This, however, is a rather heavy solution if all you require is the option to detect collisions. In this recipe, we provide a simple approach that you can use if you want to detect collisions without having to use an external library.

Getting ready

In this recipe, we use `THREE.Raycaster` to check for collisions. This object is provided by the standard Three.js distribution, so you don't need any additional libraries. We've provided a simple example that shows you how this recipe can be applied. For this, open the `07.06-add-simple-detection-collision.html` example in your browser, and you will see something similar to what is shown in the following screenshot:

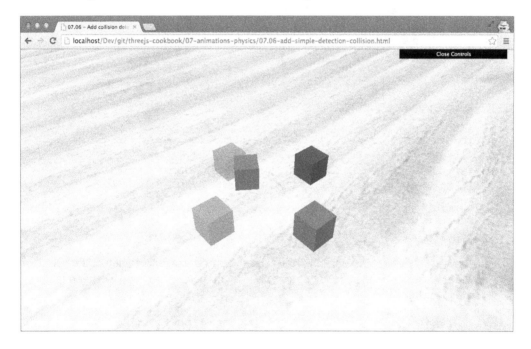

In this example, you can move the central cube around using the arrow keys and rotate it around the *y* axis with the *a* and *b* keys. Whenever a collision occurs with one of the other cubes, we change the opacity to indicate a collision.

How to do it...

To accomplish collision detection, we need to take a couple of steps:

1. Let's start simple and create the cube that we'll move around. We will detect collisions between this cube and the cubes we define in step 2:

```
var cubeGeometry = new THREE.BoxGeometry(2, 2, 2);
var cubeMaterial = new THREE.MeshLambertMaterial({color:
0xff2255});
var cube = new THREE.Mesh(cubeGeometry, cubeMaterial);
cube.name='cube';
scene.add(cube);
```

2. Now, let's create an array that will hold all the objects that we can collide with and add some cubes to that array:

```
var cubes = [];
var cubeMaterial2 = new THREE.MeshLambertMaterial({color:
0xff0000});
var cube2 = new THREE.Mesh(cubeGeometry, cubeMaterial2);
cube2.position.set(5,0,0);
cube2.name='cube-red';
scene.add(cube2);
cubes.push(cube2);
...
var cubeMaterial5 = new THREE.MeshLambertMaterial({color:
0xff00ff});
var cube5 = new THREE.Mesh(cubeGeometry, cubeMaterial5);
cube5.position.set(-5,0,0);
cube5.name='cube-purple';
scene.add(cube5);
cubes.push(cube5);
```

3. Now that we've got the object to move around and the objects to detect the collisions with, we can add the code to detect collisions. In the `render` loop, we need to add the following:

```
// reset the opacity at the beginning of the loop
cubes.forEach(function(cube){
    cube.material.transparent = false;
    cube.material.opacity = 1.0;

});
```

```
var cube = scene.getObjectByName('cube');
var originPoint = cube.position.clone();

for (var vertexIndex = 0;
        vertexIndex < cube.geometry.vertices.length;
        vertexIndex++) {
    var localVertex = cube.geometry.
    vertices[vertexIndex].clone();
    var globalVertex = localVertex.applyMatrix4(
                        cube.matrix);
    var directionVector = globalVertex.sub(
                        cube.position);

    var ray = new THREE.Raycaster(
                originPoint,
                directionVector.clone().normalize() );
    var collisionResults = ray.intersectObjects( cubes );
    if ( collisionResults.length > 0
                && collisionResults[0].distance <
                    directionVector.length() ) {
        collisionResults[0].object
                .material.transparent = true;
        collisionResults[0]
                .object.material.opacity = 0.4;
    }
}
```

In this piece of code, we simply check whether one of the vertices of our moving cube intersects with any of the cubes in the `cubes` array. If we detect a collision, we change the opacity of the cube we collided with.

With these steps, we have a rudimentary solution to detect collisions. This approach works great to detect collisions between flat objects but might miss detection with small spike-like objects. You can enhance this solution by checking collisions against more vertices. You can, for instance, add more vertices by increasing the `widthSegments`, `heightSegments`, and `depthSegments` objects of the cube, or you can calculate intermediate vertices yourself.

How it works...

To detect collisions in this approach, we shoot a ray using `THREE.RayCaster` from the center of the cube that is moving to each of its vertices. If this ray intersects with one of the other cubes from the `cubes` array in its path from the center to a vertex, it means that one of the vertices is inside one of the other cubes. We interpret this as a collision and can take appropriate action.

There's more...

This recipe is based on the great work done by Lee Stemkoski, who provided an initial implementation of this approach at `http://stemkoski.github.io/Three.js/Collision-Detection.html`. Besides a ray-based approach to collision detection, there are, of course, alternative approaches. A very common approach is to use the bounding boxes of a mesh to detect whether two meshes touch. Three.js even provides a function for this in the `THREE.Box3` object called `isIntersectionBox`. As using a ray casting approach is a rather computationally expensive way to detect collisions, often a bounding box approach is used first, followed by the more accurate ray casting method.

A couple of good resources on such an approach can be found here:

- *3D Theory - Collision Detection* at `http://www.euclideanspace.com/threed/animation/collisiondetect/`
- *AABB to AABB detection in C++* at `http://www.miguelcasillas.com/?p=30`
- *3D Collision detection and resolution using sweeping AABB bounding boxes* at `http://techny.tumblr.com/post/42125198333/3d-collision-detection-and-resolution-using-sweeping`

The physics engine we will use in the *Adding a physics engine* recipe also uses a shapes-based approach to collision detection. Besides just a bounding box, it provides a number of different shapes to detect collisions.

See also

- In the *Adding a physics engine* recipe, we detect collisions using the physics engine. For another recipe that uses `THREE.RayCaster`, you can also look at the *Dragging and dropping objects around a scene* recipe, which can also be found in this chapter.

Saving a movie of an animation in Chrome

In this chapter, we've showed you various ways to create animations. Sometimes, however, people don't have a WebGL-enabled browser, or you want to just share the resulting animation and not the WebGL website. In these cases, it would be very helpful to be able to just save the animation to your local filesystem and share it. In this recipe, we show you one approach you can use for this scenario.

Getting ready

To work with this recipe, you need to make sure that you use Google Chrome. We use an internal functionality to save the animation as a WebM file, which unfortunately, still only works on Google Chrome. We don't have to create the complete functionality for this recipe from scratch, as there is a library available that handles the low-level technical stuff for us: CCapture (`https://github.com/spite/ccapture.js/`). To work with this library, we need to load the following two JavaScript files at the top of our HTML page:

```
<script src="../libs/CCapture.min.js"></script>
<script src="../libs/Whammy.js"></script>
```

We've provided a very simple example that shows you this recipe in action. If you open up `07.07-save-a-movie-of-an-animation.html` in your browser, you'll see a slowly moving cube in your browser, as shown in the following screenshot:

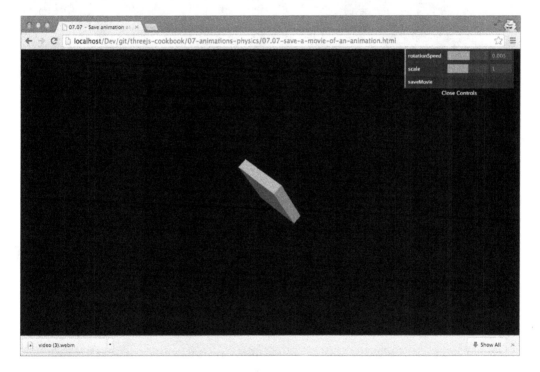

The reason this cube moves so slowly is that in the background, a movie is being saved. The libraries used slow down the animation to make sure no frames are skipped. To save the movie, click on the **saveMovie** menu button at the top of the screen.

The resulting movie can now be played in the movie player of your choice, which supports WebM (for instance, VLC or mPlayer) as shown in the following screenshot:

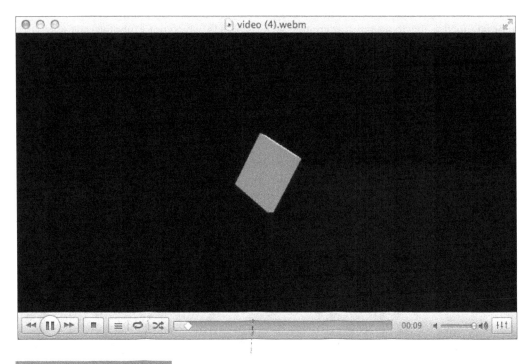

How to do it...

Once you've included the appropriate libraries in your HTML page, using this library is actually very easy:

1. The first thing we need to do is create a `capture` object:

   ```
   Var capturer = new CCapture({
     framerate: 20
   });
   ```

   Here, we create a capturer that captures 20 frames per second.

2. The next step before we start rendering the scene is to start `capturer`:

   ```
   capturer.start();
   // call the render loop
   render();
   ```

3. We also need to tell `capturer` what to capture in the `render` loop:

```
function render() {
  renderer.render(scene, camera);
  capturer.capture( renderer.domElement );
  requestAnimationFrame(render);
}
```

With these steps, the `capturer` object will start capturing the output of our WebGL canvas 20 times per second.

4. As a last step, we need to add a functionality to save the movie (in our example, this is triggered by clicking on the **saveMovie** button):

```
this.saveMovie = function() {
  var videoUrl = capturer.save();
  var link = document.createElement("a");
  link.download = 'video.webm';
  link.href = videoUrl;
  link.click();
};
```

This will download the movie as `video.webm` and save it to your local disk.

When you run this, you will notice that the frame rate in your browser drops significantly. The reason is that the CCapture library changes the behavior of the `requestAnimationFrame` function to make sure it has enough time to capture the screen and add it as a frame to the movie. The movie file that is created will look like you expected and have the number of frames per second, as specified in step 1 of this recipe.

There's more...

The approach that we showed you in the recipe works great for most types of animations. However, when you want to record a user interacting with your scene, you can't use this library as it slows down the rendering of your scene, which makes interacting with the scene difficult. An alternative way to record the scene is using a backend service that collects screenshots and creates a movie server side. An example of such a setup can be found at `http://www.smartjava.org/content/capture-canvas-and-webgl-output-video-using-websockets`.

See also

▶ If you just want to save a screenshot instead of a complete movie, you can use the *Saving WebGL output to disk* recipe, which we explained in *Chapter 6, Point Clouds and Postprocessing*.

Dragging and dropping objects around a scene

When you create an interactive environment, a common requirement is the option to use your mouse to drag objects around. This functionality isn't something that is supported out of the box by Three.js. In this recipe, we'll show you the steps that are needed to implement this functionality.

Getting ready

For this recipe, we only use the functionality that is available in the standard Three.js library. We'll use the THREE.Raycaster object together with THREE.Projector to implement the drag and drop functionality. To see the drag and drop functionality in action, you can open the 07.08-drag-n-drop-object-around-scene.html example in your browser, and you will see something similar to what is shown in the following screenshot:

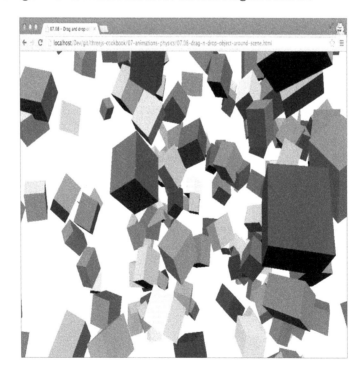

In this example, you can see a large number of cubes, which you can move individually. Just click on one with the mouse and drag it to a new position. This scene also uses THREE.OrbitControls, so when you click on the white background, you can use your mouse to rotate the scene.

How to do it...

For this recipe, we need to take a fair amount of steps:

1. The first thing we do is create a number of global variables, which we'll access in the following steps:

```
var plane;
var selectedObject;
var projector = new THREE.Projector();
var offset = new THREE.Vector3();
var objects =[];
```

We'll explain how these objects are used in the upcoming steps.

2. When we want to move an object around, we need to determine on what plane (around which axis) we're going to move the selected cube. A mouse moves in two dimensions, while our scene moves in three. For this, we'll use a invisible helper plane, which we define like this:

```
plane = new THREE.Mesh( new THREE.PlaneGeometry( 2000,
   2000, 18, 18 ), new THREE.MeshBasicMaterial() );
plane.visible = false;
scene.add( plane );
```

This plane is assigned to the global plane variable we saw in step 1.

3. The next step is to create all the cubes. For an easy understanding of this recipe, we list the code about how cubes are created:

```
for (var i = 0 ; i < 200 ; i ++) {
  var cubeGeometry = new THREE.BoxGeometry(2, 2, 2);
  var cubeMaterial = new
  THREE.MeshLambertMaterial({color:
    Math.random() * 0xffffff});
  cubeMaterial.transparent = true;
  cube = new THREE.Mesh(cubeGeometry, cubeMaterial);
  objects.push(cube);
  // randomize position, scale and rotation
  scene.add(cube);
}
```

The most interesting line is the highlighted one, where we add the created cube to the global array with the name objects. Only cubes from this array can be moved around.

4. Now that we've got the basics out of the way, we need to tell Three.js what to do when the mouse moves, when a mouse button is clicked on, and when a mouse button is released. Let's first look at the onmousemove function:

```
document.onmousemove = function(e) {

    . . .

};
```

Before we can access the information from the mouse movement, we need to register a listener. We do this, as you can see in the code snippet, by assigning a function to the document.onmousemove property. In the following steps, we'll look at the contents of this onmousemove function.

5. In the onmousemove function, we do a couple of different things. The first thing we always need to do is convert the mouse position to a position in 3D space and create THREE.Raycaster for that position:

```
// get the mouse position in viewport coordinates
var mouse_x = ( event.clientX / window.innerWidth )
  * 2 - 1;
var mouse_y = - ( event.clientY / window.innerHeight )
  * 2 + 1;
// get the 3D position and create a raycaster
var vector = new THREE.Vector3( mouse_x, mouse_y, 0.5 );
projector.unprojectVector( vector, camera );
var raycaster = new THREE.Raycaster( camera.position,
  vector.sub( camera.position ).normalize() );
```

At this point, we can use THREE.Raycaster to select objects that are the position of our mouse.

6. The next step is to either drag an object around if we've already clicked on one (see steps 7, 8, and 9 for more details on this), or reposition the plane we created in step 2:

```
if (selectedObject) {
  var intersects = raycaster.intersectObject( plane );
  selectedObject.position.copy(intersects[ 0 ]
    .point.sub( offset ) );
} else {
  var intersects = raycaster.intersectObjects(objects);
  if ( intersects.length > 0 ) {
    plane.position.copy( intersects[0]
      .object.position );
      plane.lookAt( camera.position );
  }
}
```

If we've selected an object and are dragging it around, we set the position of that object based on the position where the ray cast from our mouse intersects the invisible helper plane using the offset that we calculate in step 9. If we aren't dragging an object around, and using our ray we determine that we intersect one of the cubes, we move our helper `plane` object to the position of that object and make sure the plane faces the camera (`plane.lookAt(camera.position)`). The object, if we select it, will move alongside this helper `plane` object.

7. Next, we need to define a function to handle the `onmousedown` events:

```
document.onmousedown = function(event) {
    ...
};
```

8. Now, let's look at what to fill in for the `onmousedown` event:

```
var mouse_x = (event.clientX / window.innerWidth) * 2 - 1;
var mouse_y = -(event.clientY / window.innerHeight) *
    2 + 1;
var vector = new THREE.Vector3(mouse_x, mouse_y, 0.5);
projector.unprojectVector(vector, camera);
var raycaster = new THREE.Raycaster(camera.position,
    vector.sub(camera.position).normalize());
var intersects = raycaster.intersectObjects(objects);
```

We once again use `THREE.Raycaster` to determine whether an object intersects with a ray cast from the position of our mouse.

9. Now that we know the intersects, we can use them to select the object we're interested in:

```
if (intersects.length > 0) {
    orbit.enabled = false;
    selectedObject = intersects[0].object;
    // and calculate the offset
    var intersects = raycaster.intersectObject(plane);
    offset.copy(intersects[0].point).sub(plane.position);
}
```

As you can see in this snippet, we first disable the `orbit` controller (as we want to drag the object around and not rotate the scene). Next, we assign the first intersected object to the `selectedObject` variable, which we used in step 6 to move the selected cube around. Finally, we need to determine the offset between the point where we clicked and the center of the plane. We need this to correctly position the cube in step 6.

10. The last step we need to take is to enable the orbit controller when we release the mouse button and set the `selectedObject` property back to null:

```
document.onmouseup = function(event) {
  orbit.enabled = true;
  selectedObject = null;
}
```

As you can see, there are plenty of steps you need to take to implement this recipe. You can also look at the sources from `07.08-drag-n-drop-object-around-scene.html`, which also contain inline documentation about why certain steps are needed.

There's more...

This recipe was based on the example from the Three.js website, which you can find at `http://threejs.org/examples/#webgl_interactive_draggablecubes`. So, for another example to play around with, you can look at that implementation.

In this recipe, we showed you how you can move the complete mesh around. You can also use this same approach to move individual vertices, faces, or lines around. So, with a little bit of effort, you can use this approach to create a kind of sculpting tool with which you could directly modify a geometry from your browser. For instance, you could create something like this `http://stephaneginier.com/sculptgl/`.

See also

> ► In this chapter, we also use `THREE.Raycaster` for the *Adding simple collision detection* recipe. If you want to drag and drop external files onto your Three.js scene, you can refer to the *Dragging a file from the desktop to the scene* recipe in *Chapter 1, Getting Started*.

Adding a physics engine

In the recipes so far, we've added animations and detection collisions to the scene manually. In this recipe, we'll show you how to use an external physics engine to add gravity, collision detection, and other physics effects to your scene.

Getting ready

For this recipe, we need to use a couple of external libraries. At the top of your HTML page, you have to add the following:

```
<script src="../libs/physi.js"></script>
```

This library contains the main implementation of the physics engine. This library in itself uses two additional libraries that need to be provided. You first need to make sure the `ammo.js` library is stored in the same location as the `physi.js` library, and at the beginning of your JavaScript code, you should add this:

```
Physijs.scripts.worker = "../libs/physijs_worker.js";
```

This points to a web worker (http://www.w3.org/TR/workers/) that handles the physics calculations in a separate thread. There is, of course, a ready-to-use example of this recipe that you can use as a reference or to experiment with. The example for this recipe is called `07.09-add-a-physics-engine.html`, and when this is opened in the browser you will see something similar to what is shown in the following screenshot:

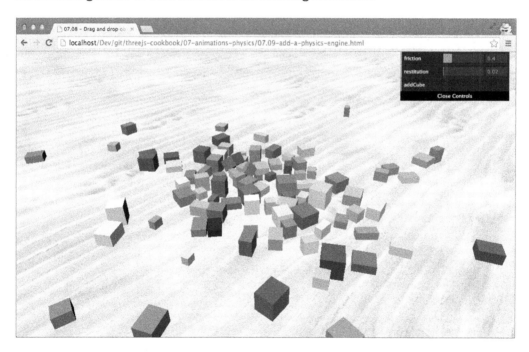

In this example, you can use the **addCube** button to add cubes to the scene. This cube will be added high above the ground plane and will drop down. The physics engine will determine how the falling cube interacts with its environment.

How to do it...

In this recipe, we only set up a basic physics-enabled scene. Refer to the *There's more...* section of this recipe for additional functionality provided by the `Physijs` library. To create a basic scene, you need to take the following steps:

1. The first thing to do is that instead of creating `THREE.Scene`, we'll create `Physics.Scene`:

   ```
   scene = new Physijs.Scene;
   scene.setGravity(new THREE.Vector3( 0, -30, 0 ));
   ```

   On this newly created scene, we also need to set the `gravity` property. In this case, we set a gravity of `-30` on the *y* axis, which means a scene where objects fall down.

2. Next, let's create `THREE.Geometry` and `THREE.MeshLambertMaterial`, which we'll use for the cubes:

   ```
   var cubeGeometry = new THREE.BoxGeometry(
     4 * Math.random() + 2,
     4 * Math.random() + 2,
     4 * Math.random() + 2);
   var cubeMaterial = new THREE.MeshLambertMaterial(
     {
       color: 0xffffff * Math.random()
     }
   );
   ```

   There is nothing special to do in this step for `Physijs`.

3. The next step is to create a mesh object. For objects to work with `Physijs`, we need to create a `Physijs` library specific mesh and a `Physijs` library specific material:

   ```
   var box_material = Physijs.createMaterial(
     cubeMaterial,
     control.friction,
     control.restitution);
   var cube = new Physijs.BoxMesh(
     cubeGeometry,
     box_material,
     10
   );
   scene.add(cube);
   ```

For the material, we use the `Physijs.createMaterial` function. This wraps our material created in step 2 and allows us to define the friction and restitution properties. The friction defines the roughness of the object and affects how far it can slide over another object. The `restitution` object is used for the bounciness of an object. To create a mesh, we use the `Physijs.BoxMesh` object, provide the geometry and the material we just created, and also add the weight of the object. `Physijs` provides differently shaped meshes; for more information on them, refer to the *There's more...* section of this recipe.

4. The final step we need to take is to update the `render` loop:

```
function render() {
  renderer.render(scene, camera);
  requestAnimationFrame(render);
  scene.simulate();
}
```

Here, we add the `scene.simulate` function. This is used to calculate the new positions of all the objects that have been wrapped in a `Physijs` library specific mesh.

With these basic steps, you've got a fully working physics-enabled Three.js scene. An important aspect to take into account when using this engine is that there is a hit on performance. For each object of the scene, `Physijs` will need to calculate its next position and rotation. This works great for tens of objects, but you'll see a severe hit when working with hundreds of Physijs-managed objects.

How it works...

We call `scene.simulate()`, which we added to the `render` loop in step 4, for each frame that is rendered. When this function is called, `Physijs` will look at all the objects it knows about, and it also looks at the gravity configured on the scene and will use that information to calculate new positions and rotations for each object if collisions between objects occur. it will use the `friction` and `restitution` properties of the `Physijs` material and the weight function of an object to determine how that object and the one it collides with should react. This is repeated in each `render` loop and gives the simulation of real physics in the scene.

There's more...

What we've done in this recipe is only a very small part of what is possible with this physics engine. You can find more information on the Physijs website at `http://chandlerprall.github.io/Physijs/`. Interesting subjects from that site are:

- Support for different object shapes: `https://github.com/chandlerprall/Physijs/wiki/Basic-Shapes`.
- How to add constraints to your object. This makes it possible to constrain the movement of an object around an axis (like a slider), a joint, or even another object. More information on this feature can be found at `https://github.com/chandlerprall/Physijs/wiki/Constraints`.

Physijs uses an external physics library for all the calculations. For more information on that engine, look at the ammo.js website (`https://github.com/kripken/ammo.js/`). Note that ammo.js itself is a JavaScript port of the Bullet physics engine. So, if you really want to dive into the details, you should look at the Bullet documentation that can be found at `http://bulletphysics.org/wordpress/`.

See also

- If you don't want to include a complete physics engine inside your project, you can also simulate parts of a physics engine yourself. How to add basic collision detection to your scene is explained in the *Adding a simple collision detection* recipe.

Index

Symbols

Thank you for buying
Three.js Cookbook

About Packt Publishing

Packt, pronounced 'packed', published its first book, *Mastering phpMyAdmin for Effective MySQL Management*, in April 2004, and subsequently continued to specialize in publishing highly focused books on specific technologies and solutions.

Our books and publications share the experiences of your fellow IT professionals in adapting and customizing today's systems, applications, and frameworks. Our solution-based books give you the knowledge and power to customize the software and technologies you're using to get the job done. Packt books are more specific and less general than the IT books you have seen in the past. Our unique business model allows us to bring you more focused information, giving you more of what you need to know, and less of what you don't.

Packt is a modern yet unique publishing company that focuses on producing quality, cutting-edge books for communities of developers, administrators, and newbies alike. For more information, please visit our website at www.packtpub.com.

About Packt Open Source

In 2010, Packt launched two new brands, Packt Open Source and Packt Enterprise, in order to continue its focus on specialization. This book is part of the Packt open source brand, home to books published on software built around open source licenses, and offering information to anybody from advanced developers to budding web designers. The Open Source brand also runs Packt's open source Royalty Scheme, by which Packt gives a royalty to each open source project about whose software a book is sold.

Writing for Packt

We welcome all inquiries from people who are interested in authoring. Book proposals should be sent to author@packtpub.com. If your book idea is still at an early stage and you would like to discuss it first before writing a formal book proposal, then please contact us; one of our commissioning editors will get in touch with you.

We're not just looking for published authors; if you have strong technical skills but no writing experience, our experienced editors can help you develop a writing career, or simply get some additional reward for your expertise.

Three.js Essentials

ISBN: 978-1-78398-086-4   Paperback: 198 pages

Create and animate beautiful 3D graphics with this fast-paced tutorial

1. Acquire thorough knowledge of the essential features of Three.js, explained using comprehensive examples.

2. Animate HTML5 elements directly from Three.js using the CSS3 3D renderer.

3. Visualize information such as sound and open data in beautiful 3D.

Learning Three.js: The JavaScript 3D Library for WebGL

ISBN: 978-1-78216-628-3   Paperback: 402 pages

Create and animate stunning 3D graphics using the open source Three.js JavaScript library

1. Create and animate beautiful 3D graphics directly in the browser using JavaScript without the need to learn WebGL.

2. Learn how to enhance your 3D graphics with light sources, shadows, and advanced materials and textures.

3. Each subject is explained using extensive examples that you can directly use and adapt for your own purposes.

Please check **www.PacktPub.com** for information on our titles

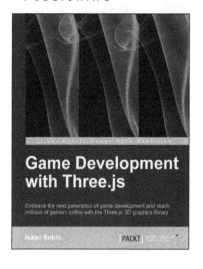

www.ingramcontent.com/pod-product-compliance
Lightning Source LLC
Chambersburg PA
CBHW060516060326
40690CB00017B/3306